HUNTING, BUTCHERING, AND COOKING WILD GAME BIBLE

[10 BOOKS IN 1]
The Ultimate Wilderness Guide for Aspiring and Seasoned Hunters
Essential Techniques and Hidden Secrets for All Game Sizes

ETHAN GREENWOOD

Outdoor Mastery Collection

Credits

Outdoor Mastery Collection: Leave by sripfoto from Noun Project (CC BY 3.0)

Background Image: Mona Eendra on Unsplash

Page 4: lizfa on Vecteezy

Page 6: terd486 on Vecteezy

TABLE OF CONTENTS

04
EXECUTION OF THE HUNT

05
ADVANCED WEAPONRY AND ARCHERY

06
FIELD DRESSING AND MEAT PROCESSING

07
PRESERVING YOUR HARVEST

08
CULINARY PREPARATIONS

09
PERFECT PAIRINGS

10
WILD GAME RECIPES

BOOK 1

THE FOUNDATIONS
OF HUNTING

CHAPTER 1
A HISTORICAL PERSPECTIVE ON HUNTING

The Evolution of Hunting Practices

Hunting has been a fundamental aspect of human existence for millennia, shaping our evolution, culture, and survival strategies. The journey from primitive hunting methods to the sophisticated techniques used today reflects not only the advancement of technology but also the deep-seated human need to connect with nature and provide for our communities.

In the earliest days of human history, hunting was a matter of survival. Prehistoric humans relied on hunting to secure the meat, hides, and bones necessary for food, clothing, and tools. Archaeological findings, such as cave paintings in Lascaux, France, depict scenes of hunters pursuing game, illustrating the central role of hunting in early human societies. These ancient hunters used rudimentary weapons like sharpened stones, wooden spears, and later, bows and arrows. These tools required significant skill to manufacture and use effectively, demonstrating early humans' ingenuity and adaptability.

As human societies evolved, so did hunting practices. During the Mesolithic and Neolithic periods, advancements in tool-making led to more effective hunting equipment. Flintknapping techniques improved, resulting in sharper, more durable arrowheads and spear points. The domestication of dogs also played a crucial role, as these animals were trained to assist in tracking and retrieving game. This symbiotic relationship between humans and dogs marked a significant step forward in hunting efficiency and success rates.

Hunting also took on a cultural and ritualistic significance in many early societies. For example, the Plains Indians of North America developed elaborate hunting rituals and dances, believing that these practices would ensure a successful hunt and honor the spirit of the animals they pursued. Similarly, ancient European tribes often held ceremonies to appease the gods and secure their favor for the hunt. These rituals highlight the deep respect early humans had for the natural world and the animals they relied upon.

The medieval period saw hunting evolve into a more structured and hierarchical activity, particularly in Europe. Hunting rights were often reserved for the nobility, and vast tracts of land were designated as royal hunting grounds. The sport of falconry, introduced from the East, became a popular pastime among the aristocracy. This period also witnessed the development of more sophisticated hunting weapons, such as the crossbow, which increased the range and accuracy of hunters. The use of trained hounds and hawks further refined hunting techniques, making it both a practical means of sustenance and a prestigious sport.

The introduction of firearms in the 16th century revolutionized hunting practices. Early matchlock and flintlock muskets allowed hunters to take down game from greater distances with improved accuracy. This technological leap not only made hunting more efficient but also changed the dynamics of predator-prey interactions. As firearms evolved, so did hunting strategies, with hunters learning to account for factors like wind direction, bullet trajectory, and the behavior of different game species.

The 19th and 20th centuries brought about significant changes in hunting practices due to industrialization and urbanization. As human populations grew and expanded into new territories, the need for regulated hunting became apparent to prevent overexploitation of wildlife. This period saw the rise of the conservation movement, with pioneers like Theodore Roosevelt advocating for sustainable hunting practices and the establishment of national parks and wildlife reserves. Laws were enacted to regulate hunting seasons, establish bag limits, and protect endangered species, ensuring that hunting could continue in a sustainable manner.

Technological advancements in the 20th century further transformed hunting. The development of high-powered rifles, advanced optics, and sophisticated camouflage gear allowed hunters to approach their prey with unprecedented stealth and precision. Innovations such as the compound bow introduced new challenges and opportunities for archers, blending ancient skills with modern engineering. These advancements not only increased hunters' success rates but also enhanced their connection to the traditions of the past.

In the contemporary era, hunting has become a blend of tradition and modernity. While the core principles of tracking, patience, and respect for nature remain unchanged, today's hunters have access to a wealth of knowledge and resources. Digital tools like GPS devices, trail cameras, and mobile apps provide hunters with real-time data on animal movements, weather conditions, and optimal hunting locations. Online forums and social media platforms have created global communities where hunters can share experiences, exchange tips, and stay informed about the latest developments in hunting gear and techniques.

Despite these advancements, the essence of hunting has remained constant. It is still a pursuit that requires skill, patience, and a deep respect for the natural world. Modern hunters continue to honor the traditions of their ancestors, whether by participating in age-old rituals, using traditional weapons, or adhering to ethical hunting practices that prioritize conservation and sustainability. Hunting remains a powerful means of connecting with nature, providing sustenance, and passing down invaluable knowledge from generation to generation.

The evolution of hunting practices is a testament to human ingenuity, adaptability, and our enduring connection to the natural world. From the primitive tools of our prehistoric ancestors to the advanced technologies of today, hunting has shaped and been shaped by human history. As we look to the future, it is essential to continue honoring these traditions while embracing new innovations that ensure hunting remains a sustainable and respected practice for generations to come.

Modern Hunting Traditions

Modern hunting traditions are a rich tapestry woven from centuries of practices, cultural heritage, and evolving societal norms. Today's hunting landscape blends ancient skills with contemporary technologies, fostering a deep connection to nature and a commitment to conservation.

One of the most distinctive aspects of modern hunting is the variation in practices across different cultures and regions. In North America, hunting is a deeply ingrained tradition, particularly evident in the big game hunting season. States like Montana and Colorado become hotspots for deer, elk, and moose hunting. The rituals associated with these hunts often include meticulous preparation and planning. Hunters spend months scouting locations, setting up trail cameras, and studying animal behavior patterns to ensure a successful hunt. The opening day of hunting season is treated almost like a holiday, with families and friends gathering to share stories, strategize, and enjoy the camaraderie that comes with the pursuit.

In Europe, hunting traditions are equally storied but differ significantly in execution. Driven hunts, where hunters stand at predetermined posts while drivers push the game towards them, are a hallmark of European hunting. Countries like Germany and Austria maintain historic hunting estates, where the experience is as much about the heritage and pageantry as it is about the hunt itself. These events often involve elaborate preparations, including traditional attire, ceremonial horns, and strict adherence to protocols passed down through generations.

Indigenous hunting practices add another layer of depth to the modern hunting landscape. For many Indigenous communities, hunting is not merely a sport but a fundamental part of their cultural and spiritual identity. Traditional methods, such as the use of bows and arrows, snares, and traps, are still employed today, not just for their effectiveness but for their cultural significance. The respect for the hunted animal is paramount, with rituals performed to honor the spirit of the animal and ensure the hunter's gratitude and respect are acknowledged. This profound connection to the land and wildlife exemplifies sustainable and ethical hunting practices that modern hunters increasingly strive to emulate.

Community and social aspects play a vital role in modern hunting traditions. Hunting clubs and organizations provide a structured environment for hunters to connect, share knowledge, and advocate for ethical hunting practices. These clubs often organize events, workshops, and hunting trips that foster a sense of community and belonging. The mentorship model is particularly significant, as experienced hunters take younger or less experienced hunters under their wing, passing down invaluable skills and wisdom. This transmission of knowledge ensures that ethical and safe hunting practices are maintained and that the next generation understands the importance of conservation and respect for wildlife.

Hunting events and competitions are another facet of modern hunting traditions. Events like deer camps and hunting derbies offer hunters the opportunity to showcase their skills and compete in a friendly, community-oriented atmosphere. These events often include categories for the largest game, best shot, and even culinary competitions for the best-prepared game dish. The competitive spirit, combined with a shared love for the outdoors, creates a vibrant community where hunters can celebrate their passion and achievements.

The integration of technology into modern hunting practices cannot be overstated. GPS devices, drones, and advanced mapping tools have revolutionized the way hunters scout and navigate hunting grounds. Real-time data on animal movements, weather conditions, and terrain changes allow hunters to plan their hunts with unprecedented precision. Innovations in hunting gear, from high-performance camouflage clothing to state-of-the-art rifles and bows, have enhanced both the efficiency and safety of hunting activities. For example, modern crossbows with advanced sighting systems and compound bows designed for greater accuracy have opened up hunting to a broader audience, including those who might not have the physical strength required for traditional archery.

The role of media and communication in modern

hunting traditions is also significant. Hunting shows, podcasts, and online forums provide platforms for hunters to share their experiences, learn new techniques, and stay informed about the latest developments in the hunting world. Social media has created communities where hunters from around the globe can connect, exchange tips, and offer support. This digital integration has not only broadened the reach of hunting traditions but also fostered a sense of global camaraderie among hunters.

Finally, sustainable practices are increasingly becoming a cornerstone of modern hunting traditions. Hunters today are more aware than ever of their impact on the environment and the importance of conservation. Sustainable hunting practices, such as selective harvesting, habitat management, and participation in conservation programs, ensure that hunting remains a viable activity for future generations. Many hunters actively engage in conservation efforts, volunteering for habitat restoration projects, participating in wildlife surveys, and advocating for policies that protect wildlife and natural habitats.

Modern hunting traditions are a complex interplay of historical practices, cultural significance, community involvement, technological advancements, and a deep-seated commitment to sustainability and ethical behavior. This rich heritage, combined with a forward-looking approach to conservation and technology, ensures that hunting remains a vital and respected practice in today's world.

CHAPTER 2
PRINCIPLES OF ETHICAL HUNTING

Conservation and Sustainability

Ethical hunting is deeply intertwined with the principles of **conservation and sustainability**. These principles guide hunters to act as stewards of the environment, ensuring that wildlife populations remain healthy and ecosystems thrive. The modern ethical hunter understands that conservation is not just about preserving game for future hunts, but about maintaining the balance of nature and protecting biodiversity for generations to come.

Conservation efforts began in earnest in the late 19th and early 20th centuries, driven by the alarming decline in wildlife populations due to unregulated hunting and habitat destruction. Notable figures like Theodore Roosevelt championed the cause, establishing national parks and wildlife refuges that served as sanctuaries for countless species. The establishment of organizations like the Boone and Crockett Club, which Roosevelt co-founded, was pivotal in promoting sustainable hunting practices and conservation principles.

A key component of conservation is **habitat management**. Healthy habitats are crucial for the survival of wildlife, providing food, shelter, and breeding grounds. Hunters often participate in habitat restoration projects, such as planting native vegetation, controlling invasive species, and creating water sources. These efforts not only benefit game species but also support a wide range of other wildlife, from insects to birds to large predators. For example, controlled burns, a technique used to manage vegetation and reduce the risk of wildfires, can rejuvenate plant growth and create diverse habitats that support robust wildlife populations.

Sustainability in hunting practices ensures that wildlife populations are not overexploited. This involves adhering to regulations that set bag limits, define hunting seasons, and restrict the hunting of certain species. These regulations are based on scientific research and population surveys conducted by wildlife biologists, who assess the health and numbers of different species. By following these guidelines, hunters help maintain the delicate balance of ecosystems and ensure that animal populations can replenish naturally.

One of the most significant aspects of sustainable hunting is **selective harvesting**. Ethical hunters focus on harvesting mature animals, often targeting older males past their prime breeding age. This practice helps maintain genetic diversity and allows younger animals to reach maturity and contribute to the population. Additionally, selective harvesting can reduce competition for resources among younger animals, promoting healthier herds overall. For instance, targeting mature bucks during deer season allows younger bucks to grow and mature, thereby supporting a stable and sustainable population structure.

Ethical hunting also involves a commitment to minimizing waste. Hunters are encouraged to utilize as much of the harvested animal as possible, turning hides into leather, bones into tools or crafts, and meat into food. This respect for the animal aligns with traditional hunting practices observed by many Indigenous cultures, who view hunting as a sacred act that demands gratitude and reverence for the life taken. Modern hunters often donate excess meat to food banks and community programs, ensuring that nothing goes to waste and that the benefits of the hunt extend beyond personal use.

Education and advocacy are crucial components of ethical hunting. Hunters play a vital role in educating the public about the importance of conservation and sustainable practices. Through participation in hunter education programs, community outreach, and conservation organizations, hunters can share their knowledge and passion for wildlife management. These efforts help dispel misconceptions about hunting and highlight the positive impact that responsible hunters have on the environment.

An example of this educational role can be seen in the North American Model of Wildlife Conservation, a set of principles that guide wildlife management in the United States and Canada. This model emphasizes that wildlife is a public resource, managed by science, and accessible to all citizens. It underscores the importance of regulated hunting as a tool for population control and habitat preservation. By supporting and promoting this model, hunters contribute to a legacy of conservation that benefits both wildlife and people.

The concept of fair chase is integral to ethical hunting. This principle emphasizes that hunting should be conducted in a manner that does not give the hunter an unfair advantage over the animal. It promotes respect for the animal, the environment, and the hunting tradition itself. Fair chase involves practices such as not hunting from vehicles, avoiding the use of electronic devices to locate game, and ensuring that the animal has a fair chance to evade the hunter. This principle fosters a sense of sportsmanship and integrity among hunters, reinforcing the idea that the hunt is about more than just the kill—it is about the experience, the challenge, and the connection to nature.

The Hunter's Role in Wildlife Management

The **role of hunters** in wildlife management is both profound and indispensable. Ethical hunters are not merely participants in the pursuit of game but are stewards of the environment, playing a critical role in maintaining the balance of ecosystems. Their active involvement in wildlife management is rooted in a deep understanding of ecology, a commitment to conservation, and a respect for the natural world.

One of the primary ways hunters contribute to wildlife management is through **population control**. In many regions, certain animal populations, such as deer or wild boar, can grow rapidly due to the absence of natural predators. Overpopulation can lead to a host of ecological problems, including habitat degradation, crop damage, and increased risk of disease. By participating in regulated hunting, hunters help to keep these populations in check, ensuring that they do not exceed the carrying capacity of their habitats. This, in turn, helps maintain the health of ecosystems and the diversity of species within them.

For example, in the United States, the overpopulation of white-tailed deer has been a significant issue in many states. Without natural predators like wolves and mountain lions, deer populations can grow unchecked, leading to overgrazing and significant impacts on plant communities. Regulated hunting seasons, determined by wildlife biologists, allow hunters to reduce deer numbers to sustainable levels. This not only helps to preserve vegetation but also supports other wildlife that depend on healthy plant communities for food and shelter.

Hunters also contribute to wildlife management through their **financial support**. The sale of hunting licenses, tags, and permits generates significant revenue that is used for conservation efforts. In the United States, the Pittman-Robertson Act, passed in 1937, imposes an excise tax on firearms, ammunition, and archery equipment. The funds collected are distributed to state wildlife agencies for habitat restoration, research, and education programs. This financial support from hunters has been instrumental in the recovery of numerous species and the restoration of critical habitats.

Moreover, hunters often engage directly in **conservation projects**. Many hunting organizations, such as Ducks Unlimited and the Rocky Mountain Elk Foundation, are actively involved in habitat preservation and restoration. These groups work to protect wetlands, forests, and grasslands that are essential for the survival of various species. Hunters volunteer their time and resources to plant trees, remove invasive species, and improve water quality. Their hands-on involvement exemplifies the deep connection between hunting and conservation.

Citizen science is another area where hunters play a vital role. Many wildlife agencies rely on data collected by hunters to monitor animal populations and assess the health of ecosystems. Hunters provide valuable information through harvest reports, surveys, and field observations. This data helps biologists make informed decisions about hunting regulations, habitat management, and conservation strategies. For instance, harvest data from waterfowl hunters have been crucial in managing migratory bird populations and ensuring sustainable hunting practices.

Education and advocacy are also important aspects of a hunter's role in wildlife management. Ethical hunters are often passionate advocates for conservation, educating the public about the importance of sustainable practices and the benefits of regulated hunting. They work to dispel myths and misconceptions about hunting, emphasizing its role in conservation and ecosystem management. By sharing their knowledge and experiences, hunters help foster a greater appreciation for wildlife and the environment.

Real-world examples illustrate the positive impact of hunters on wildlife management. In the early 20th century, North American bison were on the brink of extinction due to overhunting and habitat loss. Today, thanks to concerted conservation efforts supported by hunters, bison populations have rebounded in protected areas and on private lands. Similarly, the wild turkey, once nearly extirpated in many parts of the United States, has made a remarkable recovery due to habitat restoration and management funded by hunters.

The role of hunters extends beyond individual species to broader ecological considerations. Hunters are often involved in efforts to manage invasive species that threaten native wildlife and ecosystems. For example, feral hogs, an invasive species in the southern United States, cause extensive damage to crops and natural habitats. Hunters play a critical role in controlling feral hog populations, helping to protect native species and reduce agricultural losses.

Ethical hunters are integral to wildlife management, contributing through population control, financial support, direct conservation efforts, data collection, education, and advocacy. Their actions help ensure that wildlife populations remain healthy and ecosystems thrive. The commitment of hunters to conservation and ethical practices reflects a profound respect for the natural world and a dedication to preserving it for future generations. By fulfilling their role as stewards of the environment, hunters continue to make a significant impact on the sustainability and health of wildlife and their habitats.

CHAPTER 3
NAVIGATING HUNTING LAWS

Licensing and Permits

Navigating hunting laws is a crucial aspect of being an ethical and responsible hunter. The first step in this journey involves understanding the requirements for obtaining the necessary **licenses and permits** to hunt legally. These legal requirements are designed to ensure that hunting activities are conducted in a regulated and sustainable manner, helping to conserve wildlife populations and maintain ecological balance.

Obtaining a hunting **license** is a prerequisite for anyone wishing to hunt legally. The process typically involves several steps, including completing a hunter education course, passing a written exam, and paying a fee. Hunter education courses are comprehensive, covering essential topics such as firearm safety, wildlife conservation, and ethical hunting practices. These courses are designed to ensure that hunters are well-prepared and knowledgeable about the responsibilities and risks associated with hunting.

For instance, in the United States, each state has its own specific requirements for hunter education and licensing. In states like Colorado, prospective hunters must complete a hunter education course and pass a final exam to obtain a hunting license. The course includes both classroom instruction and practical field exercises, providing a well-rounded education on hunting safety and ethics. This rigorous training helps reduce hunting-related accidents and promotes responsible hunting practices.

Permits are often required in addition to a hunting license, especially when hunting specific types of game or in certain areas. For example, big game hunting, such as for deer or elk, usually requires special tags or permits that are often allocated through a lottery system due to high demand. These permits are critical for managing wildlife populations and ensuring that hunting pressure is distributed evenly across different regions and species. Without such regulation, certain areas could become overhunted, leading to population declines and habitat degradation.

The process of obtaining these permits can vary widely. In some states, hunters must apply for permits months in advance, while others may offer over-the-counter sales for certain species and areas. The lottery system, used in many states for highly sought-after permits, adds an element of chance, ensuring a fair distribution among applicants. This system helps maintain sustainable wildlife populations by limiting the number of hunters in specific areas and seasons.

Understanding the different types of permits is also essential. There are often separate permits for archery, muzzleloader, and rifle seasons, each with its own set of regulations and time frames. Some permits may also restrict hunters to specific zones or units within a state, requiring them to hunt only in designated areas. This zoned approach helps manage wildlife populations more effectively by targeting areas with higher or lower densities of certain species.

It's also important to recognize that hunting regulations are not static; they can change annually based on wildlife population surveys and environmental conditions. Therefore, hunters must stay informed about the latest regulations each year. State wildlife agencies typically publish annual hunting guides that detail the current regulations, permit requirements, and season dates. These guides are invaluable resources for hunters, providing up-to-date information to ensure compliance with all legal requirements.

Failure to obtain the necessary licenses and permits can result in severe penalties, including fines, loss of hunting privileges, and even criminal charges. These consequences underscore the importance of understanding and adhering to hunting laws. Ethical hunters take these regulations seriously, recognizing that they are in place to protect wildlife and ensure the sustainability of hunting as a practice.

Real-world examples highlight the importance of proper licensing and permits. In states like Montana, where elk hunting is a major activity, the allocation of permits through a lottery system ensures that hunting pressure is controlled and sustainable. Hunters who receive permits are also required to report their harvests, providing valuable data for wildlife management. This data helps biologists assess population health and

make informed decisions about future hunting seasons and permit allocations.

Moreover, international hunting trips often involve additional layers of complexity regarding licensing and permits. Hunters traveling to countries like Canada or African nations must navigate both their home country's export regulations and the host country's import and hunting laws. This often includes obtaining CITES (Convention on International Trade in Endangered Species) permits for species listed under international protection agreements. The intricate process requires careful planning and adherence to multiple sets of regulations to ensure legal compliance.

Understanding Bag Limits and Seasons

Understanding bag limits and hunting seasons is crucial for every ethical hunter. These regulations are designed to ensure the sustainable management of wildlife populations, prevent overhunting, and maintain ecological balance. By adhering to these rules, hunters contribute to the conservation of species and the preservation of habitats for future generations.

Bag limits refer to the maximum number of animals that a hunter is legally allowed to harvest during a specific period. These limits can be set daily, seasonally, or annually, depending on the species and the region. The primary purpose of bag limits is to prevent the overharvesting of wildlife, which could lead to population declines and disrupt the natural balance of ecosystems. Wildlife biologists and management agencies carefully determine these limits based on population surveys, reproductive rates, and other ecological factors.

For example, in many states across the United States, deer hunting seasons come with strict bag limits. A common regulation might allow a hunter to harvest one buck and one doe per season, or sometimes only one deer total. These limits help ensure that deer populations remain stable and that there is a healthy balance of males and females in the herd. Overharvesting bucks, for instance, could lead to a skewed sex ratio, impacting the reproductive success of the population.

In addition to overall bag limits, there are often specific rules regarding the types of animals that can be harvested. These rules might include antler restrictions for deer, where only bucks with a certain number of antler points can be legally taken. This regulation helps protect younger bucks, allowing them to mature and contribute to the genetic diversity and health of the population. Similar restrictions can apply to other species, such as requiring hunters to target mature bulls during elk season to preserve the herd's social structure and breeding success.

Hunting **seasons** are another critical component of wildlife management. These designated periods are timed to coincide with the natural life cycles of game species, ensuring that hunting activities do not interfere with key biological processes such as breeding, nesting, and migration. By establishing specific seasons, wildlife agencies can manage hunting pressure and distribute it in a way that minimizes impact on wildlife populations.

For instance, many waterfowl hunting seasons are scheduled to align with the migratory patterns of ducks and geese. These seasons are often divided into multiple segments to allow hunting opportunities at different stages of migration while ensuring that the birds have sufficient time to rest and feed. This careful timing helps maintain the health and sustainability of waterfowl populations, providing hunting opportunities year after year.

Understanding the reasons behind hunting seasons is essential for ethical hunters. These regulations are not arbitrary; they are based on extensive research and monitoring of wildlife populations. For example, hunting seasons for upland game birds like pheasants and quail typically begin after the nesting season has concluded and the young birds have had time to mature. This timing ensures that hunters do not disrupt the breeding cycle and that there are healthy populations available for future seasons.

Hunters must also be aware of special regulations that can affect bag limits and seasons. Some areas may have specific rules for certain types of hunting equipment, such as archery-only seasons or muzzleloader hunts. These regulations can influence the timing and method of hunting, adding another layer of complexity to understanding the laws. For instance, archery seasons often start earlier than rifle seasons, allowing bowhunters to pursue game with less competition and in a different phase of the animal's behavior.

Moreover, certain regions may implement additional restrictions or opportunities based on local wildlife management goals. For example, urban areas experiencing issues with overpopulation of deer might have extended seasons or additional permits to encourage population control. Conversely, areas with declining populations might have more restrictive seasons and lower bag limits to aid in recovery efforts. Hunters need to stay informed about these local variations and adjust their plans accordingly.

Real-world examples highlight the importance of adhering to bag limits and hunting seasons. In Alaska, the management of caribou herds involves intricate regulations to balance subsistence hunting by Indigenous communities, recreational hunting, and the needs of the ecosystem. Bag limits and hunting seasons are carefully set to ensure that caribou populations remain robust and that all stakeholders can benefit from the resource sustainably.

Ethical hunters take these regulations seriously, recognizing that they play a critical role in wildlife conservation. By following bag limits and observing hunting seasons, hunters help maintain healthy wildlife populations and preserve the natural heritage for future generations. Staying informed about these regulations requires diligence and a commitment to continuous learning, but it is a fundamental aspect of responsible hunting.

Local and Federal Hunting Regulations

Understanding local and federal hunting regulations is essential for every hunter. These laws are put in place to ensure sustainable hunting practices, protect wildlife populations, and maintain ecological balance. They vary significantly depending on the region, the species being hunted, and the time of year. Navigating these regulations can be complex, but it is crucial for ethical and legal hunting.

Federal regulations often set the overarching guidelines that apply to all hunters within a country. In the United States, federal laws are designed to protect migratory birds, endangered species, and certain game animals. One of the primary pieces of legislation is the **Migratory Bird Treaty Act (MBTA)**, which was enacted in 1918. This law makes it illegal to hunt, capture, kill, or sell migratory birds, their nests, or their eggs unless permitted by regulations. The MBTA is a result of treaties between the United States and several other countries, emphasizing international cooperation in wildlife conservation.

Another significant federal regulation is the **Endangered Species Act (ESA)**, which was passed in 1973. The ESA provides protection for species that are at risk of extinction. It makes it illegal to hunt, harm, or trade these species and mandates conservation efforts to help recover their populations. Hunters must be aware of the ESA listings in their area to avoid accidentally targeting protected species.

In addition to federal regulations, each state has its own set of hunting laws tailored to local wildlife management needs. These laws cover a wide range of topics, including hunting seasons, bag limits, licensing requirements, and specific hunting methods. For example, in California, the Department of Fish and Wildlife sets regulations that include zones, seasons, and quotas for different game species. These rules are designed based on population surveys, habitat conditions, and conservation goals.

Local regulations can vary even more narrowly, down to county or municipal levels. These local laws may impose additional restrictions or permissions based on specific community needs and environmental conditions. For instance, in some urban or suburban areas, special regulations may be in place to manage deer populations that have become a nuisance or pose a risk to traffic safety. These regulations might include extended hunting seasons or special permits for archery hunting to reduce the risk to nearby residents.

Compliance with local and federal regulations requires hunters to stay informed and diligent. It is not enough to know the rules in one's home state; hunters who travel to hunt in other regions must familiarize themselves with the laws of those areas. Ignorance of the law is not a defense, and violations can result in significant penalties, including fines, loss of hunting privileges, and even criminal charges.

For example, waterfowl hunting in the United States is regulated under both federal and state laws. **The U.S. Fish and Wildlife Service** sets the framework for waterfowl hunting seasons, bag limits, and shooting hours. Each state then adjusts these regulations within the federal framework to suit local conditions. Hunters must purchase both federal and state duck stamps, which fund conservation efforts and habitat restoration projects. Failure to comply with these regulations can result in hefty fines and the confiscation of hunting equipment.

Hunters must also be aware of specific regulations regarding hunting methods and equipment. Some areas may have restrictions on the types of firearms or ammunition that can be used, such as prohibiting the use of lead shot for waterfowl hunting due to its toxic effects on wildlife. Other regulations may include restrictions on hunting with dogs, the use of bait, or hunting from motorized vehicles. These rules are designed to ensure fair chase principles and minimize the environmental impact of hunting activities.

Real-world examples highlight the importance of adhering to local and federal regulations. In Alaska, for instance, hunting regulations are crucial for managing the state's abundant wildlife resources. The Alaska Department of Fish and Game sets regulations for hunting big game species like moose, caribou, and bears, which include specific seasons, bag limits, and reporting requirements. Hunters are required to report their harvests to help biologists track population trends and make informed management decisions. Compliance with these regulations ensures that Alaska's wildlife populations remain healthy and that hunting opportunities are available for future generations.

Similarly, in Africa, hunting regulations are critical for the conservation of iconic species like elephants, lions, and rhinoceroses. Countries like Namibia and South Africa have implemented strict hunting regulations and permit systems to ensure that hunting contributes to conservation efforts rather than undermines them. These regulations include quotas, mandatory guides, and significant fees that fund anti-poaching efforts and community development projects. Hunters traveling to Africa must navigate these complex regulations to participate in legal and ethical hunting activities.

Understanding and adhering to local and federal hunting regulations is a fundamental aspect of ethical hunting. These laws are designed to protect wildlife populations, ensure sustainable hunting practices, and maintain ecological balance. Hunters must stay informed about the regulations in their hunting areas, comply with licensing and permit requirements, and follow the specific rules for hunting methods and equipment. By doing so, hunters contribute to the conservation of wildlife and the preservation of natural habitats, ensuring that hunting remains a sustainable and respected tradition for future generations. This commitment to legal compliance upholds the integrity of hunting as a vital part of human culture and environmental stewardship.

BOOK 2

PREPARING FOR THE WILDERNESS

CHAPTER 1
ESSENTIAL SAFETY PRACTICES

Safe Firearm Handling

Safe firearm handling is the cornerstone of responsible hunting. Ensuring safety not only protects the hunter but also those around them, promoting a culture of respect and vigilance. Understanding and implementing the fundamental principles of safe firearm handling is essential for every hunter, whether novice or experienced.

One of the primary rules of firearm safety is to always treat every gun as if it is loaded. This mindset instills a habit of caution and respect for the weapon. Regardless of whether you are handling a rifle, shotgun, or handgun, this rule is non-negotiable. By assuming a firearm is always loaded, you naturally avoid careless handling that could lead to accidental discharge.

- **Treat Every Gun as Loaded:** This mindset instills caution and respect, preventing careless handling and potential accidents.

Keeping the muzzle pointed in a safe direction is another critical aspect of firearm safety. This means never pointing the firearm at anything you do not intend to shoot. When in the field, this practice ensures that even if an accidental

discharge occurs, it will not result in injury. This rule applies whether you are loading, unloading, cleaning, or simply carrying the firearm.

- **Point the Muzzle in a Safe Direction:** Ensures that accidental discharges do not result in injury, crucial during all firearm handling activities.

Finger placement is also crucial. Always keep your finger off the trigger until you are ready to shoot. This practice helps prevent accidental discharges caused by an inadvertent squeeze of the trigger. Instead, keep your finger alongside the trigger guard or on the firearm's frame until you are prepared to fire.

- **Keep Finger Off the Trigger:** Prevents accidental discharges by maintaining proper finger placement until ready to shoot.

Proper identification of your target and its surroundings is fundamental. Before pulling the trigger, positively identify your target and ensure there are no obstacles or unintended targets in the line of fire. This practice prevents tragic accidents caused by mistaken identity or poor visibility.

- **Identify Target and Surroundings:** Ensures

that you are shooting at the correct target and that the area behind it is safe, preventing tragic accidents.

Storing firearms safely when not in use is another essential practice. Firearms should be unloaded and securely stored in a locked cabinet or safe. Ammunition should be stored separately to prevent unauthorized access. These precautions are vital in households with children or when guests unfamiliar with firearms are present.

- **Safe Storage:** Unload firearms and store them in a locked cabinet or safe, with ammunition stored separately to prevent unauthorized access.

Real-world examples underscore the importance of these principles. Consider a hunter who failed to follow the rule of treating every gun as loaded. Assuming the firearm was unloaded, they accidentally discharged the weapon while cleaning it, resulting in a severe injury. This incident highlights the necessity of maintaining a mindset that prioritizes safety at all times.

Tree stand safety is equally crucial for hunters. Falls from tree stands are a leading cause of hunting-related injuries. Ensuring the stand is securely installed and regularly inspected for wear and damage is essential. Use a safety harness at all times when climbing, sitting, or descending from the stand. This equipment can prevent falls and save lives.

- **Secure Tree Stand Installation:** Regularly inspect for wear and damage, ensuring the stand is safe to use.
- **Use a Safety Harness:** Prevents falls and injuries when climbing, sitting, or descending from the stand.

Climbing into and out of a tree stand should be done with caution. Maintain three points of contact (two hands and one foot or two feet and one hand) to ensure stability. Avoid carrying equipment while climbing; instead, use a haul line to raise and lower your gear once you are safely in the stand.

- **Three Points of Contact:** Ensures stability and safety when climbing into and out of the tree stand.
- **Use a Haul Line:** Safely raise and lower gear, avoiding the risk of losing balance while climbing.

Environmental awareness is a critical aspect of navigating and surviving in the wild. Understanding the terrain, weather conditions, and potential hazards can make the difference between a successful hunt and a dangerous situation. Always inform someone of your hunting plans, including your expected return time and location. Carry a map, compass, or GPS device to avoid getting lost, and familiarize yourself with the area beforehand.

- **Inform Someone of Plans:** Provides a safety net in case of an emergency, ensuring someone knows your location and expected return.
- **Carry Navigation Tools:** Map, compass, or GPS device prevents getting lost, enhancing safety in unfamiliar terrain.

Preparation for unexpected situations is vital. Carrying a well-stocked first aid kit can address injuries sustained in the field. Include items such as bandages, antiseptics, a tourniquet, and any personal medications. Knowing basic first aid procedures can be lifesaving in remote areas where immediate medical assistance is not available.

- **First Aid Kit:** Essential items like bandages, antiseptics, and a tourniquet for addressing injuries in the field.
- **Basic First Aid Knowledge:** Lifesaving in remote areas where immediate medical assistance is not available.

Hydration and nutrition are also crucial for maintaining energy and focus. Carry sufficient water and high-energy snacks to sustain you throughout the hunt. Dehydration and hunger can impair judgment and reaction times, increasing the risk of accidents.

- **Hydration and Nutrition:** Carry sufficient water and high-energy snacks to maintain energy and focus.

Emergency preparedness includes knowing how to build a shelter and start a fire. These skills are essential if you become lost or injured and need to spend an unexpected night in the wilderness. Practice these skills before heading out on your hunt, ensuring you can rely on them if needed.

- **Shelter Building and Fire Starting:** Essential skills for emergency preparedness, ensuring safety in unexpected situations.

Wildlife encounters can be unpredictable. Understanding animal behavior and maintaining a respectful distance can prevent dangerous situations. Bears, for example, can be particularly dangerous if surprised or if they feel threatened. Carry bear spray and know how to use it effectively. Making noise while moving through dense vegetation can help alert animals to your presence, reducing the chance of a surprise encounter.

- **Respectful Distance:** Prevents dangerous situations by understanding animal behavior and maintaining distance.
- **Bear Spray:** Carry and know how to use it effectively, ensuring safety during potential bear encounters.
- **Make Noise in Dense Vegetation:** Alerts animals to your presence, reducing the chance of surprise encounters.

Essential safety practices in hunting encompass safe firearm handling, tree stand safety, and navigating and surviving in the wild. These principles are not just theoretical; they are practical measures that protect lives and ensure a successful, enjoyable hunting experience. By adhering to these practices, hunters demonstrate respect for the sport, the environment, and the safety of themselves and others.

Tree Stand Safety Measures

Tree stands are a popular choice among hunters for their ability to provide a better vantage point, reduce scent dispersion, and increase visibility. However, they also pose significant risks if not used properly. Understanding and implementing tree stand safety measures is critical for preventing accidents and ensuring a successful and injury-free hunt.

First and foremost, selecting a sturdy, reliable tree stand is crucial. Hunters should opt for stands that meet the standards set by the Treestand Manufacturers Association (TMA). These stands are designed and tested to ensure they can support the weight and stress they will be subjected to in the field. Always check for the TMA certification when purchasing a tree stand.

- **Select TMA-Certified Tree Stands:** Ensure your tree stand meets safety standards and can support the required weight and stress.

Before heading out into the field, thoroughly inspect your tree stand for any signs of wear or damage. Look for cracks in the metal or plastic components, frayed straps, or any other issues that could compromise the stand's integrity. Regular maintenance and inspection can prevent accidents caused by faulty equipment.

- **Inspect Tree Stands Regularly:** Check for cracks, frayed straps, and other signs of wear to prevent equipment failure.

The installation of the tree stand is another critical step. Always follow the manufacturer's instructions carefully. Ensure that the stand is secured to the tree with all provided straps and safety devices. It is essential to choose a tree that is healthy and robust, as dead or diseased trees can be unstable and pose a significant risk.

- **Follow Installation Instructions:** Secure the tree stand with all provided straps and safety devices, and choose a healthy, robust tree.

Once the tree stand is installed, the use of a safety harness is non-negotiable. A full-body harness is recommended over a simple belt, as it provides better support and reduces the risk of injury in case of a fall. The harness should be worn at all times when climbing, sitting, or descending from the tree stand. Ensure that the harness is properly fitted and adjusted to your body size.

- **Use a Full-Body Harness:** Provides better support and reduces the risk of injury, ensuring it is properly fitted and adjusted.

Climbing into and out of a tree stand requires careful attention to safety. Always maintain three points of contact—two hands and one foot, or two feet and one hand—while climbing. This technique provides better stability and reduces the likelihood of slipping or losing balance. Avoid carrying equipment while climbing; instead, use a haul line to raise and lower your gear once you are securely in the stand.

- **Maintain Three Points of Contact:** Ensures stability while climbing, reducing the risk of slipping or losing balance.
- **Use a Haul Line:** Safely raise and lower gear to avoid losing balance while climbing.

The positioning of the tree stand also plays a crucial role in safety. Place the stand at a height that provides a good vantage point but is not excessively high. A height of 15 to 20 feet is generally sufficient for most hunting scenarios. Position the stand to allow for a clear view and shooting lane, free from obstructions like branches and foliage.

- **Optimal Tree Stand Height:** Generally, 15 to 20 feet provides a good vantage point without excessive risk.

- **Clear View and Shooting Lane:** Position the stand to avoid obstructions like branches and foliage.

Weather conditions can significantly impact tree stand safety. Wet or icy conditions can make climbing and standing on a tree stand extremely hazardous. Always check the weather forecast before your hunt and avoid using a tree stand in adverse conditions. If you find yourself in a tree stand during a sudden change in weather, descend carefully and find safer ground-level options.

- **Monitor Weather Conditions:** Avoid using tree stands in wet or icy conditions, and descend carefully if weather changes.

Communication is another essential aspect of tree stand safety. Always inform someone of your hunting location and expected return time. Carry a fully charged cell phone or a two-way radio to maintain communication with others in case of an emergency. In areas with poor cell reception, consider carrying a personal locator beacon (PLB) or satellite messenger.

- **Inform Someone of Your Plans:** Provides a safety net in case of an emergency, ensuring someone knows your location and expected return.
- **Carry Communication Devices:** Cell phone, two-way radio, or PLB to maintain communication in emergencies.

Additionally, be aware of your physical limitations and health conditions. Climbing into a tree stand and sitting for extended periods can be physically demanding. Ensure you are in good physical condition and take regular breaks to stretch and move around. If you experience any dizziness, fatigue, or discomfort while in the stand, descend safely and assess your condition.

- **Assess Physical Condition:** Ensure you are fit for climbing and sitting for long periods, taking breaks to stretch and move around.

Accidents can also occur when descending from a tree stand. Always take your time and use the same three points of contact method. Do not rush, even if you are eager to track a shot animal. Descending safely is more important than hurrying and risking a fall.

- **Safe Descent:** Use three points of contact and take your time, prioritizing safety over speed.

In addition to personal safety, hunters should also consider the environmental impact of their tree stand use. Avoid damaging trees by using proper straps and padding to prevent the stand from cutting into the bark. Choose locations that minimize disruption to wildlife habitats and avoid setting up stands in areas that are heavily trafficked by other hunters.

- **Minimize Environmental Impact:** Use proper straps and padding to avoid damaging trees and choose locations that minimize habitat disruption.

Lastly, educating oneself on tree stand safety is an ongoing process. Take advantage of available resources such as safety courses, instructional videos, and literature provided by reputable hunting organizations. Staying informed and up-to-date on the latest safety practices can significantly reduce the risk of accidents.

- **Continuous Education:** Stay informed through safety courses, instructional videos, and literature from reputable hunting organizations.

Tree stand safety measures are a vital component of hunting responsibly. By selecting a reliable stand, using proper installation techniques, wearing a safety harness, maintaining three points of contact, and being mindful of weather conditions, hunters can significantly reduce the risk of accidents. Additionally, effective communication, assessing physical condition, minimizing environmental impact, and continuous education further enhance safety. Implementing these measures ensures a safe and enjoyable hunting experience, allowing hunters to focus on the thrill and satisfaction of the hunt without unnecessary risks.

Navigating and Surviving in the Wild

Successfully navigating and surviving in the wilderness requires more than just basic knowledge; it demands preparation, situational awareness, and practical skills. When hunters venture into the wild, they must be prepared for a variety of challenges, from getting lost to facing unexpected weather conditions. Understanding essential navigation and survival techniques can make the difference between a safe, enjoyable hunting experience and a potentially dangerous situation.

The first step in navigating the wild is thorough preparation. Before heading out, always inform someone of your hunting plans, including your intended location and expected return time. This crucial step ensures that someone knows where to look for you if you do not return as planned. Preparation also involves studying maps and familiarizing yourself with the terrain. Understanding the topography, water sources, and potential hazards in the area will help you navigate more effectively.

- **Inform Someone of Your Plans:** Provides a safety net in case of an emergency, ensuring someone knows your location and expected return.
- **Study Maps and Terrain:** Familiarize yourself with the topography, water sources, and potential hazards.

Carrying essential navigation tools is non-negotiable. A topographic map and a reliable compass are fundamental tools that every hunter should carry. Learning how to read a topographic map and use a compass accurately is a skill that must be practiced before venturing into the wild. In addition to traditional tools, modern technology like GPS devices and smartphone apps can be valuable aids. However, technology should never replace traditional navigation skills, as batteries can die and devices can fail.

- **Carry Essential Navigation Tools:** Topographic map, compass, and GPS devices or smartphone apps for backup.

Understanding how to use these tools is just as important as having them. A compass, for example, can help you find your direction and navigate to a specific point. To use a compass effectively, you must be able to take a bearing, which involves aligning the compass with a map and determining the direction to travel. Practicing these skills regularly will ensure you can rely on them when needed.

- **Practice Using Navigation Tools:** Regularly practice taking bearings and navigating with a map and compass.

Situational awareness is a critical component of wilderness navigation and survival. Always be aware of your surroundings and take note of landmarks, such as distinctive trees, rock formations, or water features. These landmarks can serve as reference points if you need to retrace your steps or find your way back to a specific location. Regularly checking your position on the map and comparing it to the physical landmarks around you will help you stay oriented.

- **Maintain Situational Awareness:** Note landmarks and regularly check your position on the map to stay oriented.

Weather conditions can change rapidly in the wilderness, and being prepared for these changes is essential. Always check the weather forecast before your hunt and be prepared for unexpected changes. Carry appropriate clothing and gear for the expected conditions, including rain gear, extra layers for warmth, and a hat and sunscreen for sun protection. Hypothermia and heat exhaustion are serious risks that can be mitigated with proper preparation and awareness.

- **Prepare for Weather Changes:** Check the forecast, carry appropriate clothing and gear, and be aware of hypothermia and heat exhaustion risks.

Water is a critical resource in the wilderness, and knowing how to find and purify water is essential for survival. Carrying enough water for the duration of your hunt is important, but you should also be prepared to find and purify additional water if needed. Water sources such as streams, rivers, and lakes can be contaminated, so always carry a water purification method, such as a filter, purification tablets, or a portable UV purifier.

- **Water Purification:** Carry enough water and have a purification method for additional water sources.

Fire is another essential survival tool that can provide warmth, cook food, and signal for help. Knowing how to start a fire in various conditions is a crucial skill. Always carry multiple fire-starting tools, such as waterproof matches, a lighter, and a fire starter. Practice building fires in different weather conditions and with different types of tinder and kindling to ensure you can start a fire when needed.

- **Fire-Starting Tools:** Carry waterproof matches, a lighter, and a fire starter, and practice building fires in various conditions.

Building a shelter is vital if you need to spend an unexpected night in the wilderness. A well-constructed shelter can protect you from the elements and help maintain body heat. Learn how to build different types of shelters using natural materials and carry a lightweight emergency shelter, such as a bivy sack or emergency blanket, in your gear. Practice building shelters before your hunt to ensure you can do it quickly and efficiently if needed.

- **Shelter Construction:** Learn to build shelters using natural materials and carry an emergency shelter in your gear.

First aid knowledge is crucial for handling injuries or medical emergencies in the wild. Carry a well-stocked first aid kit and know how to use its contents. The kit should include items such as bandages, antiseptics, pain relievers, a tourniquet, and personal medications. Taking a wilderness first aid course can provide valuable skills and knowledge for handling common hunting injuries, such as cuts, sprains, and fractures.

- **First Aid Kit:** Carry a well-stocked kit and know how to use it, including bandages, antiseptics, and a tourniquet.

Wildlife encounters can be both exhilarating and dangerous. Understanding animal behavior and maintaining a respectful distance can prevent dangerous situations. Bears, for example, can be particularly hazardous if surprised or if they feel threatened. Carry bear spray and know how to use it effectively. Making noise while moving through dense vegetation can help alert animals to your presence, reducing the chance of a surprise encounter.

- **Respectful Distance from Wildlife:** Prevent dangerous situations by understanding animal behavior and maintaining distance.
- **Bear Spray:** Carry and know how to use it effectively, ensuring safety during potential bear encounters.
- **Make Noise in Dense Vegetation:** Alerts animals to your presence, reducing the chance of surprise encounters.

In conclusion, navigating and surviving in the wild involves thorough preparation, situational awareness, and practical skills. By informing someone of your plans, carrying essential navigation tools, and understanding how to use them, you can navigate effectively and safely. Preparing for weather changes, knowing how to find and purify water, and building a fire and shelter are crucial survival skills. Additionally, carrying a first aid kit and understanding wildlife behavior can further ensure your safety. Implementing these practices will help you navigate the wilderness with confidence and handle any challenges that may arise, making your hunting experience safe and enjoyable.

CHAPTER 2
SELECTING YOUR GEAR

Clothing for Various Environments

Choosing the right clothing for hunting is a critical component of ensuring both safety and success in the field. The environment you'll be hunting in greatly influences the type of clothing you'll need. From extreme cold to intense heat, the right clothing can make all the difference in your comfort and effectiveness as a hunter. Understanding how to layer your clothing and select materials that suit different weather conditions and terrains is essential.

Layering is the foundation of dressing for any hunting environment. It allows hunters to adjust their clothing based on activity level and changing weather conditions. The three primary layers are the base layer, mid-layer, and outer layer. Each serves a specific purpose and contributes to overall comfort and protection.

- **Base Layer:** The base layer is crucial for moisture management. It should be made from moisture-wicking materials such as merino wool or synthetic fabrics. These materials draw sweat away from your skin, keeping you dry and preventing chills. For instance, merino wool is excellent because it is both warm and breathable, making it suitable for a variety of conditions.
- **Mid-Layer:** The mid-layer provides insulation. Its primary function is to trap body heat. Fleece and down are popular choices for mid-layers. Fleece is lightweight, breathable, and quick-drying, making it ideal for active hunting. Down offers superior warmth-to-weight ratio but can lose its insulating properties when wet. A practical example is wearing a fleece jacket for early morning hunts when temperatures are low but activity levels are high.
- **Outer Layer:** The outer layer protects against wind, rain, and snow. It should be waterproof and windproof yet breathable to allow moisture from sweat to escape. Materials like Gore-Tex are widely used for their waterproof and breathable qualities. For instance, a hunter might wear a Gore-Tex jacket during a rainy hunt to stay dry and comfortable.

Camouflage is another critical aspect of hunting clothing. The pattern and color of your camo should match the environment you'll be hunting in. Different terrains and seasons require different camo patterns. For example, woodland camo works well in forested areas with lots of greenery, while desert camo is suited for arid, sandy environments. During winter hunts, snow camo with white and grey patterns helps hunters blend into snowy landscapes.

In addition to layering and camouflage, specific environments demand unique considerations:

- **Cold Environments:** In extremely cold conditions, additional insulation is necessary. Consider wearing insulated jackets and pants, thermal gloves, and a warm hat. Heated insoles or socks can also be beneficial for keeping feet warm. Always ensure that your clothing allows for freedom of movement despite the extra layers.
- **Hot Environments:** In hot weather, staying cool and protected from the sun is crucial. Lightweight, breathable fabrics that offer UV protection are ideal. Long sleeves and pants can protect your skin from the sun and insects while still being comfortable. Light-colored clothing can also help reflect sunlight and keep you cooler.
- **Wet Environments:** Hunting in wetlands or during rainy seasons requires waterproof clothing. Waterproof boots are essential to keep your feet dry, while a poncho or waterproof jacket can protect your upper body. Quick-drying materials are beneficial in these environments to prevent prolonged dampness, which can lead to discomfort and health issues.

Footwear is another essential component of your hunting gear. The right boots can prevent injuries, keep your feet comfortable, and improve your overall hunting experience. When selecting hunting boots, consider the following:

- **Terrain:** Choose boots that are appropriate for the terrain you'll be navigating. For rocky or mountainous areas, boots with good ankle support and a rugged sole are essential. In marshy or wet conditions, waterproof boots are a must.

- **Weather:** Insulated boots are crucial for cold weather hunts, while breathable boots are better for hot conditions. Look for materials that offer both comfort and protection.
- **Fit and Comfort:** Ensure that your boots fit well and are broken in before heading out on a hunt. Blisters and foot pain can ruin a hunting trip, so prioritize comfort and fit.

Real-world examples highlight the importance of selecting the right clothing. For instance, during a late-season elk hunt in the Rocky Mountains, temperatures can vary drastically from pre-dawn to midday. Layering with a moisture-wicking base layer, an insulating fleece, and a waterproof outer shell allows hunters to adjust their clothing as temperatures rise and fall, ensuring comfort and safety throughout the day.

In contrast, a hunter in the swamps of Louisiana during duck season will prioritize waterproof gear and lightweight, breathable fabrics to stay dry and cool in humid conditions. Waterproof waders and a lightweight camo jacket made from quick-drying materials are essential for this environment.

Must-Have Hunting Accessories

When preparing for a hunting expedition, selecting the right accessories can greatly enhance your experience and success in the field. These accessories are not just add-ons; they play crucial roles in ensuring safety, efficiency, and effectiveness. Here, we delve into the must-have hunting accessories that every hunter should consider.

Optics are indispensable for identifying and targeting game from a distance. Good-quality binoculars and scopes are essential tools for any hunter.

- **Binoculars:** A reliable pair of binoculars helps in spotting game from afar, allowing you to plan your approach without alerting the animals. Look for binoculars with good magnification (8x to 10x) and a wide field of view. Models with anti-reflective coatings and waterproof features are highly recommended. For example, during a deer hunt in the dense forests of the Pacific Northwest, binoculars can help you spot movement in the thick underbrush, giving you an advantage in planning your next move.

- **Scopes:** A rifle scope improves accuracy and allows for precise shots at longer distances. Choose a scope that matches your firearm and hunting needs. Consider factors like magnification range, lens quality, and reticle type. A variable power scope (3-9x or 4-12x) is versatile and suitable for various hunting scenarios. For instance, while hunting elk in the Rocky Mountains, a good scope can help you accurately target an animal at several hundred yards.

Rangefinders are another critical tool. These devices measure the distance between you and your target, helping you make accurate shots and improving your chances of a successful hunt.

- **Laser Rangefinders:** These devices are quick and accurate, providing the exact distance to your target. Look for rangefinders with a range of at least 500 yards and features like angle compensation, which adjusts for the incline or decline of your shot. A hunter on a steep hillside in Montana, for instance, would benefit from angle compensation to ensure the bullet hits the intended mark.

Calls and Decoys play a significant role in attracting game to your location. Understanding the proper use of these tools can greatly increase your success rate.

- **Game Calls:** These mimic the sounds of animals to lure them closer. Different calls are available for various species, such as duck calls, deer grunts, and turkey gobbles. Using

a doe bleat call during the rut can attract a mature buck into shooting range.

- **Decoys:** These visual attractants can deceive game into thinking there is a potential mate or rival in the area. Proper placement and realistic movement are key to effectiveness. For example, using a hen decoy during spring turkey season can entice a tom into your shooting lane.

Field Dressing Kits are essential for processing game after a successful hunt. A well-equipped kit can make the task quicker, cleaner, and more efficient.

- **Knives:** A sharp, durable knife is the cornerstone of any field dressing kit. A fixed-blade knife with a comfortable grip and a blade length of 4-6 inches is ideal for most game. For instance, a gut hook knife is particularly useful for deer hunters, as it simplifies opening the animal's abdomen without puncturing internal organs.
- **Game Bags:** These are used to store and transport meat after dressing. They protect the meat from dirt, insects, and contaminants. Lightweight, breathable game bags are best for keeping the meat cool and clean.

Backpacks designed for hunting can carry all your gear while distributing weight comfortably. Look for packs with multiple compartments, hydration compatibility, and sturdy, weather-resistant materials.

- **Daypacks:** For shorter hunts, a daypack can carry essentials like water, snacks, extra clothing, and basic field dressing tools. These packs are lightweight and compact, allowing for greater mobility.
- **Multi-Day Packs:** For extended hunts, larger packs that can carry additional gear, sleeping bags, and food are necessary. Features like adjustable straps and padded hip belts can enhance comfort during long treks.

Navigation Tools ensure you can find your way

in and out of the hunting area safely. Getting lost in the wilderness is a serious risk, and having reliable navigation tools can prevent this.

- **GPS Devices:** Handheld GPS units provide real-time location data and can store waypoints for tracking your route. They are particularly useful in remote areas where cellular service is unavailable.
- **Compasses and Maps:** Traditional tools like compasses and topographic maps are essential backups in case of GPS failure. Knowing how to read a map and navigate using a compass is a fundamental skill for any hunter.

Safety Gear is critical for protecting yourself and others while hunting. This includes items like first aid kits, safety harnesses, and blaze orange clothing.

- **First Aid Kits:** A compact kit with bandages, antiseptics, pain relievers, and other medical supplies can be a lifesaver in the event of an injury. Customizing your kit to include personal medications and additional trauma supplies is a good practice.
- **Blaze Orange:** Wearing blaze orange clothing is required in many regions to increase visibility to other hunters and prevent accidental shootings. A blaze orange vest and hat are the minimum essentials.
- **Safety Harnesses:** For hunters using tree stands, a safety harness is essential to prevent falls. A full-body harness connected to a lifeline ensures that you are secure from the moment you leave the ground.

Real-world examples illustrate the importance of having the right accessories. A hunter in Alaska, for example, relies on high-quality optics and a reliable GPS to navigate the vast wilderness and spot caribou from long distances. Meanwhile, a deer hunter in the Midwest might use a grunt call and doe decoy to draw a trophy buck into range, ensuring their success with a well-maintained field dressing kit to process the game efficiently.

Choosing the Right Firearms and Bows

Choosing the right firearms and bows is a critical part of preparing for a successful hunting trip. The correct selection depends on various factors, including the type of game, the environment, and the hunter's personal preferences and physical abilities. A well-chosen weapon can significantly enhance your effectiveness and enjoyment in the field.

Understanding the Game: The first step in selecting a firearm or bow is understanding the type of game you plan to hunt. Different animals require different calibers, types of ammunition, and arrow setups. For example, hunting small game like rabbits or squirrels requires a small caliber rifle or a shotgun with birdshot. In contrast, hunting large game like deer, elk, or bear necessitates a larger caliber rifle or a powerful bow capable of delivering sufficient kinetic energy for a humane kill.

- **Small Game:** For small game, a .22 caliber rifle is a popular choice due to its accuracy and low recoil. A shotgun with a 20-gauge or smaller using birdshot is also effective for upland birds and small mammals.
- **Large Game:** For larger game, calibers like .30-06 Springfield, .308 Winchester, or .270 Winchester are excellent choices. These provide the power needed to ensure a quick, humane kill. Bows with a draw weight of at least 40-50 pounds are typically recommended for deer-sized game, while larger animals like elk may require a bow with a draw weight of 60 pounds or more.

Rifles: Selecting a rifle involves considering the terrain, range, and hunting style. Bolt-action rifles are renowned for their accuracy and reliability, making them ideal for medium to long-range shots. Lever-action rifles offer faster follow-up shots, which can be beneficial in dense cover or for moving targets.

- **Bolt-Action Rifles:** These are excellent for their precision and stability. A bolt-action rifle chambered in.30-06 is versatile and suitable for a wide range of large game. For instance, a hunter in the open plains of the Midwest might choose a.30-06 bolt-action rifle for its long-range capabilities and stopping power.
- **Lever-Action Rifles:** These are favored for their quick cycling and ease of handling. A lever-action rifle in.45-70 Government is effective for hunting big game in thick woods or brush where shots are typically closer and quick follow-up shots may be necessary.
- **Shotguns:** Shotguns are versatile weapons suitable for both small and large game, depending on the ammunition used. They are particularly effective for bird hunting and close-range encounters.

Pump-Action Shotguns: These are popular for their reliability and ability to handle various types of ammunition. A 12-gauge pump-action shotgun is a versatile choice for waterfowl, turkey, and even deer hunting with the appropriate slug.

- **Semi-Automatic Shotguns:** These offer faster follow-up shots and reduced recoil, which can be advantageous during fast-paced hunting scenarios. For instance, a semi-automatic 12-gauge shotgun with a duck load is ideal for waterfowl hunting in marshlands.
- **Bows:** Bow hunting requires careful selection based on draw weight, draw length, and the hunter's strength and skill level. Compound bows, recurve bows, and crossbows each have their unique advantages.

Compound Bows: These are the most popular for hunting due to their mechanical advantage and accuracy. A compound bow with an adjustable draw weight and let-off provides the power and precision needed for various game. For example, a compound bow with a 70-pound draw weight

is effective for hunting deer and elk, offering a balance of power and accuracy.

- **Recurve Bows:** These are simpler and often preferred by traditional archers. They require more skill and strength but can be highly effective in the hands of an experienced hunter. A recurve bow with a 50-pound draw weight can be suitable for deer hunting.
- **Crossbows:** These are increasingly popular due to their ease of use and power. Crossbows are effective for hunters who may have physical limitations that prevent them from using a traditional bow. A crossbow with a draw weight of 150 pounds or more is ideal for large game hunting.

Optics: The right optics can enhance your shooting accuracy and effectiveness. Scopes and rangefinders are essential accessories for both rifles and bows.

- **Scopes:** A quality rifle scope improves accuracy by providing a clear and magnified view of the target. Variables like magnification range, reticle type, and lens quality are important considerations. For instance, a scope with a 3-9x magnification range is versatile and suitable for most hunting scenarios.
- **Rangefinders:** These devices measure the distance to the target, allowing for precise shot placement. A laser rangefinder with angle compensation is particularly useful in mountainous terrain where shots may be at steep angles.

Real-World Examples: Consider a hunter in the rugged mountains of Colorado pursuing elk. This hunter might choose a.300 Winchester Magnum bolt-action rifle equipped with a high-quality scope for long-range shooting in open terrain. The rifle's power ensures a humane kill, while the scope's magnification helps in identifying and targeting game at a distance.

Alternatively, a bowhunter in the dense forests of the Eastern United States might opt for a compound bow with a 70-pound draw weight. Paired with carbon arrows and broadhead tips, this setup provides the necessary power and accuracy for a clean kill on whitetail deer.

Selecting the right firearms and bows is a nuanced process that involves understanding the type of game, the hunting environment, and personal preferences. By considering these factors and choosing appropriate weapons and accessories, hunters can enhance their effectiveness, safety, and overall hunting experience. This preparation not only increases the chances of a successful hunt but also ensures ethical and responsible hunting practices.

CHAPTER 3
ADVANCED EQUIPMENT INSIGHTS

Scopes and Binoculars for Precision

Using the right equipment can make a significant difference in your hunting success. Scopes and binoculars are essential tools that enhance your ability to spot and accurately target game from a distance. These optical devices provide clarity, magnification, and precision, which are crucial for effective hunting. Understanding the different types of scopes and binoculars, their features, and how to use them can significantly improve your performance in the field.

Firstly, let's consider scopes. A scope, also known as a telescopic sight, is mounted on a firearm to improve accuracy at long distances. The primary advantage of a scope is its magnification, which allows you to see your target more clearly and make precise shots. Scopes come in various types, including fixed-power and variable-power scopes. Fixed-power scopes have a single magnification level, which makes them simple and reliable. Variable-power scopes offer adjustable magnification, providing versatility for different hunting situations.

- **Fixed-Power Scopes:** Simple and reliable with a single magnification level, suitable for consistent environments.

- **Variable-Power Scopes:** Adjustable magnification for versatility in different hunting situations.

When selecting a scope, consider the magnification range based on your typical hunting environment. For example, a 3-9x40 scope, where 3-9x indicates the magnification range and 40 denotes the objective lens diameter in millimeters, is a popular choice for general hunting. This range offers flexibility for both close and long-range shots. For more specialized hunting, such as long-distance shooting, a higher magnification scope like a 6-24x50 may be more appropriate.

- **3-9x40 Scope:** Versatile for general hunting, suitable for both close and long-range shots.
- **6-24x50 Scope:** Higher magnification ideal for specialized long-distance shooting.

The quality of the glass and lens coatings in a scope also plays a significant role in its performance. High-quality glass provides better light transmission, resulting in brighter and clearer images. Lens coatings reduce glare and improve visibility in low-light conditions, which is particularly important during dawn and dusk hunts.

Investing in a scope with superior optics can greatly enhance your hunting experience.

- **High-Quality Glass:** Better light transmission for brighter and clearer images.
- **Lens Coatings:** Reduce glare and improve visibility in low-light conditions.

Additionally, consider the reticle or crosshair design. The reticle aids in aiming and can vary from simple duplex designs to complex mil-dot or bullet drop compensator (BDC) reticles. Duplex reticles are straightforward and easy to use, making them suitable for beginners. Mil-dot and BDC reticles provide additional reference points for adjusting aim based on distance and wind, which is beneficial for more experienced hunters.

- **Duplex Reticles:** Simple and easy to use, ideal for beginners.
- **Mil-Dot and BDC Reticles:** Provide reference points for adjusting aim, beneficial for experienced hunters.

Now, let's explore binoculars. While scopes are essential for aiming, binoculars are crucial for scouting and spotting game from a distance. Binoculars provide a wider field of view compared to scopes, making them ideal for scanning large areas. The magnification and objective lens diameter of binoculars are typically represented in a format such as 10x42, where 10x is the magnification power and 42mm is the objective lens diameter.

When choosing binoculars, balance between magnification and field of view is essential. High magnification binoculars offer detailed views but may have a narrower field of view, making it harder to scan wide areas. For general hunting, binoculars with 8x or 10x magnification are a good choice, as they provide a good balance of detail and field of view.

- **8x or 10x Magnification:** Balance of detail and field of view, ideal for general hunting.

The quality of the optics in binoculars is equally important. Look for binoculars with high-quality glass and lens coatings to ensure bright, clear images. Features such as multi-coated lenses, phase correction, and extra-low dispersion (ED) glass enhance image quality and reduce chromatic aberration, providing a sharper and more accurate view.

- **Multi-Coated Lenses:** Enhance image quality and reduce glare.
- **Phase Correction and ED Glass:** Provide sharper, more accurate views by reducing chromatic aberration.

Binoculars also come with various features to enhance usability in the field. Waterproof and fog-proof binoculars ensure reliability in different weather conditions. Ergonomic designs with comfortable grips and adjustable eyecups make extended use more comfortable. Additionally, a good neck strap or harness can reduce strain during long periods of use.

- **Waterproof and Fog-Proof:** Ensure reliability in different weather conditions.
- **Ergonomic Design:** Comfortable grips and adjustable eyecups for extended use.
- **Neck Strap or Harness:** Reduces strain during prolonged use.

Using scopes and binoculars effectively requires practice and familiarity with their features. For scopes, practice shooting at various distances to understand how magnification and reticle adjustments affect your aim. Spend time at the range to zero your scope, ensuring that it is accurately aligned with your firearm. Regular maintenance, such as cleaning the lenses and checking for any loose parts, will keep your scope in optimal condition.

- **Practice Shooting at Various Distances:** Understand how magnification and reticle adjustments affect aim.
- **Zero Your Scope:** Ensure accurate alignment with your firearm.

- **Regular Maintenance:** Clean lenses and check for loose parts to keep the scope in optimal condition.

For binoculars, practice using them to scan large areas efficiently. Hold them steady by bracing your elbows against your body or using a tripod for extended viewing sessions. Familiarize yourself with the focus adjustments to quickly bring objects into sharp view. Proper care, such as keeping the lenses clean and storing them in a protective case, will prolong the life of your binoculars.

- **Efficient Scanning:** Practice scanning large areas and holding binoculars steady.
- **Focus Adjustments:** Quickly bring objects into sharp view.
- **Proper Care:** Clean lenses and store in a protective case to prolong life.

Real-world examples highlight the importance of these tools. Imagine a hunter using a high-quality 3-9x40 scope to spot and accurately shoot a deer from 200 yards away. The clear image and precise reticle ensure a clean shot, making the hunt successful. Similarly, another hunter uses 10x42 binoculars to scan a dense forest, spotting a group of elk grazing in a distant clearing. The bright, clear image provided by the binoculars allows the hunter to plan an effective approach.

Scopes and binoculars are indispensable tools for hunters, providing the precision and clarity needed for successful hunting. By selecting the right equipment, understanding their features, and practicing their use, hunters can enhance their ability to spot and accurately target game. Investing in high-quality optics and maintaining them properly will ensure reliable performance in the field, contributing to a more enjoyable and successful hunting experience.

Effective Use of Game Calls and Decoys

Game calls and decoys are crucial tools in a hunter's arsenal, designed to lure game animals into close range by mimicking their natural sounds and appearances. Mastering the use of these tools can significantly increase your chances of a successful hunt. Understanding the types of game calls and decoys, how to use them effectively, and common mistakes to avoid are key aspects that can enhance your hunting experience.

Game calls come in various forms, each designed to replicate specific sounds made by animals. These calls can be broadly categorized into mouth calls, electronic calls, and friction calls. Mouth calls require the hunter to blow air through them, producing sounds that mimic vocalizations like grunts, bleats, or gobbles. They are lightweight, easy to carry, and offer the hunter great control over the sound's pitch and duration.

- **Mouth Calls:** Lightweight and easy to carry, offering control over pitch and duration.

Examples: Duck calls, turkey diaphragm calls, and deer grunt calls.

Electronic calls, on the other hand, use pre-recorded sounds that can be played at the push of a button. These calls are incredibly realistic and can replicate a wide range of sounds, from predator calls to distress calls of prey animals. They are particularly useful in scenarios where a hunter needs to produce loud or continuous sounds without fatigue.

- **Electronic Calls:** Use pre-recorded sounds, ideal for loud or continuous calls without fatigue.

Examples: Predator calls, fawn distress calls, and crow calls.

Friction calls, such as box calls or slate calls, produce sound through the friction created by rubbing two surfaces together. These calls are primarily used in turkey hunting but can be effective for other game as well. They offer the advantage of producing consistent, natural-sounding calls with minimal practice.

- **Friction Calls:** Produce sound through friction, offering consistent, natural-sounding calls.

Examples: Turkey box calls and slate calls.

Using game calls effectively requires understanding the behavior and vocalizations of your target species. For instance, during the rut, bucks respond well to grunt calls that mimic the sounds of other bucks challenging them. Similarly, hens can be attracted by clucking and purring sounds during the spring turkey season. Practicing these calls and learning the appropriate times to use them can greatly enhance their effectiveness.

- **Understanding Behavior:** Tailor calls to the specific behavior and vocalizations of the target species.

Examples: Grunt calls during the rut for deer, clucking for turkeys in spring.

Real-world examples illustrate the impact of effective game calling. Consider a hunter using a grunt call during the peak of the rut season. By mimicking the sound of a rival buck, the hunter can draw a dominant buck out of cover, offering a clear shot. Similarly, a predator hunter using an electronic call can simulate the distress call of a rabbit, attracting coyotes into the open for a better shot.

Real-World Examples: Grunt call during the rut to draw out a dominant buck, distress calls to attract predators.

Decoys, like game calls, are designed to lure game animals into range by mimicking the appearance of their species or prey. Decoys can be highly effective, especially when used in combination with calls. There are various types of decoys, including full-body decoys, silhouette decoys, and motion decoys.

Full-body decoys are three-dimensional representations that closely resemble the animal in size and shape. They are often used in waterfowl hunting, where lifelike decoys can draw ducks and geese into shooting range. These decoys can be positioned in realistic patterns to create the illusion of a safe and attractive landing area.

- **Full-Body Decoys:** Three-dimensional and lifelike, used to create realistic patterns for attracting waterfowl.

Examples: Duck and goose decoys in a spread.

Silhouette decoys are two-dimensional and are usually made of lightweight materials. They are easy to carry and set up, making them ideal for hunts where mobility is important. While they lack the depth of full-body decoys, they can be highly effective when used in large numbers to create the illusion of a flock.

- **Silhouette Decoys:** Lightweight and easy to carry, effective in large numbers.

Examples: Field decoys for geese and ducks.

Motion decoys add an element of movement to your setup, making them particularly attractive to game. These decoys can mimic the motion of feeding or landing birds, adding realism to the scene. Motion decoys are especially effective in waterfowl and turkey hunting, where the slightest movement can draw attention and interest.

- **Motion Decoys:** Add realism with movement, highly effective for waterfowl and turkey hunting.

Examples: Spinning wing decoys and feeding motion decoys.

The placement and setup of decoys are critical to their effectiveness. When setting up decoys, consider the natural behavior and movement patterns of the game. For example, when setting up for waterfowl, place decoys in a U or J-shaped pattern to create a landing zone. Ensure that decoys are facing into the wind, as birds typically land into the wind. For turkey hunting, place decoys within shooting range and use a combination of hen and jake decoys to create a convincing scene.

- **Placement and Setup:** Mimic natural behavior and movement patterns.

Examples: U or J-shaped patterns for waterfowl, combination of hen and jake decoys for turkeys.

Using game calls and decoys together can significantly enhance their effectiveness. By calling and using decoys simultaneously, you can create a more convincing scenario that appeals to the instincts of your target. For instance, using a hen call in conjunction with a hen decoy can attract gobblers during turkey season. Similarly, combining predator calls with motion decoys can entice cautious predators into the open.

- **Combined Use:** Enhance effectiveness by using calls and decoys together.

Examples: Hen call with hen decoy for turkeys, predator call with motion decoy for coyotes.

To maximize success, avoid common mistakes such as overcalling, improper decoy placement, and lack of patience. Overcalling can spook game, so it's important to call sparingly and adjust your volume and frequency based on the animal's response. Improper decoy placement can create suspicion, so always ensure that decoys are arranged naturally. Finally, patience is key; give the game time to respond to your setup and avoid making sudden movements that could give away your position.

- **Avoid Overcalling:** Call sparingly to avoid spooking game.
- **Proper Decoy Placement:** Arrange decoys naturally to avoid suspicion.

- **Patience:** Give the game time to respond and avoid sudden movements.

Mastering the effective use of game calls and decoys requires understanding the types of calls and decoys available, practicing their use, and setting them up correctly. By combining these tools and strategies, hunters can create realistic and convincing scenarios that draw game animals into range. Investing time in learning and perfecting these techniques will lead to more successful and enjoyable hunting experiences.

Tools for Successful Tracking and Navigation

Navigating the wilderness and tracking game effectively requires more than just basic skills and intuition. Advanced tools and technology have become integral to modern hunting, providing hunters with the precision and reliability needed to maximize success in the field. From GPS devices and trail cameras to high-quality compasses and advanced tracking apps, these tools enhance your ability to move through the wilderness, locate game, and make informed decisions. Understanding how to use these tools effectively can significantly improve your hunting experience.

One of the most valuable tools for navigation in the wilderness is a GPS device. Unlike traditional maps and compasses, GPS devices provide real-time location data, making it easier to navigate unfamiliar terrain. Handheld GPS units are specifically designed for outdoor use, offering features such as topographic maps, waypoint marking, and route tracking. These devices allow hunters to mark important locations like hunting spots, water sources, and camp sites, which can be revisited with precision.

- **Handheld GPS Units:** Provide real-time location data, topographic maps, waypoint marking, and route tracking.

Examples: Garmin GPSMAP 64st, Garmin eTrex 30x.

Trail cameras are another essential tool for successful tracking. These motion-activated cameras are placed in strategic locations to monitor wildlife activity. By capturing photos and videos of animals as they pass by, trail cameras provide invaluable insights into animal behavior, movement patterns, and population density. This information allows hunters to plan their hunts more effectively, selecting optimal times and locations based on observed activity.

- **Trail Cameras:** Capture photos and videos of wildlife, providing insights into behavior and movement patterns.

Examples: Bushnell Trophy Cam HD, Browning Strike Force Pro.

Advanced tracking apps have also revolutionized the way hunters navigate and track game. These apps can be installed on smartphones and tablets, turning them into powerful tracking tools. Many tracking apps offer features such as offline maps, weather updates, waypoint marking, and animal activity logging. Some even allow hunters to share data with others, facilitating collaborative tracking and planning efforts.

- **Tracking Apps:** Turn smartphones into powerful tracking tools with features like offline maps, weather updates, and waypoint marking.

Examples: onX Hunt, HuntStand.

High-quality compasses remain a crucial tool for navigation, especially when GPS signals are weak or unavailable. Modern compasses come with additional features such as clinometers, sighting mirrors, and global needles that work accurately in both hemispheres. Learning to use a compass effectively is a fundamental skill for any hunter, providing reliable navigation regardless of technology limitations.

- **High-Quality Compasses:** Provide reliable navigation with features like clinometers, sighting mirrors, and global needles.

Examples: Suunto MC-2, Silva Ranger 2.0.

In addition to these primary tools, various other equipment can enhance tracking and navigation efforts. Rangefinders, for example, are used to measure the distance to a target accurately. This information is crucial for making precise shots, particularly at long distances. Rangefinders can also help hunters estimate distances when planning routes or marking waypoints.

- **Rangefinders:** Measure the distance to a target accurately, aiding in precise shots and route planning.

Examples: Leica Rangemaster CRF 2400-R, Vortex Ranger 1800.

Using these tools effectively requires practice and familiarity. For GPS devices, hunters should spend time learning the interface and features, such as setting waypoints and creating routes. Practicing with the device in various terrains and weather conditions ensures that you can rely on it when it matters most. Similarly, mastering trail camera placement involves understanding animal behavior and selecting locations that maximize the chances of capturing useful data.

- **Practice with GPS Devices:** Learn the interface, set waypoints, and create routes in various terrains.
- **Master Trail Camera Placement:** Understand animal behavior and select strategic locations for optimal data capture.

Combining traditional navigation skills with modern technology is the best approach for successful tracking and navigation. While GPS devices and tracking apps provide precise location data, traditional skills like reading topographic maps and using a compass are invaluable backups. Understanding how to integrate these tools ensures that you can navigate effectively even when technology fails.

- **Combine Traditional and Modern Skills:** Integrate GPS and tracking apps with map reading and compass use for reliable navigation.

Real-world examples demonstrate the effectiveness of these tools. Consider a hunter using a handheld GPS device to navigate dense forest terrain. By marking waypoints and tracking their route, the hunter can move confidently and efficiently, reducing the risk of getting lost. In another scenario, a hunter sets up trail cameras along a known deer trail, capturing images that reveal peak activity times. Using this information, the hunter plans their hunt during these peak periods, increasing the likelihood of success.

Real-World Examples: Use GPS for efficient navigation in dense forests, and trail cameras to identify peak activity times.

Furthermore, advanced tracking tools can assist in post-hunt analysis. Reviewing data from GPS devices, trail cameras, and tracking apps can provide insights into what worked well and what could be improved. This analysis helps hunters refine their strategies and make more informed decisions in future hunts.

- **Post-Hunt Analysis:** Review data from GPS, trail cameras, and tracking apps to refine strategies and improve future hunts.

Safety is another critical aspect of using these tools. Ensuring that your GPS device and smartphone are fully charged before heading out is essential. Carrying spare batteries or a portable charger can prevent your devices from dying in the field. Additionally, always have a backup plan in case of technology failure, such as a physical map and compass.

- **Safety Precautions:** Keep devices charged and carry spare batteries or a portable charger, along with a physical map and compass as backup.

Tools for successful tracking and navigation have become indispensable in modern hunting. GPS devices, trail cameras, tracking apps, high-quality compasses, and rangefinders provide hunters with the precision and reliability needed to navigate the wilderness and track game effectively. By practicing with these tools and integrating traditional navigation skills, hunters can enhance their performance and safety in the field. Real-world examples highlight the practical benefits of these tools, from efficient navigation to informed hunt planning. Embracing these advanced equipment insights will lead to more successful and enjoyable hunting experiences.

BOOK 3

MASTERING HUNTING TECHNIQUES

CHAPTER 1
TRACKING SKILLS

Reading Animal Signs

Mastering the ability to read animal signs is a fundamental tracking skill that every hunter must develop. This skill involves interpreting various physical indicators left behind by animals, such as tracks, scat, rubs, and other subtle signs. By learning to read these clues, hunters can locate and follow game, understand animal behavior, and predict movements, significantly increasing their chances of a successful hunt. Let's delve deeper into how to effectively read and interpret these signs.

Tracks are the most obvious and commonly used animal signs. They provide crucial information about the type of animal, its size, direction of travel, and even its behavior.

Identifying tracks begins with recognizing different prints. Each species leaves distinct tracks, and learning these differences is essential. For example, deer tracks are heart-shaped with two pointed tips, while bear tracks show a broad, flat print with distinct toes and claws. The size of the tracks can also offer clues about the animal's age and size. Larger tracks typically indicate older, larger animals. Analyzing the gait, or the distance between each track, can provide

insights into the animal's speed and behavior. A long stride may suggest the animal was running, while a shorter stride might indicate walking or grazing.

A hunter in the Rocky Mountains might come across fresh deer tracks in the snow. Noticing the depth and spread of the tracks, they could infer that a sizable buck had recently passed through, possibly on the move from one feeding area to another. Following these tracks might lead the hunter to a prime location to set up a stand or ambush point.

Scat, or animal droppings, is another valuable indicator. Different animals produce distinct types of scat, which can reveal much about their diet, health, and recent activity.

- **Identification:** The size, shape, and content of scat can help identify the animal. For instance, deer scat is typically pellet-shaped, while bear scat can be large and contain remnants of their varied diet, such as berries or hair.
- **Freshness:** The freshness of the scat indicates how recently the animal was in the area. Fresh, moist scat suggests the animal passed through recently, while older, dried

scat indicates it has been some time since the animal was present.

- **Real Example:** In the dense forests of the Pacific Northwest, a hunter might find bear scat filled with berry seeds. This could indicate the bear has been feeding heavily in preparation for winter hibernation and might be nearby. Understanding this, the hunter can be more cautious and alert for signs of the bear's presence.

Rubs and scrapes are particularly important for tracking deer, especially during the rut when bucks are most active.

- **Rubs:** Bucks rub their antlers against trees to mark their territory and strengthen their neck muscles. Fresh rubs on trees indicate active bucks in the area. The size and height of the rub can suggest the size of the buck.
- **Scrapes:** Bucks also create scrapes by pawing the ground and urinating in the cleared area. These scrapes are used to mark territory and communicate with does. Fresh scrapes with wet soil and visible urine indicate recent activity.
- **Real Example:** A hunter during the rut might find a series of fresh rubs along a trail, indicating a dominant buck's territory. Setting up near these rubs could provide an excellent opportunity to encounter the buck as it patrols its domain.

Other physical signs, such as broken branches, trampled vegetation, and bedding areas, also provide valuable clues.

- **Broken Branches:** Branches broken at specific heights can indicate animals like deer or elk have passed through. For example, branches broken at about shoulder height might suggest a passing elk.
- **Trampled Vegetation:** Flattened grass or disturbed leaves can indicate recent animal activity. The size and pattern of the disturbed

area can suggest the type of animal and its behavior.

- **Bedding Areas:** Areas where vegetation is flattened in a specific pattern often indicate where animals have rested. Deer beds, for instance, are typically oval-shaped and found in sheltered areas.
- **Real Example:** In the meadows of Wyoming, a hunter might find a series of flattened grass patches indicating elk beds. These signs suggest that the herd uses the area regularly, providing the hunter with valuable information on where to set up an ambush.

To enhance these tracking skills, hunters should spend time practicing and observing in different environments. Each ecosystem presents unique challenges and signs, and familiarity with these can greatly improve tracking proficiency.

Environmental Clues and Indicators

Successfully tracking game requires a deep understanding of the environment and the various clues it offers. Environmental indicators can provide critical information about the presence and behavior of animals, helping hunters to anticipate their movements and locate them more efficiently. These indicators include natural signs such as disturbed vegetation, bedding areas, feeding sites, and even subtle changes in the landscape that suggest recent animal activity. Let's explore these environmental clues in detail and see how they can enhance your tracking skills.

Vegetation disturbances are one of the most telling environmental indicators. When animals move through an area, they often leave subtle changes in the vegetation that can reveal their presence and movements.

- **Trampled Grass and Broken Branches:** Flattened grass or leaves can indicate a recent animal trail. Broken branches at various heights can suggest the type of animal and its size. For example, branches broken at a height of about four to five feet might indicate elk or moose activity. Observing the direction of the disturbed vegetation can help track the animal's movement through the area.

- **Bent Grass and Pathways:** Animals create pathways through repeated use of the same routes. Bent grass and consistently disturbed pathways can indicate a frequently used game trail. A hunter in the Midwest might notice a well-trodden path through a field, indicating a route that deer use regularly to move between feeding and bedding areas. Setting up near these paths can increase the likelihood of encountering game.

Bedding areas are another critical clue. These are places where animals rest and sleep, and they provide significant insights into the daily habits of the game.

- **Flattened Areas:** Look for areas of flattened grass or leaves, often with indentations where the animal's body lay. These areas are typically found in sheltered spots that offer protection from the elements and predators. A deer bed, for example, is usually an oval-shaped depression in tall grass or leaves, often on a hillside where the animal can watch for danger below.
- **Sheltered Spots:** Bedding areas are usually located in places that offer both cover and a vantage point. They may be near food sources but are often in more secluded areas. Identifying these spots can reveal where animals are likely to be during different times of the day. For instance, finding a bedding area in a dense thicket might indicate where deer rest during the day, allowing hunters to plan ambushes along the paths leading to these beds.

Feeding sites provide another set of valuable indicators. The presence of specific types of vegetation and signs of feeding can point to the kinds of animals frequenting the area.

- **Nibbled Vegetation and Droppings:** Areas with vegetation that shows signs of being eaten, such as nibbled leaves or stripped bark, indicate recent feeding activity. The type of vegetation affected can help identify the animal. Deer, for instance, often leave behind cleanly nibbled plants and shrubs, while beavers leave more gnawed, rough edges on trees and branches.
- **Scratched Ground and Digging:** Some animals, like wild boar, will dig or root in the ground to find food. Scratches and overturned soil indicate their presence. A hunter might find areas where the ground has been disturbed by wild boars searching for roots and insects, suggesting a prime spot for setting up a blind.

Water sources are vital for wildlife, and areas around them can provide numerous clues.

- **Tracks and Trails:** Animals frequently visit water sources, leaving behind tracks and trails. Examining the banks of a river or pond can reveal a multitude of tracks, indicating the types and sizes of animals that visit. A well-worn trail leading to a water source can be a strategic location for a hunting stand.
- **Mud and Sand Imprints:** Soft mud or sand near water sources captures clear imprints of animal tracks. These prints can provide precise information about the direction and frequency of animal visits. For instance, in a muddy creek bed, a hunter might find fresh bear tracks, indicating recent activity and suggesting that the bear might return to this water source.

Environmental sounds and smells also serve as crucial indicators.

- **Sounds:** Listening to the natural sounds of the environment can alert hunters to the presence of animals. The rustling of leaves, breaking branches, or animal calls and movements can all provide clues. For example, the distant bugle of an elk or the rustle of leaves underfoot can direct a hunter's attention to a particular area.

- **Smells:** Certain smells, like the musky odor of a large mammal or the scent of fresh scat, can indicate the presence of game. An experienced hunter can use these olfactory cues to determine the proximity of animals. The strong, pungent smell of a wild boar, for example, might alert a hunter to its nearby presence, even if the animal is not yet visible.

Real-world example: A hunter in the dense forests of the Pacific Northwest might use a combination of these environmental indicators. Spotting trampled ferns and broken branches at shoulder height, they follow a faint game trail to a sheltered spot where they find fresh deer beds. Nearby, nibbled vegetation and deer droppings confirm the area as a frequent resting and feeding site. Setting up a tree stand along this trail increases the hunter's chances of a successful encounter.

Understanding and interpreting environmental clues and indicators are crucial for effective tracking. By paying close attention to vegetation disturbances, bedding areas, feeding sites, water sources, sounds, and smells, hunters can gain invaluable insights into the presence and behavior of game. This knowledge not only enhances the chances of a successful hunt but also deepens the hunter's connection with the natural world, fostering a greater appreciation and respect for the environment and its inhabitants.

CHAPTER 2
STALKING STRATEGIES

Effective Camouflage Techniques

Mastering the art of stalking requires understanding and implementing effective camouflage techniques. Camouflage is not just about wearing the right clothing; it involves blending into your environment in various ways to avoid detection by your prey. Whether you are stalking deer through dense woods or approaching waterfowl in an open marsh, effective camouflage can make the difference between success and failure. Here, we explore different aspects of camouflage, offering detailed strategies and real-world examples to enhance your stalking skills.

Blending in with the environment is the first and most crucial step in effective camouflage. This involves matching your clothing and gear to the colors and patterns of the surrounding terrain. Different environments require different camouflage patterns.

- **Woodland Camouflage:** In forested areas, use camouflage patterns that incorporate greens, browns, and blacks. These colors mimic the leaves, branches, and shadows of the forest floor. A hunter moving through the dense forests of the Eastern United States might choose a camouflage pattern like Realtree or Mossy Oak, which are specifically designed for woodland environments.
- **Desert and Grassland Camouflage:** In open, arid environments like deserts or grasslands, lighter colors such as tans and beiges are more effective. Patterns that break up your outline against the open sky and sparse vegetation are crucial. For example, a hunter in the American Southwest might use a pattern like MultiCam, which blends well with sandy and rocky terrains.
- **Snow Camouflage:** In snowy conditions, white and gray patterns help you blend into the winter landscape. Specialized snow camo patterns reduce contrast and mimic the texture of snow. A hunter in the Rocky Mountains during winter would benefit from wearing snow camouflage to remain undetected against the bright, reflective snow.

Movement can easily give away your position, even if you are well-camouflaged. Minimizing movement is essential for effective stalking. When you do need to move, do so slowly and deliberately. Sudden movements can catch the eye of your prey and alert them to your presence.

- **Controlled Movements:** Move only when the animal's head is down or when it is obscured by vegetation. This reduces the chances of being seen. For instance, a deer hunter might move only when the deer is feeding and its head is down.

- **Using Cover:** Use natural cover such as trees, bushes, and terrain features to hide your movements. Stay low and move along the edges of cover whenever possible. A turkey hunter might crawl behind a fallen log or through tall grass to stay hidden while approaching a flock.

Scent control is another critical aspect of effective camouflage. Animals like deer and elk have a highly developed sense of smell and can detect human scent from a considerable distance. Managing your scent involves both reducing your scent and understanding wind patterns.

- **Scent Reduction:** Use scent-free soaps and detergents to wash your body and clothing. Store your hunting clothes in a sealed bag with natural cover scents like pine needles or earth. Applying scent eliminators to your gear before heading out can also help. For example, a hunter might use a scent eliminator spray on their boots and clothing to reduce their scent trail.
- **Wind Management:** Always hunt with the wind in your face. This prevents your scent from being carried towards the game. Understanding local wind patterns and how they change throughout the day can help you plan your approach. A hunter in the rolling hills of the Midwest might set up their stand or blind on the downwind side of a field where deer are likely to enter.

Visual camouflage goes beyond clothing and includes modifying your appearance to break up your outline and reduce shine. Human shapes and smooth surfaces are easily recognizable to animals.

- **Face and Hands:** Use camo face paint or wear a camo mask to cover exposed skin.

Hands can be hidden with gloves. For example, a waterfowl hunter might wear a face mask and gloves to blend in with the reeds along a marshy shoreline.

- **Gear and Equipment:** Cover shiny surfaces on your gear with camo tape or wraps. This includes your rifle scope, binoculars, and any other equipment that might catch the light. A bowhunter might wrap their bow and arrows in camo tape to prevent them from reflecting sunlight.

Using decoys and calls can enhance your camouflage by diverting the animal's attention away from you and towards the decoy or sound.

- **Decoys:** Proper placement of decoys can draw the game into shooting range while keeping their attention off you. For instance, a hunter might place a buck decoy in an open field to attract territorial bucks during the rut.
- **Calls:** Using animal calls can create a sense of normalcy and lure the game closer. Ensure your calls are realistic and used at appropriate times. A duck hunter might use a feeding chuckle call to simulate the sounds of ducks feeding, attracting other ducks to land nearby.

Real-world example: A hunter in the dense forests of Pennsylvania during the fall might employ a combination of woodland camouflage, scent control, and strategic movement. By wearing camo that blends with the autumn leaves, using scent eliminators, and moving only when the deer are feeding, the hunter increases their chances of getting within range undetected.

Effective camouflage techniques are vital for successful stalking. By blending with the environment, minimizing movement, controlling scent, and using visual modifications, hunters can significantly improve their stealth. Incorporating decoys and calls can further enhance your ability to remain undetected. Mastering these techniques requires practice and a keen understanding of your environment, but the rewards are well worth the effort, leading to more successful and fulfilling hunts.

Utilizing Terrain and Wind to Your Advantage

Effective stalking requires a deep understanding of how to use the terrain and wind to your advantage. By mastering these elements, hunters can move stealthily through the environment, reducing the chance of detection and increasing their opportunities for a successful hunt. Understanding and manipulating the terrain and wind conditions can significantly enhance your stalking strategy. Let's explore these concepts in detail and see how they can be applied in various hunting scenarios.

Different types of **terrain** offer unique challenges and opportunities for hunters. Understanding the landscape and how to use its features to your advantage can make a significant difference in your stalking success.

- **Natural Cover:** Trees, bushes, rocks, and other natural features can provide excellent cover, allowing you to move closer to your prey without being seen. For example, when stalking deer in a forested area, use the trees and underbrush to break up your outline and mask your movements. Move slowly and stay low, using the natural cover to remain hidden. A hunter in the dense woods of the Pacific Northwest might crawl through thick ferns and undergrowth to get within range of a deer, using every available tree trunk and bush to stay concealed.
- **Elevation:** High ground offers a vantage point that can be advantageous for spotting game from a distance. Conversely, moving through low ground, such as valleys or creek beds, can keep you out of sight. When hunting elk in the mountainous regions of Colorado, use ridgelines and hills to your advantage. Moving along the crest of a ridge allows you to scan the opposite slope for game, while staying low in the valleys keeps you hidden from sight.
- **Waterways:** Rivers, streams, and lakes can serve as natural pathways for both hunters and game. Animals frequently travel along water sources, making them prime areas for setting up ambushes. Additionally, moving through water can help mask your scent and noise. A hunter might follow a riverbank, using the sound of the flowing water to cover their approach and reduce the risk of being detected by animals.
- **Game Trails:** Animals often use specific trails to travel between feeding, bedding, and watering areas. Identifying these trails and using them to your advantage can improve your stalking effectiveness. Positioning yourself along a well-used game trail increases the likelihood of encountering animals moving through the area. In the hardwood forests of the Midwest, a hunter might set up near a heavily used deer trail that runs between a cornfield and a bedding area, capitalizing on the predictable movement patterns of the deer.

Understanding and managing **wind direction** is crucial for successful stalking. Animals, especially deer and elk, have a highly developed sense of smell and can detect human scent from a considerable distance. By paying attention to wind patterns, hunters can avoid detection and increase their chances of getting close to their prey.

- **Hunting with the Wind:** Always position yourself so that the wind is blowing in your face, carrying your scent away from the direction you are stalking. This prevents your scent from reaching the game and alerting them to your presence. In open plains or grasslands, where there is little cover, hunting with the wind in your face is even more critical. A pronghorn hunter in Wyoming might plan their stalk carefully, moving into the wind to avoid spooking the sensitive animals.

- **Wind Indicators:** Use tools like wind checkers, which release a fine powder to show the wind direction, or observe natural indicators such as the movement of leaves, grass, or smoke. These can help you determine the prevailing wind direction and adjust your approach accordingly. For instance, a bowhunter in a thickly wooded area might use a wind checker to ensure they are downwind of a whitetail deer, maintaining their stealth as they close the distance.
- **Thermals:** In hilly or mountainous terrain, thermal winds caused by temperature changes throughout the day can affect scent dispersal. In the morning, as the sun rises and warms the ground, thermals rise, carrying scent upwards. In the evening, as the ground cools, thermals fall, causing scent to drift downhill. Understanding these patterns can help you plan your stalk. An elk hunter in the Rocky Mountains might wait until late morning to approach a herd, using the rising thermals to carry their scent away from the animals.

Real-World Example: consider a hunter in the rolling hills of Kentucky. This hunter needs to approach a herd of deer grazing in an open field surrounded by patches of woodland. By using the terrain to their advantage, the hunter starts their approach from the downwind side, moving through a low-lying creek bed that provides natural cover. As they get closer, they stay low and use the scattered trees and bushes along the edge of the field to conceal their movements. By carefully watching the wind direction and using the natural features of the terrain, the hunter is able to get within range without alerting the deer.

Patience and Precision in Stalking

Stalking game requires a combination of **patience and precision**. These two elements are crucial for successfully closing in on your target without alerting it to your presence. Patience ensures you don't rush the process and make mistakes, while precision in your movements and actions guarantees that each step you take brings you closer to your prey without being detected. Mastering these skills can significantly increase your chances of a successful hunt.

Patience is often the most challenging aspect of stalking for many hunters, especially those who are new to the discipline. It requires an understanding that haste can ruin a hunt and that success often comes to those who wait. Developing patience means learning to move slowly and deliberately, sometimes taking hours to cover what seems like a short distance. This slow pace minimizes noise and allows you to blend more naturally into your surroundings.

For example, a bowhunter stalking a whitetail deer through a dense forest must be willing to take each step cautiously. This means pausing frequently to scan the surroundings and listen for any signs of the deer. Quick, hurried movements can easily snap a twig or rustle leaves, alerting the deer to the hunter's presence. By moving slowly, the hunter reduces the risk of making such mistakes. Additionally, this deliberate pace allows the hunter to adjust their strategy based on the behavior of the deer, such as changing direction or finding better cover.

Precision in stalking involves being meticulous about every aspect of your approach. This starts with planning your route based on the wind direction, terrain, and the behavior patterns of the game you are hunting. Knowing when to move and when to stay still is critical. Each step should be placed carefully to avoid making noise or stepping on anything that could give away your position.

In an open field scenario, a hunter might use available cover such as tall grass, small depressions in the ground, or rocks to stay hidden. The precision here lies in choosing the right cover at the right time and knowing how to move between these points without being seen. This might involve crawling on your stomach to stay low or freezing in place when the animal looks in your direction.

One real-world example of patience and precision can be seen in the techniques used by hunters in the wide plains of the Midwest, where cover is sparse. Here, hunters often use ghillie suits to blend into the grasslands. The key to success in this environment is to move extremely slowly, sometimes covering just a few feet over several minutes. By doing so, the hunter remains virtually invisible to the game, allowing for a closer approach. This level of precision requires intense focus and control over every movement.

Patience and precision also play a crucial role in the final moments of the stalk, when the hunter is within range of the game. At this point, any mistake can result in the animal bolting and the hunt being unsuccessful. The hunter must maintain their composure, ensuring their breathing is steady and their heart rate is controlled. This helps in making an accurate shot. Whether using a bow or a rifle, the precision in aiming and timing the shot is the culmination of all the patient stalking efforts.

For instance, an elk hunter in the Rocky Mountains might spend hours getting within bow range of a herd. The final moments involve getting into a shooting position without making any sudden movements that could startle the elk. Drawing the bow must be done smoothly and slowly, ensuring that the elk do not notice the movement. This requires not only physical precision but also mental calmness and patience.

Another crucial aspect of precision is the ability to read the behavior of the game. Understanding animal body language can provide clues about their next move. For example, if a deer suddenly raises its head and looks intently in a direction, it might have sensed something unusual. A patient hunter will wait and observe, rather than moving and risking detection. This attentiveness allows the hunter to adjust their strategy accordingly, either waiting for the deer to relax or using the distraction to move closer.

Patience and precision in stalking are also about knowing when to let opportunities pass. Sometimes the conditions are not right, or the animal is too alert. In such cases, forcing the situation can lead to failure. A skilled hunter recognizes these moments and is willing to wait for a better opportunity, even if it means extending the hunt or trying again another day. This mindset is often what separates a successful hunter from an unsuccessful one.

Mastering patience and precision in stalking is essential for any serious hunter. These skills require practice, discipline, and a deep understanding of both the environment and the behavior of the game. By moving slowly and deliberately, using the terrain and cover effectively, and maintaining composure during the final moments of the hunt, a hunter can significantly increase their chances of success. The art of stalking is a blend of physical skill and mental toughness, and those who master it will find themselves more often rewarded in the field.

CHAPTER 3
OBSERVATION AND DETECTION

Enhancing Observation Skills

Observation is one of the most crucial skills for any hunter. The ability to notice and interpret subtle signs in the environment can make the difference between a successful hunt and going home empty-handed. Enhancing observation skills involves training your senses to detect movement, sounds, and other indicators of game presence. By honing these abilities, hunters can become more effective and increase their chances of success. Let's delve into the techniques and strategies that can enhance observation skills in the field.

To start with, keen observation begins with an awareness of your surroundings. This involves constantly scanning the environment and being mindful of any changes or anomalies. Instead of focusing solely on a single point, use a broad, sweeping gaze to take in the entire landscape. This method helps in detecting movement, which is often the first clue to the presence of game. For instance, the flicker of a deer's tail or the rustling of leaves caused by a moving animal can be easily missed if your focus is too narrow.

Using **optical aids** like binoculars and spotting scopes can significantly enhance your ability to observe at greater distances. High-quality binoculars allow you to spot game from afar, giving you the advantage of planning your approach without disturbing the animals. Spotting scopes, with their higher magnification, are particularly useful for open terrains where you need to scan vast areas. Imagine a hunter in the open plains of Montana, using a spotting scope to locate a herd of pronghorns several miles away. This early detection allows the hunter to strategize and approach from the best possible direction.

Sound plays a vital role in observation. Training your ears to pick up on the subtle noises of the forest can alert you to the presence of game long before you see it. The snapping of a twig, the rustle of leaves, or the distant call of an animal are all sounds that can provide valuable information. Practicing attentive listening can be done even when you are not hunting. Spend time in the woods, closing your eyes and focusing solely on the sounds around you. Over time, you'll become better at distinguishing between the different noises and identifying which ones are caused by animals.

Another key aspect of enhancing observation skills is learning to recognize **animal signs**. Tracks, scat, rubs, and other physical evidence can indicate the presence of game and their recent activities. For example, finding fresh deer tracks in a muddy area suggests that the animal has passed through recently. Similarly, a freshly broken branch might indicate a deer's path. By regularly studying and familiarizing yourself with these signs, you can become adept at interpreting them quickly and accurately.

Camouflage can be both an advantage and a challenge when it comes to observation. While it helps you remain unseen, it also means that the game can blend into the environment. Training your eyes to detect patterns and colors that stand out can help in spotting camouflaged animals. This is particularly useful in environments like dense forests or fields with tall grass, where animals can easily hide. An experienced hunter in the woodlands of the Northeast might spot a deer by noticing the unusual shape of its antlers against the backdrop of tree branches.

Incorporating a systematic approach to scanning the environment can enhance your observation skills. Divide the area into sections and scan each systematically, from left to right or top to bottom. This method ensures that you cover the entire area thoroughly without missing any crucial details. For example, when glassing a hillside, start from the bottom and slowly work your way up, ensuring that you check every possible hiding spot.

Patience is a critical component of effective observation. Rushing through the process can cause you to overlook important signs and miss opportunities. Taking the time to sit quietly and observe can reveal much about the movements and behavior of game in the area. Imagine a hunter waiting patiently at the edge of a clearing, watching a group of deer feeding. By staying still and observing, the hunter can learn the deer's habits and choose the best moment to make a move.

Practicing **mindfulness** can also improve your observation skills. Being fully present in the moment, without distractions, allows you to notice even the smallest details. This level of awareness can be developed through various mindfulness exercises, such as focusing on your breathing or paying close attention to the sensations in your body. By incorporating mindfulness into your hunting routine, you can enhance your ability to stay alert and aware.

In real-world scenarios, enhancing observation skills can lead to greater success. Consider a bowhunter in the Rocky Mountains who spends hours scanning the rugged terrain for signs of elk. By using binoculars to spot distant movement, listening for the bugle of a bull elk, and interpreting fresh tracks and scat, the hunter can accurately locate and approach the herd. This combination of visual, auditory, and interpretive skills increases the likelihood of a successful hunt.

The Role of Scent in Hunting

The role of scent in hunting is paramount, influencing both the hunter's success and the behavior of game animals. Animals like deer, elk, and wild boar possess an incredibly keen sense of smell, often detecting hunters from a considerable distance. Understanding how scent works and learning to manage it effectively can significantly enhance a hunter's ability to remain undetected and improve their chances of a successful hunt.

Scent plays a crucial role in how animals perceive their environment. For many game species, the sense of smell is their primary defense mechanism against predators. They rely on it to detect danger, locate food, and communicate with each other. For instance, a deer can pick up human scent from hundreds of yards away and will often react by fleeing the area immediately. This heightened sense of smell means that hunters must be meticulous in managing their scent to avoid detection.

Managing scent begins long before setting foot in the hunting grounds. Hunters must take steps to reduce their scent profile, starting with personal hygiene. Using scent-free soaps, shampoos, and detergents is essential. Regular soaps and detergents contain fragrances that can be easily detected by game animals. Washing hunting clothes in scent-free detergents and storing them in airtight containers with natural cover scents, like leaves or pine needles, can help mask human odors. For example, a hunter might wash their gear in a scent-free detergent and store it in a sealed bag with cedar chips to infuse a natural scent that blends with the forest environment.

In the field, maintaining scent control requires ongoing diligence. Applying scent eliminators to clothing and gear before the hunt helps reduce residual odors. These products often come in spray form and can neutralize a wide range of scents, making the hunter less detectable. Additionally, wearing scent-blocking clothing made from advanced materials that contain activated carbon or other scent-absorbing technologies can further reduce the hunter's scent profile.

Wind direction is a critical factor in managing scent during a hunt. Always position yourself so that the wind carries your scent away from the game. This means understanding the prevailing wind patterns in your hunting area and adjusting your position accordingly. For instance, if the wind is blowing from the north, approach your hunting spot from the south to ensure your scent is not carried towards the game. Using wind checkers, which release a fine powder or smoke to show wind direction, can help you constantly monitor and adjust your position in relation to the wind.

Thermals, or temperature-driven air movements, also affect how scent travels. In mountainous areas, thermals rise in the morning as the ground warms up and fall in the evening as it cools down. Knowing how thermals work can help you plan your movements and set up your stand or blind in the best possible location. A hunter in the Rocky Mountains, for example, might choose to stalk elk in the early morning when the thermals are rising, ensuring their scent is carried upwards and away from the game.

Cover scents are another tool hunters use to mask their odor. These scents mimic natural smells in the environment, such as earth, pine, or animal urine. Applying cover scents to your clothing, boots, and gear can help you blend into the surroundings. However, it's crucial to choose a cover scent that matches the environment. Using deer urine in a pine forest may raise suspicion among the animals. A more appropriate choice would be a pine or earth scent to blend naturally with the surroundings.

Scent lures, on the other hand, can attract game animals to your location by mimicking the scents of food or other animals. During the rut, for instance, using doe estrus scent can lure bucks looking for mates. Proper placement of scent lures is key to their effectiveness. Place them upwind of your position so that the wind carries the scent towards the game. Additionally, using scent drags or wicks can create a scent trail that leads animals to your location.

Real-world examples highlight the importance of scent management in hunting. A whitetail deer hunter in the Midwest might take extensive measures to reduce their scent, including using scent-free hygiene products, storing clothes in airtight containers with natural cover scents, and wearing scent-blocking clothing. In the field, they constantly monitor the wind direction using a wind checker and position themselves downwind of where they expect the deer to approach. By doing so, they minimize the chances of detection and increase the likelihood of a successful shot.

In another scenario, an elk hunter in the Rockies might use thermals to their advantage, planning their approach based on the rising and falling air currents. By understanding how the morning thermals rise, they position themselves below the elk herd, ensuring their scent is carried upwards and away from the animals. Additionally, they use cover scents that match the alpine environment, further masking their presence.

Scent plays a critical role in hunting, significantly impacting the behavior of game animals and the success of the hunter. By managing personal scent through hygiene, using scent-eliminating products, understanding wind and thermal patterns, and employing cover scents and lures appropriately, hunters can effectively reduce their scent profile and remain undetected. Mastering the art of scent control requires knowledge, preparation, and constant vigilance, but it is an essential skill for any serious hunter. With these techniques, hunters can increase their chances of a successful and rewarding hunt.

BOOK 4

EXECUTION OF THE HUNT

CHAPTER 1
TACTICS FOR VARIOUS GAME

Techniques for Hunting Deer

Hunting deer requires a blend of knowledge, patience, and skill. Each hunt is unique, influenced by factors such as the terrain, weather conditions, and deer behavior. Here, we explore various techniques to increase your chances of a successful deer hunt.

Understanding **deer behavior** is crucial. Deer are crepuscular animals, meaning they are most active during dawn and dusk. Knowing this helps you plan your hunt more effectively. Arriving at your hunting spot before dawn and staying until after dusk maximizes your chances of encountering deer. During the rut, bucks are more active throughout the day, chasing does and marking territory, making this period an excellent hunting opportunity. Bucks become less cautious and more mobile, offering more chances for sightings and shots.

Scouting is an essential part of deer hunting. Before the season begins, spend time in the field locating signs of deer activity. Look for:

- **Tracks and Droppings:** Indicate travel routes and feeding areas.
- **Rubs on Trees:** Where bucks have rubbed their antlers to mark territory.
- **Scrapes on the Ground:** Areas where bucks have pawed the ground and marked with scent.

Using trail cameras can provide valuable information on deer movement patterns, helping you identify prime hunting spots. Placing cameras along well-used trails, feeding areas, and water sources can give insights into deer behavior and timing.

Stand hunting is one of the most popular methods for hunting deer. This technique involves setting up a tree stand or ground blind in an area where deer are likely to pass.

- Position your stand downwind of deer trails or feeding areas to avoid detection.
- Ensure your stand is well-concealed and provides a clear line of sight to your target area.

For example, setting up a tree stand along the edge of a field where deer enter to feed at dusk can provide an excellent vantage point. Elevation gives you a better view and keeps your scent above the deer's nose level.

Still hunting involves moving slowly and quietly

through the woods, stopping frequently to scan the surroundings for deer. This technique requires patience and awareness.

- Move into the wind to prevent deer from catching your scent.
- Use natural cover to break up your outline and blend into the environment.

A hunter might slowly work their way through a dense thicket, taking a few steps at a time, then pausing to listen and look for any signs of deer. The key is to mimic the natural movements and sounds of the forest, remaining as unobtrusive as possible.

Calling and rattling can be effective techniques, especially during the rut. Using a grunt call to mimic the sounds of a buck or doe can attract deer to your location. Rattling antlers together simulates the sound of bucks fighting and can draw in curious or territorial bucks.

- Ensure you are well-hidden and ready to take a shot when using these techniques.
- Combine grunt calls with rattling to increase effectiveness.

For instance, using a grunt call followed by a series of rattles can entice a buck into a shooting lane, as they come to investigate the source of the sounds.

Hunting waterfowl, such as ducks and geese, requires specific strategies tailored to the birds' habits and aquatic environments. Success in waterfowl hunting depends on understanding bird behavior and using the appropriate gear. Let's delve into effective strategies for waterfowl hunting.

Recognizing the feeding and resting patterns of waterfowl is crucial. Ducks and geese typically feed in agricultural fields during early morning and late afternoon, while they rest on water bodies during midday. Positioning yourself in these feeding areas during peak times increases your chances of a successful hunt.

Setting up decoys is a fundamental tactic in waterfowl hunting. Decoys attract birds by simulating a safe and attractive landing zone.

- Use a variety of decoys to mimic different species and increase realism.
- Arrange decoys in natural-looking patterns such as the "U" or "J" formation to guide birds into shooting range.

A hunter might set up a dozen duck decoys in a shallow pond, ensuring they are spread out to avoid looking unnatural. Adding motion decoys can create ripples, enhancing the illusion of a live flock.

- Calling is another essential strategy. Effective calling can lure birds towards your decoys and into shooting range.
- Use a variety of calls to match the species and situation, including feeding calls, mating calls, and distress calls.
- Practice different calling techniques to sound as realistic as possible.

For example, using a feeding chuckle to simulate ducks actively feeding can attract others to join, while a comeback call can bring back birds that might have initially passed over your spread.

Camouflage and concealment are critical in waterfowl hunting. Birds have excellent vision and can easily spot unnatural movements and colors.

- Wear appropriate camo that matches the environment, whether it be reeds, grass, or open water.
- Use a well-concealed blind to hide movements and stay out of sight.

In a marsh setting, a hunter might use a layout blind covered with local vegetation to blend seamlessly with the surroundings, ensuring that ducks or geese flying overhead do not spot any movement.

Adapting to changing conditions is vital for waterfowl hunting. Weather, light, and bird behavior can all affect your success.

- Be prepared to adjust your setup based on wind direction and bird flight patterns.
- Stay flexible and move locations if birds are not responding to your decoys or calls.

A hunter might notice that ducks are landing in a different part of the field due to wind changes and will need to relocate the blind and decoys to that new area to stay effective.

Strategies for Waterfowl

Waterfowl hunting, including ducks and geese, requires specialized strategies that account for the birds' behavior, the aquatic environments they inhabit, and the equipment needed to effectively lure and harvest them. Here, we delve into the tactics that can significantly enhance your chances of a successful waterfowl hunt.

Understanding the feeding and resting patterns of waterfowl is fundamental. Ducks and geese typically feed in agricultural fields or wetlands during the early morning and late afternoon, then rest on larger bodies of water during midday. Timing your hunt to coincide with these peak activity periods increases your chances of encountering birds.

Decoy placement is a cornerstone of successful waterfowl hunting. Decoys attract birds by simulating a safe and attractive landing zone. Using a variety of decoys to mimic different species and increase realism can be particularly effective. Arranging decoys in natural-looking patterns, such as the "U" or "J" formation, helps guide birds into shooting range.

For example, a hunter might set up a spread of a dozen duck decoys in a shallow pond. The decoys should be spaced out naturally to avoid looking artificial. Adding a few motion decoys that create ripples can enhance the illusion of a live flock, attracting more ducks to land. Additionally, incorporating some geese decoys can add realism and increase the chances of attracting both ducks and geese.

Calling is another essential strategy in waterfowl hunting. Effective calling can lure birds toward your decoys and into shooting range. Using a variety of calls to match the species and situation, including feeding calls, mating calls, and distress calls, is crucial. Practicing different calling techniques to sound as realistic as possible will improve your effectiveness.

For instance, using a feeding chuckle to simulate ducks actively feeding can attract others to join. When ducks are circling but not committing, a comeback call can bring them back towards your spread. Geese calls, such as honks and clucks, can be used similarly to attract geese.

Camouflage and concealment are critical in waterfowl hunting due to the birds' excellent vision. Wearing appropriate camouflage that matches the environment, whether reeds, grass, or open water, helps you blend in. Using a well-concealed blind to hide movements and stay out of sight is essential.

In a marsh setting, a hunter might use a layout blind covered with local vegetation to blend seamlessly with the surroundings. This ensures that ducks or geese flying overhead do not spot any movement. Properly concealing your blind with natural materials found in the environment can make a significant difference.

Weather conditions play a significant role in waterfowl hunting. Birds are more likely to be active during windy or overcast days, as they feel safer from predators. Adapting to changing conditions is vital.

Being prepared to adjust your setup based on wind direction and bird flight patterns is necessary. For example, if the wind shifts, you may need to reposition your decoys and blind to ensure that approaching birds land into the wind, providing optimal shooting opportunities. In areas like the Chesapeake Bay, hunters often face rapidly changing weather and must be adept at adjusting their strategies on the fly.

Patience and adaptability are key traits for successful waterfowl hunters. Sometimes birds will not respond immediately to your calls or decoys. Waiting them out and making small adjustments can turn the tide in your favor.

Real-world examples highlight the importance of these strategies. A hunter in the flooded timber of Arkansas might place a dozen mallard decoys around a small opening in the trees, creating a natural-looking spread. They use a combination of feeding calls and quacks to attract passing ducks, ensuring their blind is well-concealed with natural materials. As the sun rises and ducks begin to move, the hunter remains patient, adjusting calls and decoys as needed to bring birds within range.

In another scenario, a hunter in the rice fields of California might use a spread of both duck and goose decoys, setting them up in a large U-shape to guide birds into the center. They wear camo that blends with the golden hues of the rice stubble and use a layout blind for concealment. When the wind shifts, they quickly reposition their decoys to keep the birds landing into the wind. By adapting to the changing conditions and maintaining patience, they increase their chances of a successful hunt.

Successful waterfowl hunting requires a combination of understanding bird behavior, effective decoy placement, skilled calling, proper camouflage, and adaptability to weather conditions. By employing these strategies and being prepared to make adjustments in the field, hunters can significantly enhance their chances of success. Whether in marshes, fields, or open water, the principles of timing, realism, and patience are fundamental to bringing home waterfowl.

Methods for Upland Birds

Hunting upland birds, such as pheasants, grouse, quail, and partridges, requires a distinct set of tactics and techniques tailored to these birds' unique behaviors and habitats. Effective upland bird hunting combines keen observation, strategic movement, and the use of well-trained dogs. Here, we delve into the methods that can enhance your success in upland bird hunting.

Understanding the habitat preferences of upland birds is crucial for locating them. These birds typically inhabit grasslands, brushy fields, agricultural edges, and forest clearings. Early morning and late afternoon are prime times for hunting, as birds are most active during these periods. Observing these habitats and identifying likely spots where birds might be feeding or roosting can set the stage for a successful hunt.

Employing well-trained bird dogs significantly enhances upland bird hunting. Dogs such as pointers, setters, and retrievers are trained to locate, flush, and retrieve birds. They use their keen sense of smell to find birds hidden in dense cover, making them invaluable hunting partners.

- **Pointers and Setters:** These breeds are adept at locating birds and holding a point, indicating the bird's location without flushing it. This allows the hunter to approach and prepare for a shot.
- **Retrievers:** Once a bird is shot, retrievers are trained to bring the bird back to the hunter, ensuring that no game is lost.

For example, a hunter in the Midwest might use a well-trained English Pointer to work a field of tall grass. The dog zigzags through the cover, pausing and pointing whenever it scents a bird.

The hunter then approaches, ready to take a shot when the bird flushes.

Walking and flushing is another common method for hunting upland birds. This technique involves walking through the bird's habitat, either alone or with a group, to flush birds into the open. It's important to move slowly and methodically, watching for any signs of birds taking flight.

- **Solo Hunting:** When hunting alone, move quietly and maintain a steady pace. Pause frequently to listen for any sounds of movement.
- **Group Hunting:** In a group, hunters often walk in a line abreast, maintaining a safe distance between each other. This ensures that the entire area is covered, and birds flushed by one hunter can be taken by another.
- **Real-world example:** In the rolling hills of the Dakotas, a group of hunters might walk in a line through a field of CRP (Conservation Reserve Program) grassland. As they move forward, pheasants flush from the cover, providing opportunities for shots from multiple angles.

Effective shooting techniques are essential for upland bird hunting. Birds often flush suddenly and fly rapidly, requiring quick reflexes and accurate shooting. Practicing shooting clays can help improve your skills before heading into the field.

- **Lead the Bird:** When a bird flushes, aim slightly ahead of it to account for its speed and direction. The distance you lead the bird depends on its speed and angle of flight.
- **Swing Through:** Start your gun behind the bird and swing through it, firing as you pass it. This method helps ensure that you stay on target and maintain a smooth motion.
- **Follow Through:** After pulling the trigger, continue the swing to avoid stopping short and missing the shot.

Covering different types of upland birds requires adapting your strategies. Each species has unique behaviors and habitat preferences that influence hunting tactics.

- **Pheasants:** These birds prefer dense cover like tall grasses and cornfields. They often run before flushing, so be prepared for sudden, close-range shots.
- **Grouse:** Found in forested areas with thick underbrush, grouse can be difficult to spot until they flush. They are known for their explosive flight, requiring quick shooting.
- **Quail:** Typically found in brushy areas and fields, quail often flush in coveys, providing multiple targets at once. Quick, accurate shooting is essential as they scatter in different directions.

Maintaining ethical hunting practices is paramount. This includes respecting bag limits, ensuring accurate shooting to minimize wounded birds, and retrieving all downed game. Ethical hunting ensures the sustainability of upland bird populations and maintains the integrity of the sport.

- **Bag Limits:** Always adhere to the legal bag limits for each species. This helps maintain healthy bird populations and ensures future hunting opportunities.
- **Clean Shots:** Aim for clean, quick kills to reduce suffering. Properly trained dogs can assist in retrieving birds, ensuring none are left behind.
- **Habitat Conservation:** Supporting habitat conservation efforts helps protect the environments where upland birds thrive. This can include participating in conservation programs and supporting organizations dedicated to preserving natural habitats.

Successful upland bird hunting relies on understanding the birds' habitats, employing well-trained dogs, using effective shooting techniques, and maintaining ethical practices. By adapting your methods to the specific behaviors and environments of different upland bird species, you can increase your chances of a successful and rewarding hunt. Whether walking through fields with a trusty pointer or working with a group to flush birds from cover, the strategies outlined here provide a comprehensive approach to upland bird hunting. With practice and experience, these techniques become second nature, leading to more successful and enjoyable hunting experiences.

Tips for Small Game Hunting

Hunting small game, such as rabbits, squirrels, and hares, requires a unique set of skills and techniques. Unlike big game hunting, small game hunting involves quicker reactions and a more intimate knowledge of the environment and the habits of your prey. Here, we delve into effective strategies and tips that can enhance your success when hunting small game.

First and foremost, understanding the behavior and habitat of the small game you are targeting is crucial. Rabbits and hares, for instance, are often found in brushy areas, fields, and forest edges where they can find both food and cover. Squirrels, on the other hand, are typically found in wooded areas with plenty of trees and a reliable food source, such as acorns or nuts. Knowing where to look and what signs to watch for can significantly increase your chances of success.

- **Rabbits and Hares:** These animals tend to stay close to thick cover where they can quickly escape from predators. Look for them in areas with dense underbrush, along the edges of fields, or near hedgerows. Pay attention to signs like droppings, tracks, and gnawed vegetation, which can indicate their presence.
- **Squirrels:** Squirrels are most active during the early morning and late afternoon. Look for them in mature hardwood forests where they forage for nuts and seeds. Listen for the sounds of rustling leaves or the chatter of squirrels communicating with each other.

Scouting is an essential part of small game hunting. Before heading out, spend time observing the areas where you plan to hunt. Look for signs of activity, such as tracks, droppings, and feeding sites. This can help you identify the best spots to focus your efforts.

Using the right equipment is also key to successful small game hunting. A lightweight, accurate firearm is ideal for quick, precise shots.

- **Rifles:** A .22 caliber rifle is a popular choice for small game hunting due to its accuracy and low recoil. It allows for precise shots at small targets without causing excessive damage to the meat.
- **Shotguns:** A 20-gauge shotgun is also effective, especially when hunting in areas with dense cover where quick, close-range shots are necessary. Using small shot sizes, such as #6 or #7.5, helps to avoid over-penetration and meat damage.

Stealth and patience are critical when hunting small game. Move slowly and quietly through the hunting area, taking care to avoid making noise that could alert your quarry. Wear camouflage or earth-toned clothing that blends with the surroundings to reduce visibility. Pay attention to the wind direction to prevent your scent from alerting animals.

For example, when hunting squirrels, move slowly through the forest, stopping frequently to listen and watch for movement. Squirrels often freeze when they sense danger, making them difficult to spot. By remaining still and patient, you can catch them moving again and take a shot.

Hunting with dogs can be highly effective for certain types of small game, particularly rabbits and hares. Dogs can flush game out of cover, making it easier to take a shot.

- **Beagles:** This breed is particularly well-suited for rabbit hunting. Beagles use their keen sense of smell to track and flush rabbits from dense cover.
- **Terriers:** These dogs are also effective for flushing small game from burrows and thick vegetation.

For instance, hunting rabbits with a pack of beagles involves releasing the dogs to search through brushy areas and hedgerows. The dogs' barking alerts the hunter to the location of the rabbits as they flush out, providing opportunities for a shot.

Seasonal considerations are important in small game hunting. Different seasons offer varying challenges and opportunities.

- **Fall and Winter:** These are prime seasons for hunting squirrels and rabbits. The lack of foliage makes spotting game easier, and animals are more active as they forage for food to store for winter.
- **Spring and Summer:** Hunting during these seasons can be more challenging due to thick vegetation, but it can also be rewarding. Young animals are more abundant, and some species, like squirrels, may have multiple litters per year.

Adapting your techniques to the season and weather conditions can enhance your success. In the fall, for instance, focus on areas with abundant food sources like acorn-bearing oak trees for squirrel hunting. In the winter, look for rabbit tracks in the snow leading to cover.

Maintaining ethical hunting practices is paramount in small game hunting. This includes ensuring accurate shots to minimize suffering, retrieving all downed game, and adhering to bag limits and hunting regulations. Ethical hunting helps sustain healthy wildlife populations and ensures the future of the sport.

- **Accurate Shots:** Aim for the head or vital areas to ensure a quick, humane kill. Practice shooting regularly to maintain accuracy.
- **Retrieving Game:** Use dogs or your own tracking skills to locate and retrieve all downed game, ensuring nothing is wasted.
- **Adhering to Regulations:** Familiarize yourself with local hunting laws and regulations, including season dates and bag limits. This helps maintain sustainable wildlife populations.

Hunting small game requires a unique blend of knowledge, skill, and patience. By understanding the behavior and habitat of your quarry, using the appropriate equipment, and employing effective stealth and scouting techniques, you can increase your chances of success. Hunting with dogs, adapting to seasonal changes, and maintaining ethical practices are all part of a comprehensive approach to small game hunting. With practice and experience, these methods will become second nature, leading to more rewarding and enjoyable hunts.

CHAPTER 2
BEHAVIORAL INSIGHTS

Seasonal Behavior Patterns

Understanding the seasonal behavior patterns of game animals is crucial for any hunter aiming to increase their success in the field. Game animals, like deer, waterfowl, and upland birds, exhibit distinct behaviors throughout the year that are influenced by changes in weather, food availability, and breeding cycles. By recognizing these patterns, hunters can better predict animal movements and behaviors, making their hunts more strategic and effective.

In the **spring**, many game animals enter a period of increased activity. This season is characterized by mild weather and an abundance of new growth, providing ample food sources. For deer, the spring is a time for recovery and growth after the harsh winter months. Bucks begin to regrow their antlers, and does focus on nurturing their fawns. This period of growth and renewal means that deer are often found in areas with abundant forage, such as fields and forest edges. Hunters can take advantage of this by scouting these areas for signs of deer activity, such as tracks, droppings, and browsing marks on vegetation.

Waterfowl behavior in the spring is dominated by migration and breeding. Ducks and geese return to their northern breeding grounds, and they can be seen in large flocks during this period. Hunters looking to capitalize on spring waterfowl opportunities should focus on staging areas where birds rest and feed during their migration. Wetlands, marshes, and flooded fields are prime locations for setting up decoys and blinds. Observing flight patterns and timing your hunts to coincide with peak migration periods can greatly enhance your success.

During the **summer**, many game animals become more reclusive due to the heat and increased human activity in their habitats. Deer, for example, often retreat to shaded, cooler areas during the hottest parts of the day. Early morning and late evening are the best times to observe and hunt deer in the summer, as they are more active during these cooler periods. Additionally, water sources become critical during the summer months. Hunters should focus on areas near rivers, streams, and ponds where deer and other game animals are likely to visit for hydration.

For upland birds such as grouse and pheasants, the summer is a time for raising their young. These birds often remain hidden in dense cover to protect their chicks from predators. Scouting for these birds can be challenging, but focusing on areas with thick vegetation and abundant insect life can increase your chances of locating them. Hunters should be mindful of the delicate nature of this season and take care to avoid disturbing nests and young birds.

The fall is arguably the most critical season for hunters, as it coincides with the rut for many big game species and the migration of waterfowl. The rut is the breeding season for deer, and it brings about significant changes in behavior, particularly for bucks. During the rut, bucks become more active and less cautious as they search for does. This increased movement and aggression make them more visible and approachable. Hunters can use calls, scents, and decoys to attract bucks during this period. Setting up near travel corridors, rub lines, and scrapes can also be effective strategies.

Waterfowl migration in the fall provides hunters with ample opportunities to harvest ducks and geese. As birds move southward to their wintering grounds, they stop at various feeding and resting areas along the way. Hunters should focus on these staging areas and use decoys and calls to attract birds within range. Understanding the timing of migration and weather patterns that influence bird movements, such as cold fronts, can significantly enhance your hunting success.

In the **winter**, game animals adapt to the harsh conditions by altering their behavior and habitat use. Deer, for instance, tend to congregate in areas with good cover and reliable food sources. They become more predictable in their movements, often using the same trails to travel between bedding and feeding areas. Hunters can take advantage of this by focusing on these travel routes and setting up stands or blinds in strategic locations. Snow can also be an asset, as it makes tracking deer easier and highlights their movements through the landscape.

Waterfowl hunting in the winter focuses on late-season strategies. As lakes and ponds freeze over, ducks and geese concentrate on remaining open water areas. These spots can become prime hunting locations. Hunters should also pay attention to agricultural fields where birds feed on leftover grain. Using larger decoy spreads and ensuring your blind is well-camouflaged can help attract wary late-season birds.

For small game such as rabbits and squirrels, winter is a time of increased visibility as the leaves fall and cover becomes sparse. These animals must remain active to find food, making them easier to locate and hunt. Focusing on areas with dense brush piles, fallen trees, and other cover that provides shelter can increase your chances of success. Using snow to track movements and locate feeding areas can also be highly effective.

Real-world examples highlight the importance of understanding seasonal behavior patterns. In the Midwest, hunters might focus on cornfields during the fall, where deer are attracted to the abundant food. In the northern states, late-season waterfowl hunters might target open water areas on large rivers, where ducks and geese congregate as smaller bodies of water freeze over. Each season presents unique opportunities and challenges, and adapting your strategies to these changes is key to successful hunting.

Feeding and Mating Habits of Game

Understanding the feeding and mating habits of game animals is critical for hunters who want to maximize their success in the field. These behaviors are key determinants of animal movement and activity patterns, and they vary significantly across species. By comprehending these habits, hunters can better predict where and when to find their quarry, enhancing their chances of a successful hunt.

Feeding habits are often dictated by the

availability of food sources, which can change with the seasons. Deer, for instance, exhibit varied feeding behaviors based on the time of year. During the spring and summer, they primarily consume green vegetation, such as leaves, grasses, and forbs. This period of abundant food allows them to gain weight and prepare for the leaner months ahead. Hunters can find deer in open fields and forest edges where this vegetation is plentiful. As autumn approaches, their diet shifts to mast, such as acorns, nuts, and fruits, which are high in energy and essential for building fat reserves for winter.

- **Key Food Sources:** Understanding the primary food sources during different seasons can help hunters locate deer. In the fall, oak trees that produce acorns are prime locations to find deer feeding. Setting up near these areas can provide excellent hunting opportunities.
- **Feeding Times:** Deer typically feed during the early morning and late afternoon. Knowing these peak feeding times can help hunters plan their outings more effectively.

Waterfowl, such as ducks and geese, have feeding habits that are closely tied to their migratory patterns. These birds require high-energy foods to sustain their long flights. During migration, they stop at various staging areas to feed and rest. Wetlands, flooded fields, and coastal marshes are prime feeding grounds, where they consume grains, aquatic plants, and invertebrates. Hunters targeting waterfowl should focus on these areas during migration periods.

- **Migration Timing:** Understanding the timing of migration is crucial. Cold fronts and changing weather patterns often trigger migrations, providing hunters with the best opportunities to intercept birds.
- **Feeding Behavior:** Waterfowl often feed in large groups, which can make them easier to spot. Using decoys and calls to mimic feeding flocks can attract birds to your hunting area.

Upland birds, such as pheasants, grouse, and quail, have feeding habits that are influenced by their habitat. These birds forage for seeds, insects, and berries in grasslands, brushy areas, and forest clearings. Their feeding activity is often concentrated in the early morning and late afternoon, similar to deer.

- **Habitat Preferences:** Knowing the preferred habitats of upland birds can help hunters locate them. For example, pheasants are often found in agricultural fields and grassy areas, while grouse prefer dense forest cover.
- **Feeding Patterns:** Upland birds move frequently while foraging, covering large areas in search of food. Hunters should be prepared to walk and flush birds from cover.

The mating habits of game animals are equally important for hunters to understand. The rut, or breeding season, for deer is a time of heightened activity and movement. Bucks become more aggressive and less cautious as they search for does, making them more visible and easier to hunt. This period varies by region but typically occurs in the fall.

- **Rut Behavior:** During the rut, bucks create rubs and scrapes to mark their territory and attract does. Hunters can use this behavior to their advantage by setting up near these signs of activity.
- **Calling and Rattling:** Using calls and rattling antlers to mimic the sounds of other deer can attract bucks looking for a fight or a mate. This can be an effective strategy during the peak of the rut.

For waterfowl, mating habits influence their behavior during the spring and fall migrations. During the spring, ducks and geese return to their breeding grounds and engage in courtship displays. Understanding these behaviors can help hunters identify the best times and locations to hunt.

- **Courtship Behavior:** Observing courtship

behavior, such as mating calls and displays, can provide clues about where waterfowl are congregating. Hunters can use decoys and calls to mimic these behaviors and attract birds.

- **Breeding Grounds:** Knowing the locations of key breeding grounds can help hunters anticipate where waterfowl will be during migration.

Upland birds also exhibit distinct mating behaviors that can be exploited by hunters. For instance, male grouse engage in drumming displays to attract females, while male pheasants crow and display their colorful plumage.

- **Displaying Behavior:** Identifying areas where males display can lead hunters to concentrations of birds. Setting up in these areas during the breeding season can increase hunting success.
- **Nesting Habits:** Understanding the nesting habits of upland birds can also be beneficial. During the nesting season, females stay close to their nests, and males are often nearby.

Hunters can focus their efforts in areas with suitable nesting cover.

Real-world examples illustrate the importance of understanding feeding and mating habits. In the Midwest, hunters often focus on oak groves during the fall to take advantage of deer feeding on acorns. Similarly, waterfowl hunters on the Mississippi Flyway use knowledge of migratory patterns and feeding habits to set up decoy spreads in flooded fields, attracting large numbers of ducks and geese.

A deep understanding of the feeding and mating habits of game animals is essential for successful hunting. By knowing what and where animals eat, as well as their breeding behaviors, hunters can better predict animal movements and position themselves for optimal hunting opportunities. Whether it's setting up near a feeding area, using calls to attract a mate-seeking buck, or mimicking courtship displays to lure waterfowl, these insights are invaluable tools for any hunter.

BOOK 5

ADVANCED WEAPONRY AND ARCHERY

CHAPTER 1
EXPLORING FIREARMS

Bolt-Action, Semi-Automatic, and Lever-Action Rifles

Understanding the different types of rifles and their respective mechanisms is fundamental for any hunter. Each rifle type—bolt-action, semi-automatic, and lever-action—has unique characteristics, advantages, and limitations. Choosing the right one can significantly impact your hunting experience and success.

Bolt-action rifles are renowned for their accuracy and reliability. These rifles operate by manually manipulating the bolt, which opens the breech, ejects the spent cartridge, and chambers a new round. This design allows for a solid lock-up, contributing to the rifle's precision. Bolt-action rifles are commonly used in big game hunting where long-range accuracy is crucial.

For instance, a hunter pursuing elk in the wide-open spaces of the Rocky Mountains might prefer a bolt-action rifle chambered in a powerful caliber like.30-06 Springfield or.300 Winchester Magnum. The bolt-action's inherent accuracy helps make precise shots at extended ranges, which is often necessary in such expansive terrains.

- **Accuracy:** The bolt-action mechanism ensures a secure lock-up, enhancing accuracy.
- **Reliability:** With fewer moving parts compared to semi-automatics, bolt-action rifles are less prone to jamming and are easier to maintain.
- **Versatility:** Available in a wide range of calibers, making them suitable for various types of game.

Semi-automatic rifles offer a different set of advantages, primarily in their ability to quickly fire consecutive shots. These rifles automatically cycle the action, ejecting the spent cartridge and chambering a new round with each pull of the trigger. This feature is particularly beneficial in situations where follow-up shots may be necessary.

A semi-automatic rifle chambered in.308 Winchester, for example, might be ideal for hunting wild boar in dense forests. The quick follow-up shots can be crucial when dealing with fast-moving or multiple targets. Moreover, the semi-automatic action can be advantageous in predator control scenarios, where swift successive shots are often needed to manage the situation effectively.

- **Rapid Fire Capability:** Allows for quick follow-up shots, which can be essential in certain hunting scenarios.
- **Ease of Use:** Semi-automatic rifles are often easier to shoot accurately for beginners due to the reduced recoil and smooth operation.
- **Modern Features:** Many semi-automatic rifles come with advanced features like adjustable stocks, rails for optics, and ergonomic designs.

Lever-action rifles hold a nostalgic appeal and offer unique advantages. These rifles operate by manipulating a lever located around the trigger guard, which cycles the action. Lever-action rifles are often associated with classic American hunting and are particularly effective in thick brush or wooded areas.

For example, a hunter chasing whitetail deer in the dense woods of the eastern United States might choose a lever-action rifle chambered in .30-30 Winchester. The compact size and quick cycling action of the lever gun allow for fast handling and quick follow-up shots in tight, close-range encounters.

- **Handling and Speed:** Lever-action rifles are known for their quick cycling and ease of handling, making them ideal for close-range hunting.
- **Compact Design:** The shorter barrel and overall length make them suitable for use in dense cover where maneuverability is crucial.
- **Historical Significance:** Many hunters appreciate the traditional aspect of lever-action rifles, which have been a part of American hunting heritage for generations.

Choosing the right caliber and action type is equally important. The caliber of the rifle determines its suitability for different types of game and hunting environments. Larger calibers are generally used for big game, offering more stopping power, while smaller calibers are suitable for varmints and small game, providing precision without excessive damage to the meat.

When selecting a rifle, consider the type of game you are hunting and the typical distances you will be shooting. A bolt-action rifle in a caliber like .270 Winchester or .308 Winchester is versatile and effective for a wide range of game, from deer to elk. These calibers offer a balance of power, accuracy, and manageable recoil.

- **Big Game Hunting:** For larger game like elk or moose, calibers such as .300 Winchester Magnum or 7mm Remington Magnum provide the necessary power and long-range performance.
- **Medium Game Hunting:** Calibers like .243 Winchester and .30-30 Winchester are excellent for deer and antelope, offering sufficient power with moderate recoil.
- **Small Game and Varmint Hunting:** For smaller game, calibers like .22 Long Rifle or .17 HMR offer precision and minimal meat damage.

Ultimately, the choice of rifle and caliber should match the hunter's experience, the game being pursued, and the hunting environment. For example, a novice hunter might start with a bolt-action rifle in .243 Winchester, which provides a good balance of power and low recoil, making it easier to handle and shoot accurately.

Choosing the Right Caliber and Action Type

Selecting the appropriate caliber and action type for your rifle is a critical decision that can significantly impact your hunting experience and success. The right combination ensures you have sufficient stopping power for the game you are pursuing, manageable recoil, and the accuracy needed for ethical kills. Here, we delve into the factors that influence this choice, offering detailed insights to help you make an informed decision.

When choosing a caliber, consider the size of the game you plan to hunt. Larger calibers are designed for big game, providing the necessary energy to ensure a quick, humane kill. Smaller calibers are suitable for varmints and small game, offering precision without causing excessive damage to the meat.

For big game hunting, such as elk, moose, or bear, you need a caliber with significant stopping power. Calibers like .300 Winchester Magnum and 7mm Remington Magnum are popular choices due to their ability to deliver high energy at long distances. These calibers are effective for taking down large animals quickly, minimizing the chances of wounding and losing the game.

- **.300 Winchester Magnum:** Known for its flat trajectory and powerful impact, this caliber is ideal for hunting large game in open terrains. It offers excellent long-range accuracy, making it suitable for shots over 300 yards.
- **7mm Remington Magnum:** This caliber provides a good balance of power and recoil, making it a versatile choice for big game hunters. Its high velocity and flat trajectory ensure precise shots at extended ranges.

For medium game, such as deer and antelope, calibers like .243 Winchester, .270 Winchester, and .308 Winchester are highly effective. These calibers offer a balance of stopping power and manageable recoil, making them suitable for a wide range of hunting scenarios.

- **.243 Winchester:** This caliber is excellent for hunters who need a light-recoiling, accurate round. It's particularly effective for deer-sized game and offers flat shooting capabilities, making it a great choice for younger or less experienced hunters.
- **.270 Winchester:** Renowned for its versatility, the .270 Winchester provides sufficient

power for medium to large game. Its flat trajectory and moderate recoil make it a favorite among hunters in North America.
- **.308 Winchester:** This is one of the most popular hunting calibers due to its versatility and effectiveness. It's suitable for a wide range of game and hunting environments, offering reliable performance with manageable recoil.

Small game and varmint hunting require calibers that provide precision without excessive power. Calibers like .22 Long Rifle and .17 HMR are ideal for these purposes, allowing for accurate shots on small targets without causing unnecessary damage.

- **.22 Long Rifle:** This classic caliber is perfect for small game hunting, such as rabbits and squirrels. It offers minimal recoil and is widely available, making it a great choice for beginners and seasoned hunters alike.
- **.17 HMR:** Known for its high velocity and flat trajectory, the .17 HMR is excellent for varmint hunting. It's capable of taking down small targets at longer distances with pinpoint accuracy.

The choice of action type—bolt-action, semi-automatic, or lever-action—also plays a crucial role in hunting effectiveness. Each action type has its own set of advantages and is suited to different hunting scenarios.

Bolt-action rifles are favored for their accuracy and reliability. The manual operation of the bolt ensures a strong lock-up, which contributes to the rifle's precision. This makes bolt-action rifles ideal for long-range shooting, where accuracy is paramount.

- **Reliability:** Fewer moving parts mean less chance of mechanical failure, making bolt-action rifles incredibly reliable in the field.
- **Precision:** The strong lock-up and solid construction contribute to consistent, accurate

shooting. This is crucial when making long-range shots on wary game.

Semi-automatic rifles offer the advantage of rapid follow-up shots, which can be essential in certain hunting situations. The ability to fire multiple rounds quickly without manually cycling the action is beneficial when hunting fast-moving or multiple targets.

- **Quick Follow-Up Shots:** Ideal for scenarios where quick successive shots are necessary, such as hunting wild boar or predator control.
- **Ease of Use:** Reduced recoil and smoother operation can make semi-automatic rifles easier to handle, especially for beginners.

Lever-action rifles are known for their speed and handling, making them suitable for hunting in thick cover or wooded areas. The lever mechanism allows for quick cycling of the action, enabling fast follow-up shots.

- **Speed and Maneuverability:** Lever-action rifles are easy to handle and quick to cycle, making them perfect for close-range hunting in dense environments.
- **Historical Appeal:** Many hunters appreciate the traditional aspect of lever-action rifles, which have a rich history in American hunting lore.

Real-world examples highlight the importance of choosing the right caliber and action type. A hunter pursuing elk in the mountainous regions might opt for a bolt-action rifle chambered in.300 Winchester Magnum, appreciating the caliber's power and the rifle's long-range accuracy. On the other hand, a hunter targeting feral hogs in the dense brush of the southern United States might choose a semi-automatic rifle in.308 Winchester, valuing the quick follow-up shots and manageable recoil for close encounters.

Selecting the right caliber and action type for your hunting rifle is essential for achieving success and ensuring ethical kills. By considering the size of the game, the hunting environment, and your personal preferences, you can choose a rifle that meets your needs and enhances your effectiveness in the field. Whether you prefer the precision of a bolt-action, the rapid fire of a semi-automatic, or the handling of a lever-action, the right combination of caliber and action type will significantly contribute to your hunting experience.

CHAPTER 2
BOWS AND ARROWS

Understanding Compound, Recurve, and Crossbows

Choosing the right bow for hunting is an essential step that can significantly influence your effectiveness and enjoyment in the field. Each type of bow—compound, recurve, and crossbow—has unique characteristics, advantages, and limitations. Understanding these differences will help you make an informed decision that aligns with your hunting style and preferences.

Compound bows are among the most popular choices for modern hunters due to their advanced technology and precision. They use a system of pulleys and cables, which provide a mechanical advantage that makes drawing and holding the bowstring easier. This let-off feature allows hunters to hold the bow at full draw for extended periods with less effort, aiding in accurate and steady aiming. Compound bows are also known for their adjustable draw weight and length, making them versatile and customizable to fit individual needs.

A hunter in the Midwest, targeting whitetail deer, might choose a compound bow for its precision and ease of use. The ability to hold the bow at full draw with minimal strain allows for

a more accurate shot when the perfect moment arises. Additionally, compound bows often come equipped with accessories like sights, stabilizers, and arrow rests, enhancing their performance and accuracy.

- **Adjustable Draw Weight and Length:** Allows for customization to fit the hunter's strength and shooting style.
- **Let-Off Feature:** Reduces the holding weight at full draw, making it easier to aim steadily.
- **Accessories:** Many compound bows come with options for adding sights, stabilizers, and other enhancements to improve accuracy and performance.

Recurve bows, in contrast, offer a more traditional and simplistic approach to archery. These bows have a classic design, with limbs that curve away from the archer when unstrung. This design stores more energy and delivers it more efficiently when the bow is shot. Recurve bows require more physical strength and skill to use effectively, as they lack the mechanical advantages of compound bows. However, many hunters appreciate the challenge and traditional feel of recurve bows.

For example, a hunter in the dense forests of

the Pacific Northwest might use a recurve bow to hunt elk. The simplicity and quiet operation of a recurve bow can be advantageous in close-range encounters where stealth is crucial. The hunter's skill in drawing and aiming the bow becomes paramount, making each successful shot a testament to their proficiency.

- **Traditional Design:** Appeals to hunters who prefer a classic and straightforward approach to archery.
- **Efficiency:** The recurve design stores and delivers energy effectively, though it requires more physical effort.
- **Stealth:** The quiet operation of a recurve bow can be beneficial in close-range hunting situations.

Crossbows combine elements of both archery and firearms, offering unique advantages for hunters. These bows have a horizontal limb assembly mounted on a stock, similar to a rifle, and are shot by pulling a trigger. Crossbows are easy to use and require less physical strength to operate, making them accessible to a wider range of hunters. They provide high accuracy and power, often with a shorter learning curve compared to other types of bows.

A hunter pursuing wild boar in the southeastern United States might opt for a crossbow due to its power and ease of use. The crossbow's ability to remain cocked and ready to shoot allows the hunter to focus on aiming without the need for physical strain. This can be particularly advantageous when hunting from a ground blind or a tree stand, where movement needs to be minimized.

- **Ease of Use:** Requires less physical strength and has a shorter learning curve.
- **Accuracy and Power:** Delivers high accuracy and powerful shots, suitable for a variety of game.
- **Versatility:** Can be used in various hunting scenarios, including from blinds and tree stands.

Each type of bow—compound, recurve, and crossbow—has specific scenarios where it excels. Understanding these contexts helps hunters choose the right tool for their specific hunting needs. For instance, compound bows are excellent for hunters who prioritize precision and customization. Recurve bows are ideal for those who value tradition and simplicity, while crossbows offer a blend of power and ease of use, suitable for various hunting situations.

Real-world examples illustrate the practical applications of these bows. A compound bowhunter in the open plains of Kansas might rely on the precision and accessories of their bow to make long-range shots on mule deer. In contrast, a traditional archer using a recurve bow in the thick brush of Florida might appreciate the bow's quiet operation and challenge of close-range hunting. A crossbow hunter in the forests of Pennsylvania might benefit from the crossbow's power and ease of use when targeting black bear.

Selecting the Best Arrows and Broadheads

Choosing the right arrows and broadheads is crucial for successful bow hunting. The correct selection not only improves accuracy and penetration but also ensures a humane kill. This involves understanding the various components of arrows, the types of broadheads available, and how these choices impact your hunting efficiency.

Arrows are made from different materials, each with its advantages. The most common materials are aluminum, carbon, and carbon-aluminum hybrids. Each type of material affects the arrow's weight, strength, and flexibility.

- **Aluminum Arrows:** These arrows are durable and provide consistent performance.

They are heavier than carbon arrows, which can be beneficial for increasing penetration on larger game. However, they can bend if they hit a hard surface, which can affect their accuracy.

- **Carbon Arrows:** Known for their lightweight and strength, carbon arrows offer excellent speed and accuracy. They are less likely to bend compared to aluminum arrows, making them more reliable over long distances. This makes them a popular choice for many hunters.
- **Carbon-Aluminum Hybrids:** These arrows combine the best features of both materials. They offer the strength and straightness of aluminum with the lightweight and durability of carbon. This combination provides a balance of speed, accuracy, and penetration.

When selecting arrows, it's essential to consider the arrow spine, which refers to the stiffness of the arrow. The spine must match the draw weight and length of your bow to ensure proper flight. An arrow that is too stiff or too flexible can result in poor accuracy and inconsistent performance.

- **Matching Arrow Spine:** Check the manufacturer's recommendations for your bow to find the appropriate spine. For example, a hunter using a compound bow with a draw weight of 70 pounds might require a stiffer arrow compared to someone using a recurve bow with a lower draw weight.

The arrow's fletching, or vanes, are also critical for stable flight. Fletchings come in different shapes and sizes, and they can be made from either plastic (vanes) or feathers. The purpose of fletching is to stabilize the arrow in flight, ensuring it flies straight and accurately.

- **Plastic Vanes:** These are durable and perform well in various weather conditions. They are less likely to get damaged and are a popular choice for many hunters.
- **Feathers:** While they offer excellent stability and accuracy, feathers are more susceptible to damage from weather and rough handling. They are often preferred by traditional archers using recurve or longbows.

Choosing the right broadhead is equally important. Broadheads come in two main types: fixed-blade and mechanical (expandable) broadheads. Each type has its pros and cons, and the choice depends on personal preference, the type of game, and the hunting environment.

- **Fixed-Blade Broadheads:** These broadheads have blades that are fixed in place and do not move. They are known for their durability and reliability, making them suitable for large game and tough conditions. Fixed-blade broadheads require careful tuning to ensure they fly accurately, as their larger surface area can affect arrow flight.

Example: A hunter pursuing elk in rugged terrain might choose a fixed-blade broadhead for its reliability and penetration power.

- **Mechanical Broadheads:** These broadheads have blades that expand upon impact. They typically fly like field points, providing better accuracy and longer range. Mechanical broadheads can cause significant damage due to their larger cutting diameter, but they may be less reliable in certain conditions, such as dense brush.

Example: A hunter targeting whitetail deer in an open field might prefer mechanical broadheads for their accuracy and the larger wound channel they create.

Weight is another crucial factor when selecting broadheads. The standard weight for broadheads is typically 100 grains, but 125 grains or heavier options are available for hunters needing more penetration. The weight of the broadhead affects the arrow's front-of-center (FOC) balance, which impacts flight stability and penetration.

- **Balancing Weight and Accuracy:** Heavier broadheads provide better penetration, especially on larger game, but may require adjustments to arrow spine and tuning. Ensuring that the broadhead weight is compatible with your arrows and bow setup is essential for maintaining accuracy and performance.

Tuning your arrows and broadheads to your bow setup is essential for achieving optimal performance. This involves adjusting your bow's settings and ensuring that the arrows fly true with the broadheads attached. Paper tuning, bare shaft tuning, and walk-back tuning are common methods used by archers to fine-tune their setup.

- **Paper Tuning:** Shooting an arrow through a piece of paper to observe the tear pattern. This helps identify any flight issues and make necessary adjustments to the bow or arrow.
- **Bare Shaft Tuning:** Shooting an unfletched arrow to see how it flies compared to a fletched arrow. This can reveal imbalances in the arrow setup or bow tuning.
- **Walk-Back Tuning:** Shooting arrows at increasing distances to ensure consistent arrow flight and grouping. Adjustments are made based on the results to achieve better accuracy.

Real-world examples highlight the importance of selecting the right arrows and broadheads. A hunter using a compound bow with carbon arrows and mechanical broadheads might achieve precise shots on whitetail deer in open fields, benefiting from the combination of speed, accuracy, and significant wound channels. In contrast, a traditional archer with a recurve bow might prefer aluminum arrows with fixed-blade broadheads, ensuring reliability and penetration on larger game like elk or moose.

Selecting the best arrows and broadheads is a critical aspect of bow hunting that requires careful consideration of various factors. The choice of arrow material, spine, fletching, and broadhead type and weight all contribute to the overall performance and success in the field. By understanding these components and how they interact with your bow setup, you can enhance your accuracy, penetration, and overall hunting effectiveness. Whether you're targeting small game with lightweight arrows and mechanical broadheads or pursuing big game with heavy-duty fixed-blade broadheads, the right combination will ensure a humane and successful hunt.

CHAPTER 3
ESSENTIAL ACCESSORIES

Ammo Selection and Maintenance

Choosing the right ammunition and maintaining it properly is crucial for any hunter aiming to ensure consistent performance and ethical kills in the field. The selection of ammo involves understanding the different types available, their intended use, and how they affect your hunting experience. Proper maintenance ensures that your ammo remains reliable and effective when it matters most.

Ammo selection begins with understanding the type of game you are hunting and matching your ammunition to your firearm and its intended use. Different calibers and bullet types are designed for various hunting scenarios, and selecting the right one can significantly impact your success.

For big game hunting, such as deer, elk, and bear, you need ammunition that delivers enough power to ensure a humane kill. This typically means choosing larger calibers and heavier bullets that offer deep penetration and controlled expansion. Common calibers for big game hunting include.30-06 Springfield,.308 Winchester, and.300 Winchester Magnum. Each of these calibers provides sufficient power to take down large animals effectively.

- **.30-06 Springfield:** Known for its versatility and effectiveness, this caliber is a popular choice for hunters targeting a variety of big game. It offers a good balance of power, accuracy, and manageable recoil.
- **.308 Winchester:** This caliber is favored for its accuracy and performance over medium to long ranges. It is suitable for deer and elk hunting and is widely available.
- **.300 Winchester Magnum:** Ideal for larger game and longer shots, this caliber offers exceptional power and penetration. It is particularly useful in open terrains where long-distance accuracy is critical.

Bullet type is another critical factor in ammo selection. Different bullets are designed for various purposes, and choosing the right one can affect both your accuracy and the effectiveness of your shot.

- **Soft Point (SP):** These bullets are designed to expand upon impact, creating a larger wound channel and ensuring a humane kill. They are suitable for big game hunting where deep penetration and controlled expansion are necessary.
- **Hollow Point (HP):** These bullets are designed to expand rapidly upon impact,

making them ideal for small game and varmint hunting. The rapid expansion minimizes over-penetration and maximizes the damage to the target.

- **Full Metal Jacket (FMJ):** These bullets are designed for target shooting and practice. They offer deep penetration but minimal expansion, making them less suitable for hunting but excellent for training and range use.

Maintaining your ammunition is just as important as selecting the right type. Proper storage and handling ensure that your ammo remains reliable and performs as expected when needed. Here are some essential tips for ammo maintenance:

- **Storage:** Store your ammunition in a cool, dry place to prevent moisture and humidity from degrading the powder and primers. Using airtight containers and silica gel packs can help keep moisture at bay.
- **Handling:** Avoid touching the bullets and primers directly with your fingers, as oils and dirt from your skin can affect their performance. Use gloves or handle them by the casing to maintain their integrity.
- **Inspection:** Regularly inspect your ammunition for any signs of corrosion, damage, or deformities. Damaged ammo can cause malfunctions and potentially harm your firearm or yourself. Discard any questionable rounds.

Cleaning your firearm regularly also contributes to maintaining your ammunition's effectiveness. A clean firearm ensures that bullets are chambered and fired correctly, reducing the risk of jams and misfires. Make sure to follow the manufacturer's guidelines for cleaning and lubricating your firearm.

Real-world examples illustrate the importance of proper ammo selection and maintenance. A hunter in the Rocky Mountains pursuing elk might choose .300 Winchester Magnum soft point bullets to ensure deep penetration and a humane kill at long distances. By storing the ammo in an airtight container with silica gel packs, the hunter ensures that the rounds remain dry and reliable throughout the hunt. Regular inspections before each outing help identify any damaged rounds, preventing potential issues in the field.

In the dense forests of the Southeast, a hunter targeting wild boar might opt for .308 Winchester hollow point bullets to ensure rapid expansion and maximum damage. Properly storing the ammunition in a climate-controlled environment helps maintain its reliability. Handling the bullets carefully and inspecting them before use ensures that each round performs as expected when the moment of truth arrives.

Additionally, hunters who engage in both target practice and hunting should consider keeping separate supplies of FMJ rounds for practice and hunting-specific rounds for the field. This ensures that practice sessions do not deplete the specialized hunting ammunition and that hunters remain familiar with the performance characteristics of both types.

Maintaining a detailed log of your ammunition usage, including purchase dates, storage conditions, and performance notes, can also be beneficial. This log helps track the age and condition of your ammo, ensuring that older rounds are used first and that any performance issues are documented for future reference.

Optimizing Sighting Systems

Optimizing your sighting system is a critical aspect of enhancing accuracy and effectiveness in hunting. A well-chosen and properly adjusted sighting system can make the difference between a successful hunt and a missed opportunity. This involves understanding the different types of sighting systems available, how to properly mount and zero them, and regular maintenance to ensure consistent performance.

Sighting systems come in various types, including iron sights, telescopic sights (scopes), red dot sights, and holographic sights. Each type has its advantages and is suitable for different hunting scenarios.

Iron sights are the most basic type of sighting system, consisting of a front sight and a rear sight. They are reliable and durable, often used as backup sights in case other systems fail. However, they require more skill and practice to use effectively, especially at longer distances.

- **Front and Rear Sights:** Proper alignment of these sights is crucial for accuracy. The shooter must align the front sight post within the rear sight aperture, ensuring that the target is in focus.

Telescopic sights, or scopes, are the most popular sighting systems among hunters. They offer magnification, which helps in identifying and aiming at distant targets. Scopes come in various magnification ranges and objective lens sizes, each suited to different types of game and hunting environments.

- **Fixed vs. Variable Power Scopes:** Fixed power scopes have a single magnification level, making them simpler and more durable. Variable power scopes allow hunters to adjust magnification, offering greater flexibility for different ranges and target sizes.
- **Objective Lens Size:** Larger objective lenses gather more light, improving visibility in low-light conditions. This is particularly useful during dawn and dusk when many game animals are most active.

Red dot sights provide a simple aiming point without magnification. They are ideal for close to medium-range shooting and are particularly effective in fast-action scenarios where quick target acquisition is essential. Red dot sights are often used in hunting situations where rapid shots are needed, such as hunting wild boar or small game in dense cover.

Reticle Options: Red dot sights come with different reticle options, including single dots, circles, and crosshairs. Choose a reticle that offers quick target acquisition without obstructing your view.

Holographic sights are similar to red dot sights but use a hologram of a reticle that appears to be projected in front of the sight. They offer the same advantages as red dot sights but often with more complex reticle options and enhanced accuracy.

- **Parallax-Free Design:** Many holographic sights are parallax-free, meaning the reticle remains on target even if your head moves slightly. This feature ensures consistent accuracy regardless of shooting position.

Proper mounting and zeroing of your sighting system are crucial steps to ensure accuracy. Mounting involves securely attaching the sight to your firearm, ensuring it remains stable and aligned. Zeroing adjusts the sight to align with the point of impact of your bullets, ensuring that your shots hit where you aim.

- **Mounting:** Use high-quality mounts and rings to attach your sight. Ensure that all screws are tightened to the manufacturer's specifications to prevent movement or misalignment.
- **Bore Sighting:** This preliminary step involves aligning the sight with the bore of the firearm. Use a bore sight tool to get the sight roughly aligned with the target before live firing.
- **Zeroing:** After bore sighting, shoot groups at a specific distance to fine-tune the sight. Adjust the windage (horizontal) and elevation (vertical) settings until the point of aim matches the point of impact. Most hunters zero their rifles at 100 yards, but

this distance can vary based on the expected hunting range.

Regular maintenance of your sighting system ensures that it remains reliable and accurate. This includes cleaning, checking for damage, and re-zeroing as necessary.

- **Cleaning:** Keep lenses clean and free of debris. Use a lens cloth and appropriate cleaning solutions to prevent scratches and maintain clarity.
- **Inspection:** Regularly inspect mounts and screws to ensure they are tight and secure. Check for any signs of wear or damage that could affect performance.
- **Re-Zeroing:** Changes in environment, handling, or accidental drops can affect zero. Re-zero your sight periodically, especially before the hunting season, to ensure continued accuracy.

Real-world examples highlight the importance of optimized sighting systems. A hunter targeting deer in dense forests might prefer a low-power variable scope or a red dot sight for quick target acquisition at short ranges. Properly mounted and zeroed, these sights allow the hunter to quickly align the reticle with the target, ensuring fast and accurate shots.

In open plains or mountainous regions where long-range shots are common, a hunter might choose a high-power variable scope with a large objective lens. The magnification allows for precise aiming at distant targets, while the larger lens improves visibility in low-light conditions. Regular maintenance and re-zeroing ensure that the scope performs reliably, even after rough handling or environmental changes.

Another example is a hunter pursuing wild boar in thick brush. A holographic sight provides a clear, quick aiming point that remains on target despite slight head movements. The parallax-free design ensures accuracy in fast-paced hunting scenarios where quick reflexes are essential.

In conclusion, optimizing your sighting system is a critical component of successful hunting. By understanding the different types of sights, properly mounting and zeroing them, and maintaining them regularly, hunters can enhance their accuracy and effectiveness in the field. Whether using iron sights, telescopic scopes, red dot sights, or holographic sights, the right sighting system tailored to the hunting environment and game pursued will significantly contribute to a successful hunt.

BOOK 6

FIELD DRESSING AND MEAT PROCESSING

CHAPTER 1
BASICS OF FIELD DRESSING

A Step-by-Step Field Dressing Guide

Field dressing is a crucial skill for any hunter, ensuring that the meat from your game is preserved in the best possible condition from the moment of the kill. Proper field dressing minimizes spoilage, reduces the weight of the animal for transport, and ensures that the meat is safe and palatable for consumption. Here is a detailed, step-by-step guide to field dressing your game, along with the essential tools and techniques you'll need.

The first step in field dressing is preparation. Make sure you have the necessary tools at hand and have a clear understanding of the process. Essential tools include a sharp knife, a bone saw, latex gloves, and a clean cloth or paper towels. Additionally, having a small tarp or a piece of plastic sheeting can help keep the carcass clean and provide a sanitary work surface.

Once you've located your downed game and ensured that it is indeed dead, approach it from behind to avoid any potential reflex movements. This is particularly important with large game, such as deer or elk. Once you've confirmed that the animal is dead, position it on its back with

its legs spread apart. This position provides the best access to the abdominal cavity.

Start by making a small incision just below the breastbone. Be careful to only cut through the skin and avoid puncturing the internal organs, as this can contaminate the meat with digestive contents or bile. Extend the incision downwards towards the pelvis. As you cut, use your free hand to gently lift the skin and abdominal muscles away from the organs to avoid accidental punctures.

- **Initial Incision:** Start below the breastbone and extend towards the pelvis, taking care to avoid puncturing internal organs.
- **Lifting Skin:** Use your free hand to keep the skin and muscles clear of internal organs, reducing the risk of contamination.

Next, extend the incision upwards towards the sternum. Again, be careful to avoid the internal organs. This incision will allow you to reach inside the chest cavity and access the heart and lungs, which need to be removed to cool the carcass quickly and prevent spoilage. At this point, you should have a clear view of the animal's internal organs.

Reaching inside the abdominal cavity, carefully

cut the diaphragm, the muscle that separates the chest cavity from the abdominal cavity. This will allow you to access the heart and lungs more easily. Pull these organs out through the chest opening, being cautious not to rupture them.

- **Diaphragm Cutting:** Slice through the diaphragm to access the chest cavity.
- **Removing Organs:** Pull out the heart and lungs gently to avoid rupturing them.

Once the chest cavity is clear, move back to the lower abdomen. Carefully cut around the anus and the urinary tract, tying off the intestines with a piece of string or a zip tie if necessary. This prevents any waste material from contaminating the meat. Continue to work methodically, pulling the intestines and stomach out of the abdominal cavity. Be mindful of the bladder, which can rupture easily and contaminate the meat with urine.

- **Securing the Intestines:** Tie off the intestines to prevent contamination.
- **Removing the Digestive Tract:** Pull out the intestines and stomach carefully, avoiding the bladder.

Once all the internal organs are removed, take a moment to inspect the cavity for any remaining debris or blood clots. Use a clean cloth or paper towels to wipe down the inside of the carcass, removing as much blood as possible. This helps cool the meat and slows the growth of bacteria.

- **Cleaning the Cavity:** Wipe down the inside of the carcass to remove blood and debris.

After the cavity is clean, consider propping open the chest cavity with sticks or using a spreader to allow air circulation. This helps the carcass cool more efficiently. If the weather is warm, you may need to pack the cavity with ice to speed up the cooling process.

Transporting the carcass is the final step. If the animal is large and needs to be quartered for transport, use a bone saw to separate the legs from the body. Always ensure that the cuts are clean to avoid splintering the bones, which can damage the meat. Once the carcass is in manageable pieces, place them in game bags or wrap them in clean cloth to keep them protected from dirt and insects during transport.

- **Propping Open the Chest:** Use sticks or a spreader to improve air circulation.
- **Cooling the Carcass:** Pack with ice if necessary to speed up cooling.

The tools you use for field dressing are just as important as the technique itself. A sharp, durable knife is indispensable. It should be easy to handle and maintain its edge throughout the entire process. Many hunters carry a small sharpening tool to keep the knife in optimal condition. A bone saw is necessary for cutting through bones when quartering the animal. It should be compact and sharp, designed specifically for the tough bones of large game.

- **Sharp Knife:** Essential for making precise cuts and avoiding accidents.
- **Bone Saw:** Useful for quartering large game and making clean cuts through bone.
- **Latex Gloves:** Keep your hands clean and reduce the risk of contamination.
- **Tarp or Plastic Sheeting:** Provides a clean surface and helps keep the carcass sanitary.
- **Cloth or Paper Towels:** Useful for cleaning the carcass and removing blood.

In summary, field dressing is a skill that requires knowledge, practice, and the right tools. By following these steps and taking care to avoid contamination, you can ensure that your game meat remains in excellent condition from the field to your freezer. Proper field dressing not only enhances the quality and safety of the meat but also honors the animal by making the most of your harvest.

Essential Tools and Techniques

Field dressing an animal is a vital skill for any hunter, ensuring that the meat is preserved in the best possible condition from the moment of the kill until it reaches the kitchen. The right tools and techniques are indispensable for performing this task efficiently and cleanly. This section will delve into the essential tools and techniques required for effective field dressing, highlighting the importance of each and providing practical tips for their use.

Having the proper **tools** is the foundation of successful field dressing. Each tool has a specific purpose and contributes to the overall efficiency and cleanliness of the process.

- **Sharp Knife:** The cornerstone of any field dressing kit. A high-quality, sharp knife is crucial for making clean, precise cuts. A fixed-blade knife is often preferred for its strength and reliability, though folding knives with locking mechanisms can also be effective. The blade should be around 4-6 inches long, offering a balance between control and cutting power. Example: The Benchmade Hidden Canyon Hunter is a popular choice among hunters for its durable steel blade and comfortable grip, ensuring precision and ease of use.
- **Bone Saw:** Necessary for cutting through bones when quartering large game. The saw should be compact and specifically designed for the tough bones of large animals. A good bone saw helps in making clean cuts without splintering, which can damage the meat. Example: The Gerber Vital Pack Saw is lightweight and efficient, making it ideal for cutting through the pelvic bone and ribcage.
- **Latex or Nitrile Gloves:** Keeping your hands clean reduces the risk of contaminating the meat. Gloves also protect your hands from the elements and from potential zoonotic diseases. Nitrile gloves are particularly durable and puncture-resistant, making them a reliable choice for field dressing.
- **Tarp or Plastic Sheeting:** This provides a clean surface to lay out the carcass, helping to keep the meat free from dirt and debris. It's especially useful in muddy or wet conditions. Example: A compact, foldable tarp like the Stansport Reinforced Multi-Purpose Tarp is easy to carry and deploy in the field.
- **Cloth or Paper Towels:** Useful for cleaning the carcass and wiping away blood. Keeping the meat clean from blood helps in the cooling process and improves the quality of the meat.
- **Game Bags:** These breathable, lightweight bags are designed to keep insects and dirt off the meat while allowing it to cool. They are essential for transporting meat back to camp or your vehicle. Example: Alaska Game Bags are renowned for their durability and effectiveness in protecting meat during transport.

Proper **techniques** are just as important as having the right tools. Each step in the field dressing process should be performed with care to ensure the meat is kept in optimal condition.

1. **Initial Incision and Evisceration:** After confirming the animal is dead, position it on its back with the legs spread apart. Make a small incision just below the breastbone. Carefully extend the cut towards the pelvis, lifting the skin and abdominal muscles away from the internal organs to avoid puncturing them. This prevents contamination from stomach contents or bile.
2. **Removing the Organs:** Once the abdominal cavity is open, carefully cut around the diaphragm to access the chest cavity. Pull out the heart and lungs through the chest opening. Move back to the lower abdomen and carefully cut around the anus and urinary tract, tying off the intestines if necessary. Remove the intestines and stomach, being mindful of the bladder.

3. **Cleaning the Carcass:** After the organs are removed, wipe down the inside of the carcass with cloth or paper towels. Removing as much blood as possible helps the meat cool and slows bacterial growth. Prop open the chest cavity with sticks or a spreader to allow air circulation.

4. **Quartering:** If the animal is large and needs to be transported in pieces, use a bone saw to separate the legs from the body. Ensure cuts are clean to avoid splintering the bones, which can affect the quality of the meat.

5. **Transporting:** Place the meat in game bags to protect it from dirt and insects during transport. Keep the meat cool by packing it with ice or placing it in a shaded, cool area.

Real-world examples can illustrate the effectiveness of these tools and techniques. For instance, a hunter in the Rocky Mountains might use a sharp knife like the Benchmade Hidden Canyon Hunter to quickly and efficiently field dress an elk. The bone saw helps in cutting through the tough pelvic bone, while the game bags ensure that the meat stays clean and cool during the hike back to camp.

In the dense forests of the Midwest, a hunter targeting whitetail deer might use latex gloves and a compact tarp to keep the carcass clean. The Gerber Vital Pack Saw makes quick work of the ribcage, and cloth towels help in cleaning the cavity before transport.

By using these tools and following proper techniques, hunters can ensure that their game meat is of the highest quality. Proper field dressing not only preserves the meat but also honors the animal by making the most of the harvest. The right tools and techniques are essential for any hunter serious about their craft, ensuring that the meat they bring home is clean, safe, and delicious.

Field dressing is a critical skill that requires the right tools and techniques. A sharp knife, bone saw, gloves, tarp, towels, and game bags are essential components of a field dressing kit. By following proper techniques, hunters can ensure that their game meat is preserved in the best possible condition from the field to the kitchen. Real-world examples illustrate the effectiveness of these tools and techniques, highlighting their importance in maintaining the quality and safety of the meat. Whether hunting in the mountains, forests, or fields, the right approach to field dressing ensures a successful and respectful harvest.

CHAPTER 2
BUTCHERING ESSENTIALS

Breaking Down Large Game Efficiently

Breaking down large game efficiently is a crucial skill for hunters. Proper butchering ensures that you maximize the yield of usable meat, maintain quality, and reduce waste. It requires a clear understanding of the animal's anatomy, the right tools, and precise techniques. Here, we will explore the essential steps and tips for butchering large game, using deer as a primary example, although these methods can be adapted for other large game animals such as elk, moose, and wild boar.

The first step in butchering large game begins with proper field dressing. Once the animal has been field dressed and transported to a suitable butchering location, the process of breaking it down can commence. Ensuring that you have a clean, sanitary workspace is vital. This can be a designated area in your garage or an outdoor space that is easy to clean and maintain.

Essential tools for butchering include sharp knives of various sizes, a bone saw, a meat cleaver, meat hooks, a cutting board or table, and a meat grinder if you plan to make ground meat. A knife sharpener is also essential to keep your blades in optimal condition throughout the process. Gloves, aprons, and cleaning supplies are also important to maintain hygiene and safety.

To begin breaking down the deer, hang the carcass by its hind legs. This position allows gravity to assist in the butchering process and provides better access to all parts of the animal. Start by removing the skin. Make incisions around the legs and carefully peel the skin away from the muscle tissue. The goal is to keep the hide intact for potential use while exposing the meat for butchering. Use your knife to cut through the connective tissues, working slowly to avoid damaging the meat.

- **Skinning:** Make incisions around the legs and peel the skin carefully. Use your knife to cut through connective tissues.
- **Gravity Assistance:** Hanging the carcass by its hind legs allows gravity to help in the skinning and butchering process.

Next, remove the head at the base of the neck using a bone saw. This step can be skipped if you plan to mount the head as a trophy. Once the head is removed, you can start breaking down the carcass into primal cuts. The primary sections of a deer include the hindquarters, loin (backstrap), ribs, and forequarters. Each section can be further divided into smaller cuts.

- **Head Removal:** Use a bone saw to remove the head at the base of the neck.
- **Primal Cuts:** The primary sections include hindquarters, loin, ribs, and forequarters.

Begin with the hindquarters. These are the largest and most valuable parts of the deer, containing the most meat. Use a sharp knife to cut through the muscle groups and separate the hindquarters from the carcass. The major cuts from the hindquarters include the sirloin, rump, and round. These cuts can be further processed into steaks, roasts, or stew meat.

- **Hindquarters:** The largest and most valuable sections, containing cuts such as the sirloin, rump, and round.
- **Major Cuts:** These cuts can be processed into steaks, roasts, or stew meat.

Next, remove the backstraps, which run along either side of the spine. These are the most tender cuts of meat on a deer, equivalent to ribeye or tenderloin in beef. To remove the backstraps, make an incision along the spine and carefully peel the muscle away, taking care not to waste any meat. Backstraps are ideal for grilling or pan-searing due to their tenderness and flavor.

- **Backstraps:** The most tender cuts, running along either side of the spine.
- **Removal Technique:** Make an incision along the spine and carefully peel the muscle away.

The ribs can be removed next. Depending on your preference, you can leave the ribs whole for slow roasting or smoking, or you can cut the meat between the bones for individual ribs. Rib meat is flavorful and can be used in various recipes, including barbecues and stews.

- **Ribs:** Can be left whole or cut into individual ribs. They are flavorful and versatile for various recipes.

Finally, focus on the forequarters. These contain the shoulder cuts, which are tougher but flavorful. Use a bone saw to separate the shoulders from the carcass. The shoulder meat is best suited for slow-cooking methods such as braising or smoking, which help tenderize the meat and bring out its rich flavor.

- **Forequarters:** Contain shoulder cuts, which are tougher but flavorful.
- **Cooking Methods:** Best suited for slow-cooking methods like braising or smoking.

After separating the primary cuts, trim any excess fat and connective tissue from the meat. Fat on venison tends to be gamey, so removing as much as possible improves the flavor. Additionally, trim the silver skin, a tough membrane that can make the meat chewy if not removed.

- **Trimming:** Remove excess fat and connective tissue to improve flavor. Trim the silver skin to avoid chewiness.

If you plan to grind some of the meat for burgers, sausages, or other recipes, use a meat grinder. The trimmings from the entire butchering process can be utilized for this purpose. Mixing venison with pork fat or beef tallow can improve the texture and flavor of the ground meat, making it more versatile for various dishes.

- **Grinding Meat:** Utilize trimmings for ground meat. Mixing with pork fat or beef tallow enhances texture and flavor.

Maintaining cleanliness and sanitation throughout the butchering process is critical. Regularly clean your knives, saws, and cutting surfaces to prevent bacterial contamination. Using a solution of water and mild detergent or a specialized meat-safe cleaner ensures that all equipment remains sanitary.

- **Sanitation:** Regularly clean knives, saws, and surfaces to prevent contamination.

Real-world examples of butchering large game

efficiently often highlight the importance of preparation and practice. Experienced hunters know that efficient butchering not only maximizes meat yield but also enhances the quality of the meat. For instance, a hunter in the Rocky Mountains who successfully brings down an elk will benefit significantly from being able to quickly and cleanly butcher the animal, ensuring that the meat remains in prime condition throughout the process. By using the right tools and techniques, the hunter can ensure that the meat is properly preserved and ready for transport back to camp.

Breaking down large game efficiently requires the right tools, knowledge of anatomy, and precise techniques. By following these detailed steps and maintaining a focus on cleanliness and efficiency, hunters can ensure that they make the most of their harvest, honoring the animal and providing high-quality meat for consumption. Whether processing deer, elk, or any other large game, these methods will help ensure a successful butchering process that maximizes yield and maintains the meat's integrity.

Techniques for Processing Small Game

Processing small game is a critical skill for hunters who want to maximize the yield and quality of their harvest. Small game, such as rabbits, squirrels, and birds, requires different techniques compared to large game due to their size and the delicacy of their meat. Proper processing ensures that the meat is preserved in the best possible condition, ready for cooking or storage. This chapter will provide detailed techniques for efficiently processing small game, focusing on practical tips and real-world examples to help you get the most out of your hunt.

The first step in processing small game begins in the field. As soon as the animal is harvested, it's important to field dress it to prevent spoilage. Field dressing involves removing the internal organs, which can harbor bacteria that cause meat to spoil. For small game, this process is relatively straightforward but must be done with care to avoid damaging the meat.

Begin by making a small incision in the abdomen, being careful not to puncture the internal organs. Use your fingers to gently separate the skin from the muscle tissue, working your way around the body. This method helps keep the meat clean and free from hair. Once the skin is loosened, make a longer incision to open the abdominal cavity, then reach in to remove the internal organs. For birds, it's often easier to remove the organs through the vent, a method known as "paunching."

- **Field Dressing:** Make a small incision in the abdomen, avoid puncturing organs, and remove them carefully.
- **Paunching Birds:** Remove organs through the vent to minimize damage to the meat.

After field dressing, the next step is to skin the animal. For rabbits and squirrels, start by making a cut around the hind legs and pulling the skin down towards the head. The skin should come off relatively easily, but you may need to use a knife to cut through tough spots. For birds, plucking is the preferred method. Plucking involves removing the feathers by hand or using a plucking machine. If you prefer skinless birds, you can make an incision and peel the skin off, similar to skinning a rabbit.

- **Skinning Rabbits and Squirrels:** Make a cut around the hind legs and pull the skin down. Use a knife for tough spots.
- **Plucking Birds:** Remove feathers by hand or with a machine, or skin them if preferred.

Once the animal is skinned or plucked, it's time to break it down into usable cuts. For rabbits, the primary cuts include the hind legs, backstrap (loin), and forelegs. Begin by separating the hind legs from the body. Use a sharp knife to cut through the muscle and joints, taking care not to splinter the bones. Next, remove the backstrap by making an incision along the spine and carefully peeling the meat away. Finally, remove the forelegs using a similar technique.

- **Breaking Down Rabbits:** Separate the hind legs, remove the backstrap, and detach the forelegs.
- **Avoiding Bone Splinters:** Use a sharp knife to cut through joints and muscles cleanly.

For squirrels, the process is similar but requires more precision due to their smaller size. Focus on removing the legs and backstrap, ensuring that you get as much meat as possible. The forelegs can be less meaty, but they are still worth keeping for stews or stock.

Birds are typically processed into whole or partial carcasses, depending on their size and your cooking plans. For small birds like doves or quail, you might prefer to leave them whole. Larger birds, such as ducks or pheasants, can be broken down into breasts, thighs, and wings. To remove the breasts, make a cut along the breastbone and peel the meat away from the bone. Thighs and wings can be separated by cutting through the joints.

- **Processing Birds:** Decide whether to leave small birds whole or break down larger birds into breasts, thighs, and wings.
- **Cutting Breasts:** Make a cut along the breastbone and peel the meat away.
- **Removing Thighs and Wings:** Cut through the joints to separate these parts.

Proper storage is essential for preserving the quality of your small game meat. Immediately after processing, rinse the meat in cold water to remove any remaining blood and debris. Pat the meat dry with paper towels and wrap it tightly in plastic wrap or vacuum-seal bags. Store the meat in a cooler with ice if you're in the field, and transfer it to a refrigerator or freezer as soon as possible. For longer storage, freezing is the best option. Label the packages with the type of meat and date of harvest to keep track of your inventory.

- **Rinsing and Drying:** Clean the meat with cold water and pat it dry.
- **Wrapping and Storing:** Use plastic wrap or vacuum-seal bags. Store in a cooler with ice, then move to a refrigerator or freezer.
- **Freezing for Long-Term Storage:** Label packages with the type of meat and date.

Real-world examples of processing small game can illustrate the effectiveness of these techniques. Imagine a hunter in the southern United States who has just harvested several squirrels during a morning hunt. After field dressing the squirrels in the field to remove the organs, the hunter skins them by making cuts around the hind legs and pulling the skin off in one motion. The legs and backstrap are then carefully cut away from the carcass using a sharp knife. The meat is rinsed, dried, and packed in vacuum-seal bags for storage in a cooler until the hunter returns home.

Another example might involve a bird hunter in the Midwest who has bagged a few ducks. The hunter decides to pluck the ducks to keep the skin intact, which enhances the flavor when cooking. Using a plucking machine, the feathers are removed quickly and efficiently. The ducks are then eviscerated by making an incision and pulling out the internal organs. The breasts, thighs, and wings are separated and stored in plastic wrap for transport back to camp.

Processing small game efficiently requires knowledge, practice, and the right tools. By following these detailed steps and maintaining a focus on cleanliness and precision, hunters can ensure that their small game meat is preserved in the best possible condition. Whether processing rabbits, squirrels, or birds, these techniques will help maximize yield, maintain meat quality, and enhance the overall hunting experience. Proper processing not only provides delicious, high-quality meat but also honors the animal by making the most of your harvest.

CHAPTER 3
MAINTAINING YOUR TOOLS

Proper Care for Knives, Saws, and Grinders

Proper care and maintenance of your butchering tools are essential for ensuring their longevity, functionality, and safety. High-quality knives, saws, and grinders can be significant investments, and with appropriate care, they can provide years of reliable service. This chapter will delve into the best practices for maintaining these crucial tools, drawing on practical tips and real-world examples to help you keep your equipment in top condition.

Knives are perhaps the most frequently used tools in butchering and meat processing. Keeping them sharp, clean, and well-maintained is vital for efficient and safe cutting. A dull knife is not only less effective but also more dangerous, as it requires more force to use and is more likely to slip.

Regular sharpening is key to maintaining a sharp edge on your knives. This can be done using a variety of tools, such as whetstones, honing rods, or electric sharpeners. The method you choose will depend on your preference and the type of knife.

- **Whetstones:** These are traditional sharpening stones that come in different grits. To use a whetstone, wet it with water or oil, then hold the knife at the correct angle (typically around 20 degrees) and draw the blade across the stone in a smooth, consistent motion.
- **Honing Rods:** Also known as sharpening steels, these are used to realign the edge of the knife. Regular honing keeps the blade sharp between more thorough sharpenings. Hold the honing rod vertically and draw the knife down and across the rod at the proper angle.
- **Electric Sharpeners:** These devices are convenient and efficient, with slots set at precise angles to ensure consistent sharpening. Follow the manufacturer's instructions for the best results.

In addition to sharpening, it's important to clean your knives thoroughly after each use. This prevents the buildup of residue that can dull the blade and harbor bacteria. Use warm, soapy water and a non-abrasive sponge to clean the blade, then dry it immediately with a soft cloth to prevent rust.

Cleaning Knives: Wash with warm, soapy water

and a non-abrasive sponge. Dry immediately to prevent rust.

Saws are essential for cutting through bone and large sections of meat. Keeping them sharp and clean is crucial for efficient butchering. Bone saws can be sharpened using a file or a specialized saw sharpener. Regular cleaning after use is also important to prevent the buildup of bone dust and meat residue.

- **Sharpening Saws:** Use a file or saw sharpener to maintain the teeth of the saw.
- **Cleaning Saws:** Remove meat and bone residue with warm, soapy water and a brush. Dry thoroughly to prevent rust.

Grinders are used to process meat into ground products or sausage. Maintaining a grinder involves regular cleaning and occasional lubrication. After each use, disassemble the grinder and clean all parts with warm, soapy water. Pay special attention to the blades and grinding plates, as these can harbor meat residue that leads to bacterial growth.

- **Cleaning Grinders:** Disassemble and clean all parts with warm, soapy water. Dry thoroughly to prevent rust.
- **Lubrication:** Apply a food-safe lubricant to the moving parts to ensure smooth operation and prevent rust.

Real-world examples illustrate the importance of proper tool maintenance. Consider a hunter who regularly processes deer during the hunting season. By keeping his knives sharp with a whetstone and honing rod, he ensures that each cut is clean and precise, reducing the effort required and minimizing the risk of accidents. After each butchering session, he thoroughly cleans his knives and saws, preventing rust and maintaining their effectiveness for future use.

In another example, a homesteader who raises and butchers rabbits and chickens uses an electric grinder to process meat for sausages and ground products. After each use, she disassembles the grinder and cleans each part meticulously, ensuring that no meat residue remains. She also applies a food-safe lubricant to the grinder's moving parts, keeping it in optimal condition for the next use.

Proper storage is another critical aspect of tool maintenance. Knives should be stored in a knife block, magnetic strip, or protective sheath to prevent damage to the blades. Saws and grinders should be stored in a dry, cool place to prevent rust and corrosion. If you use your tools infrequently, consider applying a light coating of mineral oil to the blades and metal parts to protect them during storage.

- **Storing Knives:** Use a knife block, magnetic strip, or sheath to protect the blades.

Storing Saws and Grinders: Keep in a dry, cool place. Apply a light coating of mineral oil to prevent rust.

Ensuring the sanitation of your tools is vital for food safety. After cleaning and drying your knives, saws, and grinders, use a sanitizing solution to kill any remaining bacteria. This can be a solution of one tablespoon of bleach to one gallon of water or a commercial food-safe sanitizer. Allow the tools to air dry completely before storing them.

- **Sanitizing Tools:** Use a solution of bleach and water or a commercial sanitizer. Allow tools to air dry completely before storage.

Routine inspections of your tools can help identify any potential issues before they become serious problems. Check for signs of wear, such as nicks in knife blades, worn teeth on saws, or dull grinder blades. Addressing these issues promptly ensures that your tools remain in top working condition.

- **Inspecting Tools:** Regularly check for signs of wear and address any issues promptly.

Proper care and maintenance of your butchering tools are essential for their longevity and effectiveness. Regular sharpening, thorough cleaning, and appropriate storage are key practices that every hunter and home butcher should adopt. By following these guidelines and using real-world examples as a reference, you can ensure that your knives, saws, and grinders remain reliable and safe for all your butchering needs. Taking the time to maintain your tools not only enhances your efficiency but also ensures the quality and safety of the meat you process.

Ensuring Sanitation and Longevity

Ensuring the sanitation and longevity of your butchering tools is crucial for both the safety of your meat and the durability of your equipment. Proper maintenance not only enhances the efficiency of your tools but also prevents the risk of contamination. This section delves into the best practices for keeping your knives, saws, and grinders clean and in optimal working condition.

Sanitation starts with thorough cleaning immediately after use. Blood, tissue, and fat residues can harbor bacteria that pose significant health risks. Each tool—knives, saws, and grinders—requires a specific cleaning approach.

For knives, use warm, soapy water and a non-abrasive sponge to remove any debris. Pay special attention to the area where the blade meets the handle, as this can be a breeding ground for bacteria. Rinse the knife thoroughly with clean water and dry it immediately with a soft cloth to prevent rust.

Saws, especially bone saws, can trap small particles of bone and meat in their teeth. Use a stiff brush to scrub the teeth and joints of the saw with warm, soapy water. Rinse thoroughly and dry completely to prevent rusting.

Grinders are more complex and require disassembly to clean effectively. After each use, take the grinder apart and clean all components with warm, soapy water. Use a brush to remove any trapped meat from the grinding plates and blades. Rinse and dry all parts thoroughly before reassembling.

- **Cleaning Knives:** Use warm, soapy water and a non-abrasive sponge. Rinse and dry immediately.
- **Cleaning Saws:** Scrub with a stiff brush, rinse thoroughly, and dry completely.
- **Cleaning Grinders:** Disassemble, clean each part with warm, soapy water, rinse, and dry thoroughly.

After cleaning, sanitizing your tools is the next critical step. Sanitation involves killing any remaining bacteria that may not have been removed during cleaning. Use a solution of one tablespoon of bleach to one gallon of water, or a commercial food-safe sanitizer. Submerge the tools in the solution or apply it with a clean cloth, ensuring all surfaces are covered. Let the tools air dry completely before storing them.

- **Sanitizing Tools:** Use a bleach solution or commercial sanitizer. Air dry completely.

Proper storage of your tools is essential to prevent contamination and damage. Knives should be stored in a knife block, magnetic strip, or protective sheath to protect the blades from nicks and moisture. Saws and grinders should be kept in a dry, cool place to prevent rust. If storing for an extended period, apply a light coating of mineral oil to metal parts to protect against rust.

- **Storing Knives:** Use a knife block, magnetic strip, or sheath.
- **Storing Saws and Grinders:** Keep in a dry, cool place. Apply mineral oil to prevent rust.

Regular inspection and maintenance are vital for ensuring the longevity of your tools. Check knives for nicks or dullness and sharpen as needed. Inspect saws for any bent teeth or signs of wear and sharpen or replace parts as necessary. For grinders, ensure that all moving parts are functioning smoothly and apply a food-safe lubricant to prevent friction and wear.

- **Inspecting Knives:** Check for nicks or dullness and sharpen as needed.
- **Inspecting Saws:** Look for bent teeth or wear and address as needed.
- **Inspecting Grinders:** Ensure smooth operation and lubricate moving parts.

A practical example of these principles can be seen in the practices of experienced hunters. Take, for instance, a seasoned deer hunter who processes multiple deer each season. After field dressing, he immediately cleans his knives with warm, soapy water and a sponge, ensuring all blood and tissue are removed. He then sanitizes the blades with a bleach solution and lets them air dry. Once dry, he stores them in a knife block in a dry, cool area. Before the next use, he inspects the blades for sharpness and hones them if needed, ensuring they are in optimal condition for the next hunt.

In another example, a homesteader who butchers rabbits and chickens uses a grinder to make sausage and ground meat. After each session, she disassembles the grinder and meticulously cleans each part. She sanitizes the components with a commercial food-safe sanitizer and lets them air dry. During the offseason, she applies a light coat of mineral oil to the metal parts and stores the grinder in a cool, dry place to prevent rust. Regular inspection and lubrication ensure the grinder remains in top condition, ready for use whenever needed.

Ensuring sanitation and longevity of your butchering tools is not only about maintaining their functionality but also about ensuring the safety and quality of the meat you process. By following these detailed steps, you can extend the life of your tools and protect yourself and others from potential health risks. Proper cleaning, sanitizing, and storage, combined with regular inspections, are the cornerstones of effective tool maintenance. Whether you are a seasoned hunter or a homesteader, these practices will help you maintain your tools in peak condition, ensuring efficient and safe butchering processes. Taking the time to properly care for your knives, saws, and grinders will pay off in the long run, both in terms of tool longevity and meat quality.

BOOK 7

PRESERVING YOUR HARVEST

CHAPTER 1
TRADITIONAL AND MODERN PRESERVATION

Methods for Curing and Smoking

Curing and smoking are two of the oldest and most effective methods for preserving meat. These techniques not only extend the shelf life of your harvest but also enhance the flavor, making them a favorite among hunters and outdoor enthusiasts. This section explores the traditional and modern methods of curing and smoking, providing detailed insights and practical tips for preserving your game meat.

Curing involves using salt, sugar, nitrates, or nitrites to draw moisture out of the meat, thereby inhibiting the growth of bacteria and other pathogens. There are two main types of curing: dry curing and wet curing (brining). Each method has its own set of techniques and applications, depending on the type of meat and desired flavor.

- **Dry Curing:** This method involves rubbing the meat with a mixture of salt, sugar, and spices. The meat is then left to cure in a cool, dry place. Dry curing is ideal for hams, bacon, and sausages. The process can take anywhere from a few days to several weeks, depending on the thickness of the meat and the desired level of preservation. For example, a

traditional country ham might be cured for up to a year.

Example: To dry cure a deer ham, mix salt, brown sugar, black pepper, and a bit of curing salt. Rub the mixture thoroughly over the meat, ensuring it gets into all the crevices. Place the meat on a rack in a cool, dry place and let it cure for several weeks. Turn the meat periodically to ensure even curing.

- **Wet Curing (Brining):** This method involves submerging the meat in a solution of water, salt, sugar, and spices. Brining is typically used for poultry, fish, and pork. The meat absorbs the flavors of the brine, resulting in a moist and flavorful product. The duration of brining can range from a few hours to several days, depending on the size and type of meat.

Example: For brining a wild turkey, prepare a brine with water, kosher salt, brown sugar, garlic, and bay leaves. Submerge the turkey in the brine and refrigerate for 24 to 48 hours. Rinse the turkey thoroughly before cooking to remove excess salt.

Smoking is another ancient preservation method that not only prolongs the shelf life of meat but also imparts a distinct, smoky flavor. There are two main types of smoking: hot smoking and cold smoking.

- **Hot Smoking:** This method cooks the meat while smoking it, usually at temperatures between 165°F and 225°F. Hot smoking is suitable for a wide range of meats, including fish, poultry, and sausages. The process typically takes a few hours, depending on the size and type of meat.

Example: To hot smoke venison sausage, preheat your smoker to 200°F. Hang the sausages in the smoker and smoke them for about 3 to 4 hours, or until the internal temperature reaches 160°F. Use hardwoods like hickory or apple for a rich, smoky flavor.

- **Cold Smoking:** This method involves smoking the meat at lower temperatures, typically below 85°F. Cold smoking does not cook the meat but infuses it with smoke flavor over a longer period, often several days. Cold smoking is ideal for items like smoked salmon, bacon, and ham.

Example: For cold smoking bacon, cure the pork belly with a mixture of salt, sugar, and curing salt for a week. Rinse the meat and let it dry in the fridge overnight. Smoke the bacon at 75°F to 85°F for 6 to 12 hours using a cold smoker. Slice and cook the bacon as needed.

Both curing and smoking require careful attention to detail and proper equipment. Essential tools for curing include a reliable scale for measuring ingredients, airtight containers for storing the meat, and a cool, dry place for curing. For smoking, you'll need a quality smoker, wood chips or pellets, a meat thermometer, and plenty of patience.

- **Equipment for Curing:** Use scales for accurate measurements, airtight containers, and ensure a cool, dry place for curing.
- **Equipment for Smoking:** A quality smoker, wood chips or pellets, and a meat

thermometer are essential for consistent results.

When preserving meat, it's important to follow food safety guidelines to prevent spoilage and foodborne illnesses. Always use fresh, high-quality meat, and keep your curing and smoking area clean and sanitary. Monitor the temperature and humidity closely, especially during long curing or smoking processes.

- **Food Safety:** Use fresh meat and keep the area clean. Monitor temperature and humidity closely.

Real-world examples highlight the practical application of these techniques. Consider a hunter who has just harvested a deer. After field dressing and butchering the animal, they decide to dry cure a portion of the meat for future use. Using a traditional dry curing method, they mix a blend of salt, sugar, and spices and thoroughly rub it into the meat. The meat is then placed in a cool, dry place to cure for several weeks. Periodically, the hunter checks the meat, turning it to ensure even curing. The result is a flavorful, preserved meat that can be enjoyed for months.

In another scenario, a fisherman wants to preserve a large catch of salmon. They opt for a wet brine followed by cold smoking. The salmon is submerged in a brine solution for 24 hours, then rinsed and dried. The fish is then placed in a cold smoker and smoked for several days. The end product is a rich, smoky salmon that can be enjoyed in various dishes or stored for later use.

Curing and smoking are not only effective preservation methods but also enhance the flavor and texture of the meat. By mastering these techniques, you can enjoy your harvest for extended periods, making the most of your hunting and fishing efforts. Whether you're using traditional methods passed down through generations or modern techniques with advanced equipment, curing and smoking offer a rewarding way to preserve and savor your game meat.

Techniques for Drying and Dehydrating

Drying and dehydrating are age-old methods of preserving meat that have been utilized by various cultures throughout history. These techniques not only extend the shelf life of the meat but also concentrate its flavors, making it a versatile ingredient for a variety of dishes. In this section, we will delve into the details of drying and dehydrating meat, exploring traditional practices, modern methods, and practical tips for achieving the best results.

Drying meat involves removing moisture through exposure to air, heat, or a combination of both. This method inhibits bacterial growth and enzymatic activity, which are responsible for spoilage. Traditional drying methods rely on natural air circulation and sunlight, while modern techniques often employ dehydrators or ovens to achieve consistent results.

- **Traditional Air Drying:** This method is simple and effective, especially in arid climates. The meat is sliced into thin strips and hung in a well-ventilated area away from direct sunlight. Air drying can take several days to weeks, depending on the thickness of the meat and the environmental conditions. The key to successful air drying is ensuring adequate airflow around the meat to prevent mold growth and spoilage.

Example: Indigenous peoples in North America have used air drying for centuries to preserve buffalo and venison. They cut the meat into thin strips and hang it on wooden racks or tree branches, allowing the dry, windy conditions to remove moisture naturally.

- **Using a Dehydrator:** Dehydrators are modern appliances designed to control temperature and airflow, providing a consistent drying environment. They are particularly useful for those who live in humid or unpredictable climates. Dehydrators come with adjustable trays and temperature settings, allowing for precise control over the drying process.

Example: To dehydrate venison jerky, slice the meat into thin strips, marinate it in your preferred seasoning, and place the strips on the dehydrator trays. Set the temperature to 145°F and dry for 4 to 8 hours, or until the meat is firm and dry but still pliable.

Drying meat in an oven is another effective method, especially if you don't have a dehydrator. This technique involves setting the oven to a low temperature and using the oven's fan or leaving the door slightly ajar to ensure proper airflow.

- **Oven Drying:** Arrange the meat strips on a baking sheet lined with a cooling rack to allow air circulation. Set the oven to the lowest temperature, usually around 170°F, and use the convection setting if available. Prop the oven door open with a wooden spoon to allow moisture to escape. The drying process can take 6 to 12 hours, depending on the meat's thickness and your oven's efficiency.

Example: Making beef jerky in the oven involves marinating thin strips of beef in a mixture of soy sauce, Worcestershire sauce, brown sugar, and spices. Arrange the strips on a cooling rack over a baking sheet, and dry at 170°F for 6 to 8 hours, turning the strips occasionally for even drying.

Dehydrating meat requires careful attention to food safety. It's essential to use lean cuts of meat, as fat can become rancid over time. Before drying, it's recommended to freeze the meat for at least 30 days to kill any parasites that might be present, particularly in wild game. Always slice the meat against the grain for better texture and chewability.

Food Safety Tips:

- Use lean cuts of meat to prevent rancidity.

- Freeze meat for at least 30 days before drying to kill parasites.
- Slice meat against the grain for better texture.

Dehydrating meat can also be combined with other preservation methods, such as marinating or curing, to enhance flavor and shelf life. For example, jerky is often marinated in a mixture of salt, sugar, and spices before drying, adding both flavor and preservative qualities.

- **Marinating for Flavor and Preservation:** Combine soy sauce, Worcestershire sauce, garlic powder, onion powder, and black pepper to create a flavorful marinade. Soak the meat strips in the marinade for 12 to 24 hours before drying. This not only infuses the meat with flavor but also helps to draw out additional moisture.

Example: Marinating venison strips in a blend of soy sauce, apple cider vinegar, brown sugar, and smoked paprika before dehydrating results in a smoky, sweet jerky with enhanced shelf life.

Real-world examples of drying and dehydrating meat illustrate the practicality and effectiveness of these methods. Consider a hunter who has just returned from a successful elk hunt. After field dressing and butchering the elk, they decide to preserve some of the meat using a dehydrator. They slice the meat into thin strips, marinate it in a savory mixture, and lay the strips out on the dehydrator trays. After several hours, the meat is transformed into tender, flavorful jerky that can be stored for months.

In another scenario, a homesteader aims to preserve surplus chicken from their farm. They opt for oven drying, slicing the chicken breasts into thin strips and seasoning them with a mix of herbs and spices. The strips are arranged on a cooling rack and dried in the oven at a low temperature. The resulting dried chicken can be stored in airtight containers and used as a protein-packed snack or added to soups and stews.

Combining traditional and modern techniques can also yield excellent results. For example, air drying can be used initially to reduce moisture, followed by finishing the process in a dehydrator or oven to ensure complete dryness and safety.

- **Combination Methods:** Start with air drying to reduce moisture content, then finish in a dehydrator or oven for complete dryness.

Example: Drying venison initially in a shaded, windy area for a few days, then transferring it to a dehydrator to ensure thorough drying and prevent spoilage.

The versatility of drying and dehydrating makes it an indispensable method for preserving a variety of meats. From beef and pork to wild game and poultry, these techniques allow you to enjoy the fruits of your hunt or farm throughout the year. Properly dried meat not only provides a long-lasting food source but also offers convenience and rich flavors that enhance your culinary repertoire.

Drying and dehydrating are time-tested preservation methods that, when done correctly, offer safe, flavorful, and long-lasting meat products. Whether using traditional air drying or modern dehydrators and ovens, the key to success lies in controlling temperature and airflow, ensuring food safety, and incorporating complementary techniques like marinating for added flavor and preservation. By mastering these methods, you can make the most of your harvest, enjoying the benefits of preserved meat long after the hunt.

CHAPTER 2
FREEZING AND STORAGE SOLUTIONS

Best Practices for Freezing Game Meat

Freezing is one of the most effective methods for preserving game meat, allowing hunters to enjoy their harvest long after the hunting season has ended. Properly freezing game meat involves several critical steps that ensure the meat remains fresh, flavorful, and safe to eat. This section will detail the best practices for freezing game meat, offering practical tips and real-world examples to help you maximize the quality and longevity of your frozen meat.

The first step in freezing game meat is proper preparation. This begins with field dressing and butchering the animal promptly after the kill to minimize bacterial growth and preserve the quality of the meat. Once the meat is processed, it's essential to cool it as quickly as possible to prevent spoilage. Ideally, the meat should be refrigerated at temperatures below 40°F within a few hours of butchering.

Before freezing, it's crucial to trim any excess fat, sinew, and damaged tissue from the meat. Fat can become rancid over time, even in the freezer, and sinew can affect the texture of the meat. By trimming these parts, you ensure that the meat you freeze is of the highest quality.

- **Trimming Meat:** Remove excess fat, sinew, and damaged tissue to improve the quality and longevity of frozen meat.

Once the meat is trimmed, portion it into meal-sized servings. This makes it easier to thaw only what you need and reduces waste. Use a scale to measure portions accurately and package the meat in freezer-safe bags or vacuum-sealed bags to prevent freezer burn. Vacuum sealing is particularly effective because it removes air, which is the primary cause of freezer burn.

- **Portioning Meat:** Divide meat into meal-sized portions and use a scale for accuracy.
- **Packaging:** Use freezer-safe or vacuum-sealed bags to prevent freezer burn.

Label each package with the type of meat, the cut, and the date of freezing. This helps you keep track of your inventory and ensures that you use the oldest meat first, maintaining a first-in, first-out rotation system. Proper labeling also helps you identify specific cuts for particular recipes.

- **Labeling:** Include the type of meat, cut, and

date of freezing on each package to manage inventory effectively.

Freezing meat at the correct temperature is crucial for preserving its quality. Set your freezer to 0°F or lower to ensure that the meat freezes quickly and remains at a consistent temperature. Rapid freezing prevents the formation of large ice crystals, which can damage the meat's cellular structure and affect its texture and flavor. If you have a lot of meat to freeze, consider investing in a chest freezer, which maintains a more stable temperature than a standard refrigerator freezer.

- **Freezer Temperature:** Set the freezer to 0°F or lower for optimal preservation.
- **Rapid Freezing:** Quick freezing prevents large ice crystals from forming and damaging the meat.

Proper organization of your freezer can also help maintain the quality of your game meat. Avoid overloading the freezer, as this can restrict airflow and cause temperature fluctuations. Arrange packages in a way that allows for easy access and rotation. Place newer packages behind older ones to ensure that older meat is used first.

- **Freezer Organization:** Avoid overloading and arrange packages for easy access and rotation.

It's also important to check your freezer regularly to ensure that it's maintaining the correct temperature. A freezer thermometer can help you monitor the temperature accurately. If you experience a power outage, keep the freezer door closed to retain the cold air. A full freezer will stay cold longer than a half-empty one, so consider using ice packs or bottles of water to fill empty space if needed.

- **Monitoring Temperature:** Use a freezer thermometer to ensure consistent freezing temperatures.

- **Power Outages:** Keep the freezer door closed to retain cold air during outages.

Real-world examples illustrate the effectiveness of these best practices. Consider a hunter who has just returned from a successful deer hunt. After field dressing and butchering the deer, they immediately refrigerate the meat to cool it down. They trim excess fat and sinew, then portion the meat into meal-sized servings. Each portion is vacuum-sealed, labeled with the type of cut and the date, and placed in a chest freezer set to 0°F. By following these steps, the hunter ensures that the deer meat remains fresh and flavorful for months.

In another example, a homesteader who raises and butchers rabbits uses similar practices. After processing the rabbits, they trim and portion the meat, then package it in freezer-safe bags. The packages are labeled and arranged in a dedicated chest freezer. Regular checks with a freezer thermometer ensure that the temperature remains consistent, preserving the quality of the meat.

Proper freezing techniques are not limited to just large cuts of meat. Ground meat, sausages, and even cooked game can be frozen effectively if prepared correctly. Ground meat should be packaged in thin, flat portions to allow for quicker freezing and thawing. Sausages should be individually wrapped before being placed in larger freezer bags or vacuum-sealed. Cooked game should be cooled completely before freezing to prevent condensation, which can lead to ice crystals and freezer burn.

- **Ground Meat:** Package in thin, flat portions for quicker freezing and thawing.
- **Sausages:** Individually wrap before placing in larger bags or vacuum-sealing.
- **Cooked Game:** Cool completely before freezing to prevent ice crystals and freezer burn.

The best practices for freezing game meat involve careful preparation, proper packaging, accurate labeling, and consistent temperature maintenance. By trimming excess fat and sinew, portioning meat into meal-sized servings, and using freezer-safe or vacuum-sealed bags, you can significantly extend the shelf life of your game meat. Setting your freezer to the appropriate temperature, organizing it effectively, and monitoring it regularly are also crucial steps in maintaining the quality and safety of your frozen meat. Whether you are preserving a bountiful deer harvest or a few rabbits from your homestead, these techniques will ensure that your game meat remains a delicious and valuable resource throughout the year.

Strategies for Long-Term Storage

Storing game meat for the long term involves more than just placing it in the freezer. Proper long-term storage strategies ensure that your meat remains safe, flavorful, and nutritious over extended periods. By employing the right techniques and paying attention to details, you can preserve the quality of your harvest for months, even up to a year or more. This section will explore various strategies for long-term storage, highlighting practical tips and real-world examples to help you make the most of your game meat.

To begin with, understanding the importance of packaging cannot be overstated. Packaging is the first line of defense against freezer burn and contamination. Freezer burn occurs when air reaches the food's surface and causes it to dry out, resulting in a tough, leathery texture and off-flavors. The best way to prevent this is to use high-quality, airtight packaging materials.

- **Vacuum Sealing:** Vacuum sealing is one of the most effective methods for long-term storage. By removing all the air from the packaging, vacuum sealing significantly reduces the risk of freezer burn. This method also helps retain the meat's moisture and flavor. Vacuum sealers are relatively affordable

and a worthwhile investment for any serious hunter or homesteader.

Example: After a successful hunt, you can process and portion your deer meat. Using a vacuum sealer, package each portion, ensuring all air is removed before sealing. Label each package with the type of cut and the date before placing them in the freezer.

- **Freezer Paper and Plastic Wrap:** If a vacuum sealer is not available, a combination of plastic wrap and freezer paper can be used. Wrap the meat tightly in plastic wrap, ensuring no air pockets are left. Then, wrap it again in freezer paper, which provides an additional barrier against air and moisture. Secure the package with freezer tape to maintain the seal.

Example: For smaller game like rabbits or birds, you can individually wrap each piece in plastic wrap, followed by freezer paper. This double-layer method helps protect the meat from freezer burn, even without a vacuum sealer.

Another key strategy for long-term storage is to ensure your freezer is operating at the optimal temperature. For best results, set your freezer to 0°F (-18°C) or lower. Consistent temperatures help maintain the meat's quality by preventing the growth of bacteria and slowing down enzymatic reactions that can degrade the meat over time.

- **Freezer Temperature:** Monitor your freezer's temperature regularly with a freezer thermometer. This ensures it remains consistently at or below 0°F. Avoid overloading the freezer, as this can restrict airflow and lead to temperature fluctuations.

Example: Keep a digital freezer thermometer inside your chest freezer. Check it weekly to ensure the temperature stays steady. If you notice any fluctuations, adjust the settings or redistribute the items inside to improve airflow.

Proper organization within the freezer is also crucial. An organized freezer not only helps in maintaining consistent temperatures but also makes it easier to manage your inventory and minimize waste.

- **Organizing the Freezer:** Store meat in a way that allows for easy access and rotation. Place newer packages behind older ones, using a first-in, first-out system to ensure older meat is used first. Label all packages clearly with the type of meat, the cut, and the date it was frozen.

Example: Use bins or shelves to separate different types of meat and cuts. Label each section clearly, making it easy to locate specific items and keep track of what needs to be used first.

In addition to proper packaging and organization, it's important to consider the duration for which you plan to store the meat. While game meat can remain safe indefinitely at 0°F, its quality may start to decline after a certain period.

- **Storage Duration:** For best quality, aim to use most frozen game meat within one year. Ground meat and sausages are best used within 3 to 4 months, while larger cuts like steaks and roasts can last up to a year or more if properly packaged and stored.

Example: After processing a wild hog, label packages of ground meat with a use-by date of four months from the freezing date, and larger cuts with a date one year out.

Real-world examples of long-term storage strategies can illustrate their effectiveness. Consider a hunter who processes and freezes several deer each season. By vacuum sealing each portion, labeling packages clearly, and organizing them efficiently in a chest freezer set at 0°F, the hunter ensures that the meat remains in excellent condition throughout the year. Regular checks with a freezer thermometer help maintain the ideal temperature, and the first-in, first-out system ensures that older meat is used first, minimizing waste.

Another example might involve a family who raises and processes chickens. After butchering, the meat is wrapped tightly in plastic wrap and freezer paper, then labeled and stored in an upright freezer. Each package is placed in a designated section for easy access. By using proper packaging and storage techniques, the family enjoys high-quality chicken meat throughout the year, with minimal risk of freezer burn or spoilage.

For those interested in alternative storage solutions, consider the benefits of chest freezers versus upright freezers. Chest freezers often maintain a more consistent temperature, are more energy-efficient, and offer more storage space. However, they can be more challenging to organize and access. Upright freezers, on the other hand, provide easier access and better organization options but may experience more temperature fluctuations and are generally less energy-efficient.

- **Chest Freezers vs. Upright Freezers:** Choose based on your needs and preferences. Chest freezers offer better temperature consistency and efficiency, while upright freezers provide easier access and organization.

Example: A homesteader with limited space might opt for an upright freezer to keep their game meat organized and easily accessible. They can use bins and shelves to separate different cuts and types of meat, ensuring efficient use of space.

Effective long-term storage of game meat involves a combination of proper packaging, maintaining the correct freezer temperature, and organized storage. By using vacuum sealing or a combination of plastic wrap and freezer paper, setting your freezer to 0°F, and keeping it well-organized, you can ensure that your game meat remains safe, flavorful, and nutritious for extended periods. These strategies not only preserve the quality of your harvest but also maximize the value of your hunting and butchering efforts, allowing you to enjoy the fruits of your labor throughout the year.

BOOK 8

CULINARY PREPARATIONS

CHAPTER 1
THE QUALITIES OF GAME MEAT

Nutritional Benefits and Unique Characteristics

Game meat is a prized possession for many hunters and outdoor enthusiasts, offering a variety of nutritional benefits and unique characteristics that set it apart from conventional livestock meats like beef, pork, and chicken. Understanding these qualities can enhance your appreciation of game meat and inform your culinary preparations, ensuring you make the most of your harvest.

One of the most significant nutritional benefits of game meat is its leanness. Wild animals are typically more active than their domesticated counterparts, resulting in lower fat content. This makes game meat a healthier option for those looking to reduce their intake of saturated fats. For example, venison (deer meat) has about half the fat content of beef, making it a leaner alternative that is rich in protein. This high protein content supports muscle growth and repair, making it an excellent choice for those with active lifestyles.

- Lean Protein Game meat like venison has lower fat content compared to beef, making it a healthier protein source.

- **Active Lifestyle:** The high protein content supports muscle growth and repair, ideal for active individuals.

Additionally, game meat is often richer in certain vitamins and minerals compared to farmed meats. Wild game animals forage for a diverse diet that includes a variety of plants, nuts, and berries, which can lead to higher levels of essential nutrients in their meat. For instance, wild game is typically higher in iron and zinc, which are crucial for maintaining healthy blood and immune function. Iron from game meat is highly bioavailable, meaning it is easily absorbed by the body, which can help prevent iron deficiency anemia.

- **Higher Nutrient Density:** Game meat often contains more iron and zinc, essential for blood and immune health.
- **Bioavailable Iron:** Iron from game meat is easily absorbed, helping to prevent deficiencies.

Another unique characteristic of game meat is its flavor profile. The diet and lifestyle of wild animals contribute to a distinct taste that many people find more robust and flavorful than farm-raised meats. For example, the diet of a deer, which consists of a variety of wild plants, gives venison a rich, earthy flavor that can be quite different from the mild taste of beef. Similarly, wild turkey has a deeper, more intense flavor compared to its domestic counterpart, owing to its varied diet and active lifestyle.

- **Distinct Flavor:** The diverse diet of wild animals imparts a rich, robust flavor to game meat.

Examples: Venison has an earthy flavor, while wild turkey offers a more intense taste compared to farm-raised turkey.

The unique textures of game meat also add to its culinary appeal. Because wild game animals are more active, their muscles are more developed, which can result in a firmer texture. This makes game meat well-suited for slow-cooking methods, such as braising or stewing, which help tenderize the meat and bring out its full flavor. On the other hand, some cuts of game meat, like the tenderloin, are incredibly tender and can be cooked quickly over high heat.

- **Varied Textures:** Game meat can range from firm to tender, suitable for various cooking methods.
- **Cooking Methods:** Slow-cooking techniques like braising are ideal for tougher cuts, while tender cuts can be grilled or seared.

Identifying different cuts of game meat is crucial for proper preparation and cooking. Just like with beef or pork, different cuts of game meat vary in tenderness, flavor, and suitable cooking methods. Understanding these cuts can help you make the most of your harvest and ensure you prepare each piece of meat to its fullest potential.

Starting with venison, the most common cuts include the backstrap (loin), tenderloin, shoulder, and hindquarters. The backstrap and tenderloin are the most tender cuts and are best suited for quick cooking methods such as grilling, pan-searing, or roasting. The shoulder and hindquarters, being tougher cuts, are ideal for slow-cooking methods like braising or stewing. These cuts benefit from long, slow cooking times that break down connective tissue and render the meat tender and flavorful.

Venison Cuts:

- **Backstrap (Loin):** Best for grilling, pan-searing, or roasting.
- **Tenderloin:** Extremely tender, ideal for quick cooking.
- **Shoulder and Hindquarters:** Tougher cuts suited for braising or stewing.

For smaller game like rabbits and squirrels, the primary cuts include the legs, loins, and shoulders. Rabbit legs are particularly flavorful and are excellent when braised or slow-cooked. The loins are tender and can be grilled or pan-fried. Squirrel meat, while lean, is best used in stews and casseroles where slow cooking can help tenderize the meat and meld its flavors with other ingredients.

Rabbit and Squirrel Cuts:

- **Legs:** Flavorful and ideal for braising or slow-cooking.
- **Loins:** Tender, suitable for grilling or pan-frying.
- **Squirrel Meat:** Best used in stews and casseroles.

Birds such as wild turkey, pheasant, and duck offer different cuts, including breasts, thighs, and wings. Wild turkey breast is lean and can be dry if overcooked, so it is often brined before cooking to retain moisture. The thighs and legs, being tougher, are better suited for slow-cooking methods. Pheasant and duck also have rich, flavorful meat that benefits from careful cooking to prevent drying out. Duck, in particular, has a higher fat content, which renders well during roasting or grilling.

Bird Cuts:

- **Wild Turkey Breast:** Lean, often brined to retain moisture.
- **Thighs and Legs:** Tougher cuts ideal for slow cooking.
- **Pheasant and Duck:** Rich, flavorful meat that requires careful cooking.

Incorporating game meat into your diet can be both a nutritional and culinary adventure. The lean protein, high nutrient density, and unique flavors make it a valuable addition to any meal. Whether you're grilling a venison tenderloin, braising rabbit legs, or roasting a wild turkey, understanding the qualities of game meat will help you make the most of your harvest. Properly identifying and preparing different cuts ensures that each piece of meat is cooked to perfection, maximizing its flavor and tenderness.

For those new to game meat, experimenting with various cooking methods and recipes can open up a world of culinary possibilities. Traditional recipes, such as venison stew or rabbit fricassee, showcase the rich flavors and textures of game meat. Modern cooking techniques, like sous vide, can also be used to achieve precise cooking results, ensuring that the meat is cooked evenly and retains its moisture.

- **Experimentation:** Try different cooking methods and recipes to explore the full potential of game meat.
- **Traditional and Modern Techniques:** From classic stews to sous vide, various methods can enhance the flavors and textures of game meat.

The nutritional benefits and unique characteristics of game meat make it an exceptional choice for health-conscious individuals and culinary enthusiasts alike. By understanding its qualities and learning to identify and prepare different cuts, you can enjoy the full spectrum of flavors and textures that game meat has to offer. Whether you're a seasoned hunter or a home cook looking to expand your repertoire, game meat provides endless opportunities for delicious, nutritious meals.

Identifying Different Cuts of Meat

Understanding the different cuts of game meat is essential for preparing delicious and nutritious meals. Each cut has unique characteristics that influence its flavor, tenderness, and best cooking methods. This knowledge allows you to make the most of your harvest, ensuring that every part of the animal is utilized to its fullest potential. This section will explore the various cuts of popular game animals like deer, wild boar, rabbit, and birds, providing practical tips and real-world examples to help you identify and prepare them effectively.

Starting with deer, or venison, this animal provides a variety of cuts, each with its own culinary possibilities. The most prized cuts are the backstrap (loin) and the tenderloin. The backstrap runs along either side of the spine and is known for its tenderness and mild flavor. It is best cooked quickly over high heat, making it ideal for grilling, roasting, or pan-searing. The tenderloin, found inside the body cavity along the spine, is even more tender than the backstrap and requires minimal cooking to achieve perfection. These cuts are often reserved for special dishes due to their superior quality.

- **Venison Backstrap:** Best for grilling, roasting, or pan-searing. Known for its tenderness and mild flavor.
- **Venison Tenderloin:** Even more tender than the backstrap, requires minimal cooking.

Moving to the front of the deer, the shoulder or chuck is a tougher cut with a rich, deep flavor. This cut contains more connective tissue, which makes it ideal for slow cooking methods like braising or stewing. Cooking the shoulder low and slow breaks down the connective tissue, resulting in tender, flavorful meat perfect for hearty dishes like stews and pot roasts.

- **Venison Shoulder (Chuck):** Tougher cut, ideal for slow cooking methods such as braising or stewing.

The hindquarters of the deer provide several important cuts, including the rump, top round, bottom round, and sirloin. These cuts vary in tenderness, with the rump being the toughest and the sirloin being the most tender. The top round and bottom round are lean cuts that benefit from marinating before cooking to enhance their flavor and tenderness. These cuts can be roasted, grilled, or used for making jerky.

Venison Hindquarters:

- **Rump:** Tough, best for slow cooking.
- **Top Round and Bottom Round:** Lean, benefits from marinating, suitable for roasting, grilling, or jerky.
- **Sirloin:** Tender, versatile for various cooking methods.

Wild boar, another popular game animal, offers cuts that are similar to domestic pork but with a richer, more robust flavor. The loin and tenderloin are prized for their tenderness and are best suited for quick cooking methods. These cuts can be grilled, roasted, or pan-seared to highlight their natural flavor.

- **Wild Boar Loin and Tenderloin:** Tender cuts, best for grilling, roasting, or pan-searing.

The shoulder of a wild boar, like that of a deer, is tougher and contains more connective tissue. It is ideal for slow cooking methods that break down the tissue and infuse the meat with rich, deep flavors. This cut is perfect for making pulled pork, stews, and braised dishes.

- **Wild Boar Shoulder:** Tough, best for slow cooking methods like braising or making pulled pork.

The hindquarters of wild boar provide cuts such as the ham, which can be cured and smoked to make traditional ham, or roasted and braised. These cuts are versatile and can be prepared in a variety of ways to suit different culinary preferences.

- **Wild Boar Hindquarters (Ham):** Versatile, can be cured, smoked, roasted, or braised.

Rabbit is another game animal with distinct cuts that offer unique culinary opportunities. The legs are the most substantial and flavorful parts of the rabbit, making them ideal for braising or roasting. They benefit from slow cooking methods that tenderize the meat and allow it to absorb the flavors of accompanying herbs and spices.

- **Rabbit Legs:** Flavorful, best for braising or roasting.

The loins of the rabbit are tender and can be cooked quickly over high heat. These cuts are perfect for grilling, pan-frying, or roasting, and they pair well with a variety of sauces and seasonings.

- **Rabbit Loins:** Tender, suitable for grilling, pan-frying, or roasting.

Birds such as wild turkey, pheasant, and duck also offer a variety of cuts, each with distinct characteristics. Wild turkey breasts are lean and can dry out if overcooked, so they are often brined before cooking to retain moisture. These cuts can be roasted, grilled, or sautéed, providing a versatile base for many dishes.

- **Wild Turkey Breast:** Lean, often brined to retain moisture, suitable for roasting, grilling, or sautéing.

The thighs and legs of wild birds are tougher and benefit from slow cooking methods. These cuts are perfect for braising, stewing, or slow-roasting, which helps to tenderize the meat and enhance its flavor.

- **Wild Bird Thighs and Legs:** Tougher, ideal for braising, stewing, or slow-roasting.

Pheasant and duck offer rich, flavorful meat that can be prepared in a variety of ways. Duck, in particular, has a higher fat content, which renders well during roasting or grilling, providing a crispy exterior and juicy interior. Pheasant meat is leaner and can be grilled, roasted, or braised, depending on the cut and desired flavor profile.

- **Pheasant and Duck:** Rich, flavorful meat, duck is best roasted or grilled for a crispy exterior, pheasant can be grilled, roasted, or braised.

Incorporating these different cuts into your cooking repertoire allows you to fully appreciate the unique qualities of game meat. Whether you're grilling a venison tenderloin, slow-cooking a wild boar shoulder, or roasting a wild turkey breast, understanding the characteristics of each cut helps you choose the best cooking method and seasoning to highlight the meat's natural flavors.

Experimenting with various recipes and cooking techniques can further enhance your culinary skills and enjoyment of game meat. Traditional dishes like venison stew, rabbit fricassee, and wild boar pulled pork showcase the rich flavors and textures of these meats. Modern techniques like sous vide can also be used to achieve precise cooking results, ensuring that the meat is cooked evenly and retains its moisture.

- **Experimentation:** Try different recipes and cooking techniques to explore the full potential of game meat.
- **Traditional and Modern Methods:** From classic stews to sous vide, various methods can enhance the flavors and textures of game meat.

Identifying and understanding the different cuts of game meat is essential for making the most of your harvest. Each cut offers unique qualities that influence its flavor, tenderness, and best cooking methods. By mastering the art of butchery and culinary preparation, you can transform your game meat into delicious, nutritious meals that highlight the natural bounty of the wild. Whether you're a seasoned hunter or a home cook looking to expand your repertoire, the diverse cuts of game meat provide endless opportunities for culinary creativity and enjoyment.

CHAPTER 2
MARINADES AND SEASONINGS

Techniques for Marinating and Tenderizing

Marinating and tenderizing game meat is crucial for enhancing its natural flavors and ensuring a tender, enjoyable eating experience. Game meat, being leaner and often tougher than domesticated meats, benefits greatly from these techniques. This section explores the methods for marinating and tenderizing game meat, providing practical tips and real-world examples to help you maximize the flavor and texture of your harvest.

Marinating involves soaking the meat in a seasoned liquid mixture to impart flavor and moisture. The ingredients typically include an acid (such as vinegar, lemon juice, or wine), oil, and a blend of herbs and spices. The acid helps to break down the meat's fibers, making it more tender, while the oil keeps it moist and enhances the flavor absorption. The herbs and spices add depth and complexity to the meat's natural taste.

- **Basic Marinade Composition:** Combine an acid, oil, and herbs/spices. The acid tenderizes the meat, while the oil and spices add flavor.

For example, a classic venison marinade might include red wine, olive oil, crushed garlic, rosemary, thyme, and black pepper. The red wine's acidity helps tenderize the dense muscle fibers of the venison, while the olive oil and herbs infuse the meat with rich, savory flavors. Marinating times can vary, but for tougher cuts like venison shoulder or haunch, an overnight marinade (about 12-24 hours) is recommended to ensure the flavors penetrate deeply.

Example: Venison Marinade: Red wine, olive oil, garlic, rosemary, thyme, black pepper. Marinate for 12-24 hours.

When marinating smaller game such as rabbit or quail, the process is similar but usually requires less time due to the more delicate nature of the meat. A marinade for rabbit might include white wine, lemon juice, olive oil, and a mix of tarragon and mustard. Marinating for 4-6 hours can suffice, ensuring the meat remains tender and flavorful without becoming overly acidic.

Example: Rabbit Marinade: White wine, lemon juice, olive oil, tarragon, mustard. Marinate for 4-6 hours.

Tenderizing game meat can also be achieved through mechanical methods. Using a meat mallet to physically break down the muscle fibers is effective for tougher cuts. This method is particularly useful for cuts like wild boar shoulder or venison round steak. Lightly pounding the meat with a mallet helps to soften the fibers, making it more palatable when cooked. For tougher game birds, such as pheasant or wild turkey, spatchcocking (removing the backbone and flattening the bird) can help ensure even cooking and tenderness.

- **Mechanical Tenderizing:** Use a meat mallet to break down muscle fibers. Effective for tougher cuts like wild boar shoulder or venison round steak.
- **Spatchcocking:** Remove the backbone and flatten game birds for even cooking and tenderness.

In addition to acids and mechanical tenderizing, enzymatic tenderizers are another option. Natural enzymes found in certain fruits, such as papaya (papain) and pineapple (bromelain), can break down proteins and tenderize meat. These enzymes can be included in marinades but should be used carefully as they can over-tenderize the meat if left too long.

- **Enzymatic Tenderizing:** Use natural enzymes from fruits like papaya and pineapple. Effective but requires careful timing to avoid over-tenderizing.

A practical example of enzymatic tenderizing is using a pineapple-based marinade for wild boar. The natural bromelain in pineapple helps break down the tough muscle fibers of the boar, while the fruit's sweetness balances the meat's robust flavor. A typical pineapple marinade might include pineapple juice, soy sauce, brown sugar, and ginger. Marinate the wild boar for 2-4 hours, ensuring the meat becomes tender without becoming mushy.

Example: Wild Boar Marinade: Pineapple juice, soy sauce, brown sugar, ginger. Marinate for 2-4 hours.

Crafting flavorful rubs and seasonings is another essential aspect of preparing game meat. Dry rubs consist of a blend of herbs, spices, and sometimes sugar and salt, which are applied to the meat's surface. Rubs can create a flavorful crust when the meat is cooked, adding texture and enhancing the overall taste.

- **Dry Rubs:** Blend of herbs, spices, salt, and sugar. Creates a flavorful crust and enhances taste.

For instance, a robust dry rub for venison might include smoked paprika, garlic powder, onion powder, ground cumin, brown sugar, and a touch of cayenne pepper. This combination provides a smoky, sweet, and slightly spicy flavor that complements the gamey taste of venison. Apply the rub generously to the meat and let it sit for at least an hour before cooking to allow the flavors to meld.

Example: Venison Dry Rub: Smoked paprika, garlic powder, onion powder, ground cumin, brown sugar, cayenne pepper. Apply and let sit for at least an hour.

Seasoning game birds like pheasant or duck can involve simpler blends that highlight their natural flavors. A basic yet effective seasoning for duck might include sea salt, cracked black pepper, and finely chopped fresh herbs like thyme and sage. This blend enhances the duck's rich flavor without overpowering it. Season the duck generously and let it rest for 30 minutes before cooking.

Example: Duck Seasoning: Sea salt, cracked black pepper, thyme, sage. Season and let rest for 30 minutes.

Marinating and seasoning techniques are not only about tenderizing and flavoring but also about creating a culinary experience that highlights the unique qualities of game meat. Experimenting with different marinades, tenderizing methods, and seasoning blends can open up a world of flavors and textures, making your game meat dishes truly memorable.

Real-world application of these techniques can be seen in the preparation of a wild turkey feast. After spatchcocking the turkey to ensure even cooking, it is marinated in a mixture of apple cider, olive oil, garlic, sage, and thyme for 8-12 hours. This marinade tenderizes the meat and infuses it with a savory, aromatic flavor. Before roasting, a dry rub of smoked paprika, brown sugar, salt, and pepper is applied to create a flavorful crust. The result is a tender, juicy, and flavorful turkey that showcases the best of wild game cooking.

Example: Wild Turkey Preparation: Spatchcock, marinate in apple cider, olive oil, garlic, sage, thyme for 8-12 hours. Apply a dry rub of smoked paprika, brown sugar, salt, and pepper before roasting.

In conclusion, mastering the techniques of marinating and tenderizing game meat, along with crafting flavorful rubs and seasonings, is essential for any hunter or cook looking to elevate their culinary creations. By understanding the principles behind these methods and experimenting with various ingredients and techniques, you can enhance the natural flavors of your game meat and ensure it is tender and delicious. Whether you are preparing venison, wild boar, rabbit, or game birds, these practices will help you create meals that are both nutritious and memorable.

Crafting Flavorful Rubs and Seasonings

Creating rubs and seasonings is an art that enhances the natural flavors of game meat, transforming it into a culinary masterpiece. These blends of herbs, spices, salts, and sometimes sugars are applied to the meat's surface, imbuing it with layers of flavor that penetrate during the cooking process. Crafting the perfect rub or seasoning requires an understanding of the meat's unique characteristics and how different ingredients interact with its natural flavors. This section delves into the techniques and principles of crafting rubs and seasonings for game meat, offering practical examples and tips to elevate your culinary skills.

A good rub begins with a balance of key elements: salt, sweet, heat, and aromatics. Salt is crucial as it enhances flavor and aids in moisture retention. Common salts used in rubs include kosher salt and sea salt, both of which provide a good balance without overpowering the meat. Sweet components like brown sugar or honey powder add depth and help create a caramelized crust when the meat is cooked. Heat comes from spices such as black pepper, cayenne, or paprika, which add a bit of spice and complexity. Aromatics, including herbs like thyme, rosemary, and oregano, and spices like garlic and onion powder, round out the flavor profile.

- **Balance of Key Elements:** Salt enhances flavor and moisture retention; sweet components add depth and caramelization; heat from spices adds complexity; aromatics provide balance and depth.

For example, a basic venison rub might include two tablespoons of kosher salt, one tablespoon of brown sugar, one teaspoon of black pepper, one teaspoon of smoked paprika, and a teaspoon each of garlic powder and onion powder. This combination highlights the meat's natural flavor while adding a touch of sweetness and a smoky undertone that complements venison's robust taste.

Example: Venison Rub: 2 tbsp kosher salt, 1 tbsp brown sugar, 1 tsp black pepper, 1 tsp smoked paprika, 1 tsp garlic powder, 1 tsp onion powder.

Game birds like pheasant and duck benefit from more delicate rubs that enhance their rich, but not overpowering, flavors. A rub for pheasant might include sea salt, ground white pepper, lemon zest, thyme, and a touch of coriander. This blend brings out the pheasant's natural sweetness and adds a citrusy brightness that pairs well with its tender meat.

Example: Pheasant Rub: 2 tsp sea salt, 1 tsp ground white pepper, 1 tsp lemon zest, 1 tsp thyme, 1/2 tsp ground coriander.

Creating a rub for wild boar involves incorporating flavors that stand up to the meat's intense taste. A robust rub for wild boar could include smoked paprika, cumin, coriander, brown sugar, kosher salt, black pepper, and a pinch of cayenne. This mix offers a balance of smoky, sweet, and spicy notes that enhance the wild boar's rich flavor.

Example: Wild Boar Rub: 1 tbsp smoked paprika, 1 tbsp cumin, 1 tbsp coriander, 1 tbsp brown sugar, 2 tsp kosher salt, 1 tsp black pepper, pinch of cayenne.

In addition to dry rubs, wet rubs or pastes can also be used to season game meat. These typically include the same dry ingredients, with the addition of wet components like oil, mustard, or even yogurt. Wet rubs help the seasoning adhere better to the meat and can also add moisture, particularly beneficial for leaner cuts.

- **Wet Rubs:** Incorporate oil, mustard, or yogurt to help seasoning adhere and add moisture.

A wet rub for venison could be made by combining olive oil with the dry ingredients of the previous venison rub recipe, creating a paste that sticks to the meat and adds a deeper flavor. Letting the meat sit with the rub for a few hours, or even overnight, allows the flavors to penetrate more deeply.

Example: Venison Wet Rub: Combine previous venison rub with 2-3 tbsp olive oil to form a paste.

Crafting seasonings for game meat also involves understanding the principles of layering flavors. Applying a base layer of salt first helps to enhance the meat's natural flavor. Following with the sweet, heat, and aromatic components ensures that each bite is well-balanced and flavorful. Seasoning in stages can be particularly effective, allowing each layer to build upon the previous one.

- **Layering Flavors:** Start with a base layer of salt, followed by sweet, heat, and aromatics in stages to build depth and complexity.

In real-world applications, consider preparing a rack of venison ribs. Begin by generously salting the ribs and letting them rest for 30 minutes to draw out some moisture and enhance the natural flavors. Next, apply a rub made from brown sugar, smoked paprika, garlic powder, onion powder, and cayenne. Let the ribs sit with the rub for several hours before slow-cooking or smoking them to perfection. The result is a beautifully caramelized crust with a deep, smoky flavor that complements the tender venison.

Example: Venison Ribs Preparation: Salt ribs, rest for 30 minutes. Apply rub of brown sugar, smoked paprika, garlic powder, onion powder, cayenne. Rest with rub for several hours before cooking.

Experimentation with different herbs and spices can lead to discovering unique flavor profiles that pair well with specific types of game meat. For instance, juniper berries, often used in European game recipes, add a piney, slightly sweet flavor that pairs exceptionally well with venison and wild boar. Grinding a few dried juniper berries into your rub can introduce a new layer of flavor that enhances the meat's natural taste.

- **Unique Ingredients:** Juniper berries add a piney, sweet flavor that complements venison and wild boar.

Incorporating freshly ground spices can also

elevate the quality of your rubs and seasonings. Grinding whole spices like black pepper, coriander, or cumin just before use ensures that the spices are at their most flavorful and aromatic. This can make a significant difference in the final dish, providing a more vibrant and potent seasoning.

- **Freshly Ground Spices:** Grinding whole spices just before use ensures maximum flavor and aroma.

Finally, consider the cooking method when crafting your rubs and seasonings. Grilling and roasting benefit from rubs that create a flavorful crust, while stews and braises may require seasonings that infuse the meat and broth. Adjusting the coarseness of the rub can also affect the texture and presentation of the final dish.

- **Cooking Method Consideration:** Rubs for grilling and roasting should create a crust; seasonings for stews and braises should infuse flavors. Adjust rub coarseness for desired texture.

In conclusion, crafting flavorful rubs and seasonings for game meat is an essential skill for any hunter or cook. By understanding the balance of salt, sweet, heat, and aromatics, and experimenting with different ingredients and techniques, you can enhance the natural flavors of your game meat and create memorable dishes. Whether you're preparing venison, wild boar, rabbit, or game birds, the right rub or seasoning can elevate your culinary creations and make the most of your harvest.

CHAPTER 3
COOKING TECHNIQUES

Methods for Grilling, Roasting, and Slow Cooking

Cooking game meat requires understanding its unique qualities and selecting the appropriate techniques to highlight its flavor and texture. Game meat, unlike domesticated livestock, tends to be leaner and sometimes tougher, necessitating methods that preserve moisture and enhance tenderness. This section explores the primary cooking techniques of grilling, roasting, and slow cooking, providing detailed insights and practical examples to help you master the art of preparing game meat.

Grilling is a popular method for cooking game meat, particularly for cuts like backstrap, tenderloin, and steaks. The high heat of the grill sears the meat, locking in juices and creating a flavorful crust. To achieve the best results, it is essential to prepare the meat correctly and manage the grill's temperature effectively.

First, ensure the grill is preheated to high heat. This step is crucial for achieving a good sear. Clean and oil the grill grates to prevent the meat from sticking. Season the game meat with a blend of salt, pepper, and any preferred spices or marinades, allowing it to sit for at least 30 minutes before grilling. This resting period helps the seasoning penetrate the meat.

- **Preheating and Cleaning:** Preheat the grill to high heat and clean the grates to prevent sticking.
- **Seasoning:** Season the meat and let it rest for 30 minutes to allow flavors to penetrate.

For cuts like venison backstrap or elk steaks, grill each side for 3-5 minutes, depending on the thickness and desired doneness. Use a meat thermometer to check the internal temperature; for medium-rare, aim for 130-135°F. Let the meat rest for a few minutes after grilling to allow the juices to redistribute, ensuring a juicy and tender result.

- **Grilling Time:** Grill each side for 3-5 minutes and check the internal temperature for desired doneness.
- **Resting Period:** Let the meat rest after grilling to retain juices and enhance tenderness.

Roasting is ideal for larger cuts of game meat, such as roasts and whole birds. This method involves cooking the meat in an oven at moderate to high temperatures, which helps to develop deep, rich flavors and maintain moisture. The key to successful roasting is proper preparation and temperature control.

Begin by bringing the meat to room temperature and seasoning it generously. For added flavor, you can insert garlic cloves, rosemary, or other herbs into small incisions in the meat. Place the meat on a rack in a roasting pan to allow air circulation and even cooking. Preheat the oven to 375°F for a moderate roast or 450°F for a higher-heat approach.

- **Preparation:** Bring the meat to room temperature, season it well, and place it on a rack in a roasting pan.
- **Oven Temperature:** Preheat the oven to 375°F for moderate roasting or 450°F for higher heat.

For venison or wild boar roasts, roast the meat for 20-25 minutes per pound, adjusting the time based on the cut's size and thickness. Baste the meat periodically with its juices or a marinade to enhance flavor and prevent drying out. Use a meat thermometer to ensure the internal temperature reaches 135-140°F for medium-rare.

- **Roasting Time:** Roast for 20-25 minutes per pound and baste periodically.
- **Internal Temperature:** Check for 135-140°F for medium-rare doneness.

After roasting, let the meat rest for at least 15 minutes before carving. This resting period allows the juices to redistribute, making the meat more tender and flavorful. For game birds like wild turkey or pheasant, consider brining them beforehand to retain moisture and enhance flavor.

- **Resting Period:** Let the meat rest for 15 minutes after roasting.
- **Brining Birds:** Brine game birds to retain moisture and enhance flavor.

Slow cooking is perfect for tougher cuts of game meat that benefit from prolonged cooking times at lower temperatures. This method breaks down connective tissue, resulting in tender, flavorful meat. It is particularly well-suited for cuts like shoulder, shank, and neck.

Start by searing the meat in a hot pan to develop a rich, caramelized crust. Transfer the meat to a slow cooker or a Dutch oven. Add vegetables, herbs, and a liquid such as broth, wine, or beer to create a flavorful cooking environment. Cover the pot and cook on low heat for several hours, typically 6-8 hours, until the meat is fork-tender.

- **Searing:** Sear the meat in a hot pan to develop a caramelized crust.
- **Slow Cooking Setup:** Transfer to a slow cooker or Dutch oven, add vegetables, herbs, and liquid, and cook on low heat for 6-8 hours.

For a venison stew, sear cubed venison, then transfer it to the slow cooker with potatoes, carrots, onions, garlic, and a mixture of beef broth and red wine. Season with thyme, rosemary, salt, and pepper. Cook on low for 8 hours until the meat is tender and the flavors are well-blended.

Example: Venison Stew: Sear cubed venison, add to slow cooker with vegetables, broth, wine, and seasonings, and cook for 8 hours.

Another excellent slow-cooking option is pulled wild boar. Begin by rubbing a wild boar shoulder with a blend of spices, then sear it in a hot pan. Transfer to a slow cooker with onions, garlic, apple cider vinegar, and barbecue sauce. Cook on low for 8-10 hours until the meat is tender and can be easily shredded with a fork.

Example: Pulled Wild Boar: Rub shoulder with spices, sear, add to slow cooker with onions, garlic, vinegar, and barbecue sauce, cook for 8-10 hours.

Using these cooking techniques, you can transform your game meat into delicious, tender, and flavorful dishes. Each method has its nuances and requires attention to detail to achieve the best results. Whether you are grilling, roasting, or slow cooking, understanding the unique qualities of game meat and how to cook it properly will enhance your culinary skills and ensure you make the most of your harvest.

Mastering the methods of grilling, roasting, and slow cooking game meat involves attention to preparation, seasoning, and temperature control. Grilling works well for tender cuts, creating a seared crust while preserving juiciness. Roasting is ideal for larger cuts and whole birds, developing deep flavors and maintaining moisture. Slow cooking excels with tougher cuts, breaking down connective tissue and resulting in tender, flavorful meat. By applying these techniques, you can elevate your game meat dishes and enjoy the rich, natural flavors of your harvest.

Incorporating Modern Cooking Techniques like Sous Vide

Incorporating modern cooking techniques into the preparation of game meat can elevate your culinary results, providing precise control over temperature and texture. Sous vide, a method where food is vacuum-sealed and cooked in a water bath at a controlled temperature, is particularly effective for game meat. This technique ensures even cooking, retains moisture, and enhances the natural flavors of the meat. Understanding how to use sous vide for different cuts of game meat can help you achieve consistent, high-quality results.

Sous vide cooking begins with proper preparation. Start by seasoning the game meat with your preferred blend of spices, herbs, and aromatics. The vacuum-sealing process locks in these flavors, allowing them to infuse the meat during cooking. For example, seasoning venison with a mixture of salt, pepper, garlic, and rosemary before vacuum-sealing will infuse the meat with these flavors, enhancing its natural taste.

- **Seasoning:** Use a blend of spices, herbs, and aromatics to infuse the meat with flavor during cooking.
- **Vacuum-Sealing:** Locks in flavors and ensures even cooking.

Set your sous vide machine to the desired temperature based on the cut and type of meat. For tender cuts like venison tenderloin or backstrap, a temperature of 130°F (54°C) for medium-rare works well. Cooking time can vary, but typically 1-2 hours is sufficient for these cuts. The precise temperature control of sous vide cooking ensures the meat reaches the perfect doneness without overcooking.

- **Temperature and Time:** For tender cuts, 130°F (54°C) for medium-rare, cook for 1-2 hours.

Once the cooking time is complete, the meat can be finished with a quick sear in a hot pan or on a grill. This step adds a desirable crust and enhances the flavor through the Maillard reaction, which creates a complex, savory taste. For example, after cooking venison tenderloin sous vide, quickly searing it in a hot cast-iron skillet with a bit of butter and thyme creates a perfect crust while keeping the interior tender and juicy.

- **Finishing:** Sear in a hot pan or grill to add a crust and enhance flavor.

Example: Sear sous vide venison tenderloin in a cast-iron skillet with butter and thyme.

Tougher cuts of game meat, such as wild boar shoulder or venison shank, benefit greatly from sous vide cooking due to the extended cooking times and low temperatures. These cuts can be cooked at 165°F (74°C) for 18-24 hours. This long, slow cooking process breaks down the connective tissue, resulting in tender, flavorful meat. Season the meat with robust spices like smoked paprika, cumin, and coriander before vacuum-sealing and cooking. After sous vide, these cuts can be shredded and used in dishes like tacos or stews.

- **Tougher Cuts:** Cook at 165°F (74°C) for 18-24 hours to break down connective tissue.
- **Seasoning:** Use robust spices like smoked paprika, cumin, and coriander.

Example: Shred sous vide wild boar shoulder for tacos or stews.

Game birds, such as pheasant or wild turkey, can

also be prepared using sous vide. These meats are prone to drying out with traditional cooking methods, but sous vide retains moisture and ensures even cooking. For pheasant breasts, set the sous vide machine to 140°F (60°C) and cook for 2-4 hours. After sous vide, a quick sear in a hot pan with butter and sage adds flavor and color.

- **Game Birds:** Sous vide retains moisture and ensures even cooking.
- **Temperature and Time:** Pheasant breasts at 140°F (60°C) for 2-4 hours.
- **Finishing:** Sear with butter and sage for added flavor and color.

Sous vide also opens up possibilities for preparing game meat with complex flavor profiles. Marinating the meat before sous vide can introduce additional layers of flavor. For instance, marinate venison steaks in a mixture of red wine, garlic, and rosemary for several hours before vacuum-sealing and cooking. The sous vide process allows the marinade to penetrate deeply, resulting in a rich, flavorful dish.

- **Marinating:** Adds complex flavors. Marinate venison in red wine, garlic, and rosemary before sous vide.

Example: Red wine-marinated venison steaks sous vide for rich flavor.

For those interested in experimenting with textures, sous vide can be used to create a confit-like result with game meat. Duck legs, for example, can be cooked sous vide with a generous amount of duck fat, garlic, and thyme at 165°F (74°C) for 24 hours. This method renders the fat and results in tender, flavorful meat similar to traditional confit.

- **Confit-Style Cooking:** Cook duck legs with duck fat, garlic, and thyme at 165°F (74°C) for 24 hours.

Example: Duck leg confit sous vide for tender, flavorful meat.

The versatility of sous vide extends beyond main dishes. Game meat can also be prepared sous vide for use in charcuterie. Venison sausages, for example, can be cooked sous vide to ensure even cooking and then finished on the grill for a smoky flavor. The precise temperature control prevents the sausages from drying out or bursting.

- **Charcuterie:** Cook venison sausages sous vide, then finish on the grill.

Example: Sous vide venison sausages for even cooking, finish on the grill for a smoky flavor.

Real-world applications of sous vide for game meat are numerous. A hunter can prepare a wild boar roast by first marinating it in a blend of apple cider vinegar, mustard, and honey. After marinating, the roast is vacuum-sealed and cooked sous vide at 165°F (74°C) for 18 hours. This long, slow cooking process ensures the meat is tender and flavorful. Once cooked, the roast is seared on all sides in a hot pan to develop a caramelized crust, then served with a reduction sauce made from the marinade and pan drippings.

Example: Wild Boar Roast: Marinate in apple cider vinegar, mustard, and honey. Cook sous vide at 165°F (74°C) for 18 hours, then sear and serve with a reduction sauce.

Incorporating sous vide into the preparation of game meat offers unparalleled control over temperature and texture, ensuring consistently tender and flavorful results. Whether you are cooking tender cuts like venison backstrap or tougher cuts like wild boar shoulder, sous vide provides a reliable method to enhance the natural qualities of the meat. By mastering this modern technique, you can elevate your game meat dishes, making them not only nutritious but also a gourmet delight.

BOOK 9

PERFECT PAIRINGS

CHAPTER 1
COMPLEMENTING WILD GAME

Choosing the Right Side Dishes

Choosing the right side dishes to complement wild game is a crucial part of creating a balanced and satisfying meal. Wild game meats, such as venison, wild boar, pheasant, and rabbit, possess unique flavors and textures that can be enhanced or overshadowed by poorly chosen accompaniments. Understanding how to select and prepare side dishes that highlight the best qualities of your game meat will elevate your culinary creations, providing a harmonious and memorable dining experience.

The first step in choosing the right side dishes is to consider the specific characteristics of the game meat you are serving. Venison, for example, has a rich, slightly sweet flavor with a lean texture. It pairs well with earthy, sweet, and acidic sides that can balance and complement its natural taste. Root vegetables, such as carrots, parsnips, and beets, roasted to bring out their natural sweetness, are an excellent choice. The caramelization of the vegetables enhances their sweetness, which contrasts beautifully with the rich, gamey flavor of the venison.

- **Venison Side Dish:** Roasted root vegetables (carrots, parsnips, beets) enhance sweetness and contrast with venison's rich flavor.

Wild boar, with its robust and slightly gamey taste, benefits from sides that offer both acidity and sweetness to cut through its richness. A classic pairing for wild boar is apples, which can be prepared in various ways, such as roasted, sautéed, or even in a sauce. Apples provide a sweet and tart contrast that balances the meat's intensity. Additionally, incorporating ingredients like sage and onions can add depth and complexity to the dish, complementing the wild boar's hearty flavor.

- **Wild Boar Side Dish:** Apples (roasted, sautéed, or in a sauce) provide sweet and tart balance, enhanced by sage and onions.

For game birds like pheasant and duck, which have a rich flavor and often a higher fat content, sides that offer acidity and lightness work well. Citrus fruits, such as oranges or lemons, can be used in salads or as part of a glaze to cut through the richness. A light, refreshing salad with mixed greens, citrus segments, and a vinaigrette made with citrus juice and olive oil can be a perfect accompaniment. The acidity of the citrus helps to balance the fat, while the greens add a fresh, crisp texture.

- **Game Bird Side Dish:** Citrus salad with mixed greens, citrus segments, and a citrus vinaigrette balances the richness of pheasant or duck.

Rabbit, which has a delicate flavor and tender texture, pairs well with mild, aromatic herbs and creamy sides. A classic preparation is rabbit with mustard sauce, accompanied by creamy mashed potatoes or polenta. The mustard sauce adds a tangy, slightly spicy element that complements the rabbit's subtle taste, while the creamy potatoes or polenta provide a smooth, comforting contrast in texture.

- **Rabbit Side Dish:** Creamy mashed potatoes or polenta with rabbit in mustard sauce for a tangy and smooth textural contrast.

Balancing flavors and textures in your side dishes is also essential. The goal is to create a meal where each component enhances the others, creating a cohesive and enjoyable experience. Here are some key principles to keep in mind:

1. **Contrast and Complement:** Choose sides that either contrast or complement the main dish. For example, a rich, fatty meat like duck benefits from acidic, bright sides, while a lean meat like venison pairs well with richer, creamier sides.
2. **Texture Variety:** Incorporate a variety of textures in your meal. If the main dish is tender, add sides that offer crunch or chew. If the meat is lean and slightly dry, pair it with creamy or juicy sides.
3. **Seasonal Ingredients:** Use seasonal ingredients to enhance the freshness and flavor of your dishes. Seasonal vegetables and fruits are often at their peak flavor and can add a dynamic element to your meal.

- **Contrast and Complement:** Rich, fatty

meats with acidic sides; lean meats with creamy sides.
- **Texture Variety:** Tender meat with crunchy sides; lean meat with creamy or juicy sides.
- **Seasonal Ingredients:** Use seasonal vegetables and fruits for peak flavor and freshness.

For a complete example, consider preparing a wild boar roast with roasted apples and onions, served alongside a creamy parsnip puree. The apples and onions provide a sweet and savory balance to the boar's robust flavor, while the parsnip puree adds a smooth, creamy texture. To enhance the meal further, a side of braised red cabbage with a touch of vinegar and caraway seeds adds acidity and a slight crunch, creating a well-rounded and satisfying plate.

Complete Meal Example: Wild boar roast with roasted apples and onions, creamy parsnip puree, and braised red cabbage for a balanced and satisfying plate.

In another example, for a venison steak, you might serve it with a side of roasted Brussels sprouts and sweet potato mash. The Brussels sprouts, roasted until caramelized and slightly crispy, add a bitter and crunchy element that contrasts with the venison's richness. The sweet potato mash, with its natural sweetness and creamy texture, provides a comforting balance.

Complete Meal Example: Venison steak with roasted Brussels sprouts and sweet potato mash for a bitter, crunchy contrast and comforting balance.

Pairing game birds like duck with a wild rice pilaf and a citrus glaze can also create a harmonious dish. The wild rice pilaf, with its nutty flavor and chewy texture, complements the duck's richness, while the citrus glaze adds a bright, acidic note that cuts through the fat. A side of lightly sautéed green beans with garlic and lemon zest can add a fresh, crisp element to complete the meal.

Complete Meal Example: Duck with wild rice

pilaf and citrus glaze, sautéed green beans with garlic and lemon zest for a fresh, crisp element.

Ultimately, the key to complementing wild game with the right side dishes lies in understanding the interplay of flavors and textures. By carefully selecting and preparing sides that enhance the unique qualities of your game meat, you can create a dining experience that is both balanced and memorable. Experiment with different ingredients and techniques, and pay attention to how each component of your meal interacts with the others. With practice and creativity, you can master the art of pairing side dishes with wild game, making every meal a culinary delight.

Balancing Flavors and Textures

Creating a balanced and harmonious meal requires understanding how different flavors and textures interact. This is particularly important when preparing wild game, which has distinct characteristics that can be both highlighted and balanced through careful selection of side dishes and cooking techniques. Balancing flavors and textures involves using contrasting and complementary elements to create a dining experience where every bite is satisfying and cohesive.

When working with wild game, it's essential to balance the natural richness and robust flavors of the meat with sides that provide contrast and harmony. For example, venison has a deep, earthy flavor and lean texture, making it an excellent candidate for sides that add both moisture and brightness. A classic pairing with venison is a cranberry sauce, which provides a tart, slightly sweet contrast that cuts through the richness of the meat. The acidity of the cranberries also helps to balance the venison's earthiness, creating a well-rounded flavor profile.

Example: Venison with cranberry sauce balances the meat's richness and earthiness with tart, sweet acidity.

Textures also play a crucial role in creating a balanced meal. Serving a tender cut of venison with a side that has a contrasting texture, such as a crunchy walnut and pear salad, adds a satisfying variety to each bite. The crunchiness of the walnuts and the crispness of the pears provide a textural counterpoint to the tender meat, enhancing the overall dining experience.

Example: Tender venison with a crunchy walnut and pear salad adds textural variety.

For wild boar, which has a more pronounced flavor and a fattier texture, sides that offer both acidity and sweetness work well. A side of braised red cabbage with apples and caraway seeds provides a sweet and tangy complement to the rich boar meat. The slight bitterness of the cabbage, combined with the sweetness of the apples and the aromatic caraway, creates a balanced dish that enhances the boar's robust flavor.

Example: Wild boar with braised red cabbage, apples, and caraway seeds offers a sweet, tangy, and slightly bitter balance.

Game birds, like duck or pheasant, often have a rich, fatty quality that benefits from sides with acidity and freshness. For instance, serving duck with an orange and fennel salad can cut through the duck's fattiness while adding a refreshing, citrusy note. The slight licorice flavor of the fennel pairs well with the orange, creating a light and vibrant side that balances the richness of the duck.

Example: Duck with an orange and fennel salad adds a refreshing, citrusy balance to the rich meat.

Another effective way to balance flavors is through the use of herbs and spices. Rosemary, thyme, and sage are traditional pairings with game meats, providing aromatic depth and complexity. For example, a venison roast rubbed with rosemary and garlic, then served with a side of creamy mashed potatoes infused with thyme, creates a cohesive flavor profile. The herbs complement the meat's earthiness, while the creamy potatoes add a comforting texture.

Example: Venison roast with rosemary and garlic, served with thyme-infused mashed potatoes for aromatic depth and creamy texture.

In addition to herbs and spices, incorporating elements of sweetness can balance the savory and sometimes gamey flavors of wild meat. A glaze or sauce made with honey, maple syrup, or balsamic reduction can add a sweet counterpoint to the savory meat. For instance, a honey-balsamic glaze on grilled wild boar chops provides a caramelized sweetness that balances the meat's strong flavor.

Example: Grilled wild boar chops with a honey-balsamic glaze for a sweet and savory balance.

Balancing flavors also involves considering the overall seasoning of the dish. Ensuring that the seasoning of the main dish and sides complements rather than competes with each other is key. For a harmonious meal, the seasoning should enhance the natural flavors of the game meat and the sides without overwhelming the palate. Lightly seasoned sides can provide a contrast to more robustly flavored game meats, ensuring that each element of the dish stands out.

Seasoning Consideration: Ensure that the seasoning of the main dish and sides complements and enhances the overall meal.

Using contrasting cooking techniques can further balance flavors and textures. Pairing a slow-cooked game dish with a quick, bright side can create a dynamic meal. For example, a slow-braised rabbit stew with root vegetables, paired with a fresh, zesty arugula and citrus salad, offers a combination of hearty and light elements. The braising process tenderizes the rabbit and infuses it with deep flavors, while the fresh salad adds a bright, acidic contrast.

Example: Slow-braised rabbit stew with root vegetables, paired with an arugula and citrus salad for a hearty and light balance.

Incorporating grains and legumes into your sides can add both texture and nutritional balance to your meal. Wild rice, quinoa, or lentils provide a chewy, satisfying texture that pairs well with the tenderness of game meat. A wild rice pilaf with mushrooms and herbs, for example, adds an earthy, chewy complement to a roasted pheasant.

Example: Roasted pheasant with wild rice pilaf and mushrooms for an earthy, chewy texture.

Balancing flavors and textures is not just about pairing the right foods; it's also about understanding how different cooking methods impact the final dish. Grilling can add a smoky, charred flavor that contrasts well with sweeter or more acidic sides. Roasting can develop deep, caramelized flavors in both meat and vegetables. Slow cooking tenderizes tougher cuts and allows for the infusion of complex flavors. By combining these techniques, you can create a meal where every component enhances the others.

Cooking Method Impact: Combine grilling, roasting, and slow cooking for a meal where every component enhances the others.

For a complete example, consider a meal featuring grilled venison steaks. Serve the steaks with a side of roasted Brussels sprouts and a cranberry walnut quinoa salad. The grilled steaks provide a smoky, charred flavor that is balanced by the slightly bitter, caramelized Brussels sprouts. The quinoa salad adds a nutty, chewy texture, and the cranberries provide a tart contrast that cuts through the richness of the meat.

Complete Meal Example: Grilled venison steaks with roasted Brussels sprouts and cranberry walnut quinoa salad for a balanced, flavorful meal.

Balancing flavors and textures when preparing

wild game involves thoughtful selection and preparation of side dishes that complement the unique characteristics of the meat. By incorporating elements of acidity, sweetness, bitterness, and freshness, as well as a variety of textures and cooking methods, you can create a harmonious and satisfying dining experience. Understanding these principles will allow you to enhance the natural flavors of wild game and delight your guests with well-rounded, delicious meals.

CHAPTER 2
WINE AND BEVERAGE SELECTIONS

Pairing Wines with Game Dishes

Pairing the right wine or beverage with game dishes is an art that enhances the dining experience by balancing and complementing the flavors of the food. Wild game meats, with their robust and distinct flavors, can be perfectly matched with specific wines that elevate the meal to a new level of enjoyment. Understanding the principles of wine pairing and how different types of wines interact with various game meats will help you make informed choices that delight the palate.

When pairing wines with game dishes, consider the weight, flavor intensity, and texture of both the meat and the wine. Heavier, more robust game meats like venison, wild boar, and duck pair well with full-bodied red wines that can stand up to their intense flavors. Lighter game meats like pheasant and rabbit are better complemented by lighter red wines or even certain white wines.

Starting with venison, which has a rich, slightly sweet flavor, consider pairing it with a full-bodied red wine like Cabernet Sauvignon or Syrah. These wines have the boldness to match the intensity of the venison, with flavors of dark fruits, pepper, and sometimes a hint of smokiness that

complements the meat. For example, a venison steak with a blackberry reduction pairs beautifully with a Cabernet Sauvignon that has notes of blackberry and cedar, creating a harmonious blend of flavors.

Example: Venison steak with blackberry reduction paired with Cabernet Sauvignon enhances the rich, sweet flavor of the meat.

Wild boar, known for its robust and slightly gamey taste, pairs well with wines that have both acidity and tannins to cut through the richness. A Zinfandel, with its spicy and fruity profile, or a Chianti, with its high acidity and flavors of cherry and leather, can balance the intense flavor of wild boar. Consider a wild boar ragu served with pappardelle pasta and a glass of Zinfandel, where the wine's bold flavors complement the hearty dish.

Example: Wild boar ragu with pappardelle paired with Zinfandel balances the intense flavor of the meat with the wine's bold, spicy profile.

For game birds like duck, which is rich and fatty, a wine with good acidity is essential to balance the fat. A Pinot Noir, with its bright acidity, red fruit flavors, and earthy undertones, is an excellent choice. The acidity cuts through the richness of the duck, while the fruit and earthy notes complement the meat's flavor. Imagine a seared duck breast with a cherry glaze paired with a glass of Pinot Noir, where the wine's cherry notes echo the glaze, enhancing the overall taste.

Example: Seared duck breast with cherry glaze paired with Pinot Noir cuts through the richness and enhances the flavor with complementary cherry notes.

Pheasant, being a lighter game bird, pairs well with both light red wines and full-bodied white wines. A Chardonnay with a good balance of fruit and oak or a light Pinot Noir can work wonderfully. For a roasted pheasant with a creamy mushroom sauce, a Chardonnay with notes of apple, butter, and vanilla would complement the dish's richness while adding a layer of complexity.

Example: Roasted pheasant with creamy mushroom sauce paired with Chardonnay balances the dish's richness with fruit and oak notes.

Rabbit, with its delicate and slightly sweet flavor, pairs well with lighter red wines like Pinot Noir or even a dry Riesling. A dish like rabbit in mustard sauce benefits from the bright acidity and subtle fruitiness of a Riesling, which cuts through the creaminess of the sauce and highlights the meat's flavor. The wine's acidity also acts as a palate cleanser, making each bite refreshing.

Example: Rabbit in mustard sauce paired with dry Riesling balances the creaminess of the sauce with the wine's bright acidity and subtle fruitiness.

In addition to wines, other beverages can also complement game dishes. Beer, for instance, offers a wide range of flavors that can pair well with different game meats. A dark stout or porter, with its roasted malt flavors, pairs beautifully with game meats like venison or wild boar. The bitterness of the beer contrasts with the meat's richness, creating a balanced flavor profile. A

pheasant dish could be paired with a Belgian witbier, where the beer's citrus and spice notes enhance the bird's light, delicate flavor.

Example: Venison paired with a dark stout balances the meat's richness with roasted malt flavors.

Another example: Pheasant paired with Belgian witbier enhances the bird's delicate flavor with citrus and spice notes.

When considering the impact of cooking methods on pairings, it's essential to match the intensity of the cooking method with the intensity of the beverage. Grilled or smoked game meats, which have strong, smoky flavors, pair well with wines that have bold, robust profiles. A Syrah or Malbec, with their smoky and spicy notes, can enhance the flavors of grilled venison or wild boar.

- **Cooking Method Impact:** Grilled or smoked game meats pair well with bold wines like Syrah or Malbec.

Roasted game meats, which develop deep, caramelized flavors, pair well with wines that have a good balance of acidity and tannins. A roasted duck with a crispy skin benefits from the bright acidity of a Pinot Noir, which cuts through the richness and complements the caramelized flavors.

- **Cooking Method Impact:** Roasted game meats with caramelized flavors pair well with wines like Pinot Noir with good acidity.

Slow-cooked or braised game dishes, which become tender and flavorful over time, pair well with wines that have a complex flavor profile and good structure. A braised rabbit stew, with its rich and savory sauce, pairs beautifully with a medium-bodied red wine like Merlot, which offers soft tannins and flavors of plum and chocolate that complement the stew's depth.

- **Cooking Method Impact:** Slow-cooked or

braised game dishes pair well with medium-bodied wines like Merlot with soft tannins and complex flavors.

Ultimately, the key to successful wine and beverage pairings with game dishes is to consider the balance of flavors and textures. By understanding the unique characteristics of both the meat and the beverage, you can create pairings that enhance and elevate the dining experience. Whether you are serving a robust wild boar ragu with a bold Zinfandel or a delicate rabbit in mustard sauce with a bright Riesling, the right pairing can transform your meal into a culinary delight.

The Impact of Cooking Methods on Pairings

The way a dish is cooked can profoundly affect its flavor, texture, and overall character. When pairing wines and beverages with game dishes, understanding how different cooking methods influence the final dish is essential. This knowledge allows for more precise and harmonious pairings that can enhance both the food and the drink.

Grilling and smoking are cooking methods that impart bold, smoky, and sometimes charred flavors to game meat. These methods can enhance the natural richness and depth of flavors in meats like venison, wild boar, and duck. Pairing wines with grilled or smoked game requires selecting beverages that can stand up to these intense flavors.

A grilled venison steak, for example, benefits from a wine that can match its robust character. A full-bodied Syrah, with its smoky, peppery notes and rich fruit flavors, complements the grilled meat perfectly. The wine's complexity and depth of flavor echo the smoky, charred notes from the grill, creating a cohesive and satisfying pairing.

Example: Grilled venison steak paired with Syrah enhances the smoky, charred flavors with the wine's peppery notes and rich fruit.

Smoking adds an extra layer of complexity to game meats. For smoked wild boar ribs, consider a Malbec, which offers dark fruit flavors, a hint of spice, and a smooth finish. The wine's bold profile complements the smoky, rich taste of the ribs, while its tannins help cut through the fat.

Example: Smoked wild boar ribs paired with Malbec balances the smoky richness with dark fruit flavors and a hint of spice.

Roasting and baking are versatile cooking methods that can develop deep, caramelized flavors in game meats. These methods often create a balance of crispy, flavorful exteriors with tender, juicy interiors. When pairing wines with roasted or baked game, it's crucial to consider the caramelization and richness these methods impart.

Roasted duck with a crispy skin and tender meat pairs beautifully with Pinot Noir. The wine's bright acidity cuts through the richness of the duck, while its red fruit flavors and earthy undertones complement the caramelized skin. This pairing highlights the duck's succulent texture and enhances its savory notes.

Example: Roasted duck with crispy skin paired with Pinot Noir balances the dish's richness with bright acidity and red fruit flavors.

For baked pheasant, a Chardonnay with a balance of fruit and oak works well. The wine's creamy texture and flavors of apple, butter, and vanilla complement the pheasant's delicate meat and any accompanying creamy sauces. This combination enhances the dish's richness while adding layers of flavor.

Example: Baked pheasant paired with Chardonnay enhances the dish's richness with creamy texture and apple, butter, and vanilla notes.

Braising and stewing involve slow-cooking

game meat in liquid, resulting in tender, flavorful dishes. These methods allow the meat to absorb the flavors of the cooking liquid, creating complex and savory profiles. Wines paired with braised or stewed game should have enough body and complexity to match these rich, hearty dishes.

A classic example is braised rabbit in red wine sauce. Pair this dish with a medium-bodied Merlot, which offers soft tannins and flavors of plum, chocolate, and herbs. The wine's smooth texture and layered flavors complement the rich, savory notes of the braised rabbit, creating a harmonious pairing.

Example: Braised rabbit in red wine sauce paired with Merlot complements the dish's richness with plum, chocolate, and herb flavors.

For a venison stew with root vegetables, consider a Cabernet Sauvignon. This full-bodied wine has robust tannins and flavors of dark fruits, cedar, and spices that stand up to the hearty stew. The wine's structure and complexity mirror the stew's depth, enhancing the overall dining experience.

Example: Venison stew with root vegetables paired with Cabernet Sauvignon balances the stew's heartiness with robust tannins and dark fruit flavors.

Pan-searing and sautéing are quick cooking methods that can create a flavorful crust on game meat while keeping the interior tender. These techniques often result in dishes with a combination of crispy and juicy textures, requiring wines that can balance these characteristics.

A pan-seared venison medallion, for instance, pairs well with a Zinfandel. The wine's bold, fruity profile and peppery notes complement the seared crust and rich interior of the venison. The slight sweetness of the Zinfandel can also balance any accompanying sauces or glazes.

Example: Pan-seared venison medallion paired with Zinfandel balances the dish's crispy crust and rich interior with bold, fruity, and peppery notes.

For sautéed rabbit with a garlic and herb sauce, a Sauvignon Blanc offers a refreshing contrast. The wine's crisp acidity and citrus flavors cut through the richness of the sauce, while its herbal notes complement the garlic and herbs used in the dish.

Example: Sautéed rabbit with garlic and herb sauce paired with Sauvignon Blanc enhances the dish with crisp acidity and complementary herbal notes.

Sous vide cooking involves vacuum-sealing game meat and cooking it in a water bath at a precise, controlled temperature. This method ensures even cooking and retains the meat's moisture and flavor. Wines paired with sous vide game dishes should enhance the meat's natural flavors without overwhelming them.

A sous vide venison tenderloin, for example, pairs well with a Bordeaux blend. The wine's balanced tannins and flavors of dark fruits, tobacco, and spice complement the tender, juicy meat. The precise cooking method of sous vide allows the wine's complex profile to shine without overpowering the dish.

Example: Sous vide venison tenderloin paired with Bordeaux blend balances the tender meat with dark fruits, tobacco, and spice notes.

For sous vide pheasant, a light red wine like Gamay or a rich white wine like Viognier works well. The Gamay's light body and red berry flavors or the Viognier's floral and stone fruit notes enhance the delicate, moist pheasant without overshadowing it.

Example: Sous vide pheasant paired with Gamay or Viognier complements the delicate meat with red berry or floral and stone fruit notes.

The cooking method significantly influences how game meat pairs with wines and other beverages. Grilling and smoking require bold wines with robust flavors, while roasting and baking benefit from wines that balance caramelization and richness. Braising and stewing call for complex, full-bodied wines, while pan-searing and sautéing pair well with wines that complement crispy and tender textures. Sous vide cooking highlights the natural flavors of the meat, making it suitable for wines with balanced profiles. By understanding these principles, you can create pairings that elevate both the food and the drink, enhancing your overall dining experience.

BOOK 10

WILD GAME RECIPES

CHAPTER 1
BIG GAME SPECIALTIES

Herb-Crusted Moose Roast

Preparation Time: 20 minutes
Cooking Time: 1 hour 30 minutes
Servings: 2

INGREDIENTS

- 1 lb moose roast
- 2 tbsp olive oil
- 2 cloves garlic, minced
- 1 tbsp fresh rosemary, chopped
- 1 tbsp fresh thyme, chopped
- 1 tbsp fresh parsley, chopped
- 1 tsp salt
- 1/2 tsp black pepper
- 1/4 cup breadcrumbs
- 1 tbsp Dijon mustard

DIRECTIONS

1. Preheat your oven to 375°F (190°C). Pat the moose roast dry with paper towels. In a small bowl, combine the minced garlic, rosemary, thyme, parsley, salt, and black pepper. Rub the olive oil all over the moose roast. Spread the Dijon mustard over the entire surface of the roast. Press the herb mixture onto the mustard-coated roast, ensuring it is evenly covered. Sprinkle the breadcrumbs over the herb-coated roast and press gently to adhere.

2. Place the moose roast on a roasting rack in a shallow baking dish. Roast in the preheated oven for about 1 hour and 30 minutes, or until the internal temperature reaches 135°F (57°C) for medium-rare. Remove the roast from the oven and let it rest for 10 minutes before slicing. Slice the moose roast thinly and serve with your choice of sides.

Nutrition Values: Calories 450; Total Fat 22g; Saturated Fat 5g; Sodium 600mg; Total Carbohydrates 10g; Dietary Fiber 1g; Protein 50g; Potassium 800mg

Grilled Elk Ribeye

Preparation Time: 15 minutes
Cooking Time: 10 minutes
Servings: 2

INGREDIENTS

- 2 elk ribeye steaks (6 oz each)
- 2 tbsp olive oil
- 1 tbsp soy sauce
- 1 tbsp Worcestershire sauce
- 2 cloves garlic, minced

- 1 tsp fresh rosemary, chopped
- 1 tsp fresh thyme, chopped
- 1/2 tsp black pepper
- 1/2 tsp salt
- 1 lemon, sliced (for garnish)

DIRECTIONS

1. In a small bowl, combine the olive oil, soy sauce, Worcestershire sauce, minced garlic, chopped rosemary, chopped thyme, black pepper, and salt. Mix well to create a marinade. Place the elk ribeye steaks in a resealable plastic bag or shallow dish and pour the marinade over them, ensuring the steaks are evenly coated. Let the steaks marinate in the refrigerator for at least 1 hour, or up to overnight for a more intense flavor.
2. Preheat your grill to medium-high heat. Remove the steaks from the marinade and let any excess drip off. Place the steaks on the grill and cook for about 4-5 minutes per side, or until they reach your desired level of doneness. Use a meat thermometer to ensure the internal temperature reaches 135°F (57°C) for medium-rare.
3. Remove the elk ribeye steaks from the grill and let them rest for 5 minutes to allow the juices to redistribute. Serve the steaks garnished with lemon slices and your choice of sides, such as grilled vegetables or a fresh salad.

Nutrition Values: Calories 420; Total Fat 28g; Saturated Fat 8g; Sodium 850mg; Total Carbohydrates 3g; Dietary Fiber 1g; Protein 38g; Potassium 750mg

Venison Carpaccio with Arugula

Preparation Time: 20 minutes
Cooking Time: 0 minutes
Servings: 2

INGREDIENTS

- 8 oz venison loin, trimmed
- 2 cups fresh arugula
- 2 tbsp olive oil
- 1 tbsp lemon juice
- 1 tsp Dijon mustard
- 1 clove garlic, minced
- 1/4 cup shaved Parmesan cheese
- 1 tbsp capers, drained
- Salt and black pepper to taste
- Freshly ground black pepper for garnish
- Lemon wedges for garnish

DIRECTIONS

1. Wrap the venison loin tightly in plastic wrap and place it in the freezer for about 30 minutes, or until it is firm but not frozen solid. This will make it easier to slice the meat thinly. Remove the venison from the freezer and use a very sharp knife to cut it into paper-thin slices.
2. Arrange the venison slices evenly on a large chilled plate, slightly overlapping them. In a small bowl, whisk together the olive oil, lemon juice, Dijon mustard, and minced garlic to create a dressing. Season the dressing with salt and black pepper to taste.
3. Drizzle the dressing over the venison slices, ensuring they are lightly coated. Place the fresh arugula in the center of the plate, arranging it neatly. Sprinkle the shaved Parmesan cheese and capers over the venison and arugula.
4. Garnish the dish with freshly ground black pepper and lemon wedges on the side. Serve

immediately, allowing the flavors to meld together.

Nutrition Values: Calories 320; Total Fat 22g; Saturated Fat 5g; Sodium 420mg; Total Carbohydrates 4g; Dietary Fiber 1g; Protein 26g; Potassium 550mg

Maple-Glazed Elk Medallions

Preparation Time: 15 minutes
Cooking Time: 20 minutes
Servings: 2

INGREDIENTS

- 2 elk medallions (6 oz each)
- 1/4 cup pure maple syrup
- 2 tbsp soy sauce
- 1 tbsp Dijon mustard
- 1 tbsp olive oil
- 2 cloves garlic, minced
- 1/2 tsp black pepper
- 1/2 tsp salt
- Fresh rosemary sprigs for garnish

DIRECTIONS

1. In a small bowl, whisk together the maple syrup, soy sauce, Dijon mustard, olive oil, minced garlic, black pepper, and salt to create a marinade. Place the elk medallions in a resealable plastic bag or a shallow dish and pour the marinade over them, ensuring the meat is well coated. Marinate the elk medallions in the refrigerator for at least 1 hour, or up to 4 hours for more intense flavor.
2. Preheat your grill to medium-high heat. Remove the elk medallions from the marinade and let any excess marinade drip off. Place the medallions on the grill and cook for about 5-7 minutes per side, or until they reach your desired level of doneness. Use a meat thermometer to ensure the internal temperature reaches 135°F (57°C) for medium-rare.
3. While the elk medallions are grilling, pour the remaining marinade into a small saucepan and bring it to a boil over medium heat. Reduce the heat and let the marinade simmer until it thickens slightly, about 5 minutes. This will create a glaze to brush over the medallions.
4. Once the elk medallions are done grilling, remove them from the grill and let them rest for 5 minutes to allow the juices to redistribute. Brush the thickened glaze over the medallions before serving. Garnish with fresh rosemary sprigs and serve with your choice of sides, such as roasted vegetables or a fresh green salad.

Nutrition Values: Calories 360; Total Fat 14g; Saturated Fat 3g; Sodium 700mg; Total Carbohydrates 20g; Dietary Fiber 0g; Protein 38g; Potassium 700mg

Braised Bison Short Ribs

Preparation Time: 20 minutes
Cooking Time: 3 hours
Servings: 2

INGREDIENTS

- 4 bison short ribs (about 1.5 lbs)
- 2 tbsp olive oil
- 1 large onion, chopped
- 2 carrots, chopped
- 2 celery stalks, chopped
- 4 cloves garlic, minced
- 1 cup beef broth
- 1 cup red wine
- 1 can (14.5 oz) crushed tomatoes
- 2 tbsp tomato paste
- 1 tbsp Worcestershire sauce
- 2 sprigs fresh thyme
- 2 sprigs fresh rosemary
- 1 bay leaf
- Salt and black pepper to taste

DIRECTIONS

1. Preheat your oven to 325°F (165°C). Season the bison short ribs generously with salt and black pepper. In a large, oven-safe pot or Dutch oven, heat the olive oil over medium-high heat. Sear the short ribs on all sides until they are browned, about 3-4 minutes per side. Remove the short ribs from the pot and set them aside.

2. In the same pot, add the chopped onion, carrots, and celery. Cook until the vegetables are softened, about 5-7 minutes. Add the minced garlic and cook for another minute until fragrant. Stir in the tomato paste and cook for another 2 minutes, allowing it to coat the vegetables.

3. Pour in the beef broth and red wine, scraping up any browned bits from the bottom of the pot. Add the crushed tomatoes and Worcestershire sauce, stirring to combine. Return the short ribs to the pot, nestling them into the liquid and vegetables. Add the thyme, rosemary, and bay leaf.

4. Bring the mixture to a simmer, then cover the pot and transfer it to the preheated oven. Braise the short ribs for about 2.5 to 3 hours, or until the meat is tender and falling off the bone. Check occasionally to ensure the liquid level is sufficient, adding more broth if needed.

5. Once the short ribs are done, remove the pot from the oven. Carefully transfer the short ribs to a plate. Strain the braising liquid through a fine mesh sieve, discarding the solids, and return the liquid to the pot. Simmer the liquid over medium heat until it reduces to a thick sauce, about 10-15 minutes.

6. Serve the braised bison short ribs hot, with the reduced sauce spooned over the top. Pair with mashed potatoes or a hearty vegetable side for a complete meal.

Nutrition Values: Calories 680; Total Fat 38g; Saturated Fat 12g; Sodium 980mg; Total Carbohydrates 25g; Dietary Fiber 4g; Protein 55g; Potassium 1100mg

Honey-Garlic Marinated Venison Chops

Preparation Time: 15 minutes (plus 2 hours marinating time)
Cooking Time: 15 minutes
Servings: 2

INGREDIENTS

- 4 venison chops (about 6 oz each)
- 3 tbsp honey
- 2 tbsp soy sauce
- 2 tbsp olive oil
- 4 cloves garlic, minced
- 1 tbsp apple cider vinegar
- 1 tsp fresh thyme, chopped
- 1 tsp fresh rosemary, chopped
- Salt and black pepper to taste

DIRECTIONS

1. In a small bowl, whisk together the honey, soy sauce, olive oil, minced garlic, apple cider vinegar, chopped thyme, and chopped rosemary to create the marinade. Season the venison chops with salt and black pepper, then place them in a resealable plastic bag or shallow dish. Pour the marinade over the chops, ensuring they are well coated. Seal the bag or cover the dish and refrigerate for at least 2 hours, allowing the flavors to penetrate the meat.

2. Preheat your grill to medium-high heat. Remove the venison chops from the marinade and let any excess marinade drip off. Place the chops on the grill and cook for about 5-7 minutes per side, or until they reach your desired level of doneness. Use a meat thermometer to ensure the internal temperature reaches 135°F (57°C) for medium-rare.

3. While the chops are grilling, pour the

remaining marinade into a small saucepan and bring it to a boil over medium heat. Reduce the heat and let the marinade simmer for 5 minutes, thickening into a glaze.

4. Once the venison chops are done, remove them from the grill and let them rest for 5 minutes to allow the juices to redistribute. Drizzle the thickened glaze over the chops before serving. Pair with roasted vegetables or a fresh salad for a complete meal.

Nutrition Values: Calories 420; Total Fat 20g; Saturated Fat 5g; Sodium 600mg; Total Carbohydrates 22g; Dietary Fiber 1g; Protein 40g; Potassium 750mg

Coffee-Rubbed Caribou Steaks

Preparation Time: 15 minutes
(plus 1 hour resting time)
Cooking Time: 10 minutes
Servings: 2

INGREDIENTS

- 2 caribou steaks (about 6 oz each)
- 2 tbsp ground coffee
- 1 tbsp brown sugar
- 1 tsp smoked paprika
- 1 tsp ground cumin
- 1/2 tsp black pepper
- 1/2 tsp salt
- 1 tbsp olive oil
- 2 cloves garlic, minced

DIRECTIONS

1. In a small bowl, combine the ground coffee, brown sugar, smoked paprika, ground cumin, black pepper, and salt. Mix well to create the coffee rub. Pat the caribou steaks dry with paper towels and evenly coat them with the coffee rub, pressing it into the meat to ensure it adheres well. Let the steaks rest at room temperature for about 1 hour to allow the flavors to meld.

2. Preheat your grill to medium-high heat. Brush the caribou steaks with olive oil and sprinkle the minced garlic over them. Place the steaks on the grill and cook for about 4-5 minutes per side, or until they reach your desired level of doneness. Use a meat thermometer to ensure the internal temperature reaches 135°F (57°C) for medium-rare.

3. Remove the caribou steaks from the grill and let them rest for 5 minutes to allow the juices to redistribute. Serve the steaks with your choice of sides, such as roasted vegetables or a fresh salad, to complement the rich, smoky flavors of the coffee rub.

Nutrition Values: Calories 350; Total Fat 14g; Saturated Fat 4g; Sodium 500mg; Total Carbohydrates 8g; Dietary Fiber 1g; Protein 46g; Potassium 800mg

Wild Boar Tenderloin with Cranberry Reduction

Preparation Time: 20 minutes
Cooking Time: 30 minutes
Servings: 2

INGREDIENTS

- 2 wild boar tenderloins (about 6 oz each)
- 1 cup fresh cranberries
- 1/4 cup red wine
- 1/4 cup chicken broth
- 2 tbsp honey
- 1 tbsp balsamic vinegar
- 1 shallot, finely chopped
- 2 cloves garlic, minced
- 1 tbsp olive oil
- 1 tsp fresh thyme, chopped
- Salt and black pepper to taste

DIRECTIONS

1. Season the wild boar tenderloins with salt and black pepper, then set them aside. In a small saucepan, heat the olive oil over medium heat. Add the chopped shallot and minced garlic, cooking until softened and fragrant. Stir in the fresh cranberries, red wine, chicken broth, honey, and balsamic vinegar. Bring the mixture to a boil, then reduce the heat and let it simmer for about 15 minutes, or until the cranberries have burst and the sauce has thickened.

2. While the cranberry reduction is simmering, heat a large skillet over medium-high heat. Add a bit of olive oil to the skillet, then sear the wild boar tenderloins on all sides until they are nicely browned, about 2-3 minutes per side. Once seared, transfer the tenderloins to a preheated oven set to 375°F (190°C). Roast for about 10-12 minutes, or until the internal temperature reaches 145°F (63°C).

3. Remove the tenderloins from the oven and let them rest for 5 minutes before slicing. While the meat is resting, strain the cranberry reduction through a fine mesh sieve to remove the solids, leaving a smooth, thick sauce. Slice the wild boar tenderloins into medallions and arrange them on a serving plate. Drizzle the cranberry reduction over the top, garnishing with fresh thyme if desired. Serve with a side of roasted vegetables or a light salad.

Nutrition Values: Calories 420; Total Fat 16g; Saturated Fat 4g; Sodium 340mg; Total Carbohydrates 28g; Dietary Fiber 3g; Protein 40g; Potassium 700mg

Roasted Antelope Loin with Juniper Berries

Preparation Time: 20 minutes (plus marinating time)
Cooking Time: 30 minutes
Servings: 2

INGREDIENTS

- 1 antelope loin (about 12 oz)
- 1/4 cup olive oil
- 1/4 cup red wine
- 1 tbsp juniper berries, crushed
- 2 cloves garlic, minced
- 1 tbsp fresh rosemary, chopped
- 1 tbsp fresh thyme, chopped
- 1 tsp black pepper
- 1 tsp salt

DIRECTIONS

1. In a bowl, combine the olive oil, red wine, crushed juniper berries, minced garlic, chopped rosemary, chopped thyme, black pepper, and salt to create the marinade. Place the antelope loin in a resealable plastic bag or shallow dish and pour the marinade over it, ensuring the meat is well coated. Seal the bag or cover the dish and refrigerate for at least 2 hours, or overnight for a deeper flavor.

2. Preheat your oven to 375°F (190°C). Remove the antelope loin from the marinade and let any excess marinade drip off. In an oven-safe skillet, heat a small amount of olive oil over medium-high heat. Sear the antelope loin on all sides until it is browned, about 3-4 minutes per side.

3. Transfer the skillet to the preheated oven and roast the antelope loin for about 20-25 minutes, or until the internal temperature reaches 135°F (57°C) for medium-rare. Remove the loin from the oven and let it rest for 5-10 minutes to allow the juices to redistribute.

4. Slice the antelope loin into medallions and serve with your choice of sides, such as roasted potatoes and seasonal vegetables, to complement the rich, aromatic flavors of the juniper berries and herbs.

Nutrition Values: Calories 420; Total Fat 28g; Saturated Fat 6g; Sodium 600mg; Total Carbohydrates 5g; Dietary Fiber 1g; Protein 38g; Potassium 750mg

Spicy Bear Sausage with Peppers and Onions

Preparation Time: 20 minutes
Cooking Time: 30 minutes
Servings: 2

INGREDIENTS

- 4 bear sausages (about 8 oz each)
- 1 red bell pepper, sliced
- 1 green bell pepper, sliced
- 1 yellow bell pepper, sliced
- 1 large onion, sliced
- 2 cloves garlic, minced
- 1 tbsp olive oil
- 1 tsp crushed red pepper flakes
- 1/2 tsp smoked paprika
- 1/2 tsp black pepper
- 1/2 tsp salt
- 1/4 cup chicken broth
- 1 tbsp fresh parsley, chopped

DIRECTIONS

1. Heat the olive oil in a large skillet over medium heat. Add the bear sausages to the skillet and cook, turning occasionally, until they are browned on all sides, about 10 minutes. Remove the sausages from the skillet and set them aside.
2. In the same skillet, add the sliced red, green, and yellow bell peppers, along with the sliced onion. Cook the vegetables, stirring occasionally, until they begin to soften, about 5-7 minutes. Add the minced garlic, crushed red pepper flakes, smoked paprika, black pepper, and salt to the skillet, stirring to combine and coat the vegetables with the spices.
3. Return the bear sausages to the skillet, nestling them among the peppers and onions. Pour the chicken broth into the skillet and bring the mixture to a simmer. Cover the skillet and let it cook for another 15 minutes, or until the sausages are cooked through and the vegetables are tender.
4. Remove the skillet from the heat and let it sit for a few minutes before serving. Sprinkle the chopped fresh parsley over the top for a burst of color and freshness. Serve the spicy bear sausage with peppers and onions hot, accompanied by crusty bread or over a bed of rice.

Nutrition Values: Calories 560; Total Fat 35g; Saturated Fat 12g; Sodium 1200mg; Total Carbohydrates 20g; Dietary Fiber 4g; Protein 40g; Potassium 850mg

CHAPTER 2

DELICIOUS SMALL GAME DISHES

Pheasant and Wild Mushroom Risotto

Preparation Time: 20 minutes
Cooking Time: 30 minutes
Servings: 2

INGREDIENTS

- 1 pheasant breast, diced
- 1 cup arborio rice
- 2 cups chicken broth
- 1 cup wild mushrooms, sliced
- 1 small onion, finely chopped
- 2 cloves garlic, minced
- 1/2 cup dry white wine
- 1/4 cup grated Parmesan cheese
- 2 tbsp olive oil
- 1 tbsp butter
- 1 tsp fresh thyme, chopped
- Salt and black pepper to taste
- Fresh parsley, chopped for garnish

DIRECTIONS

1. Heat the olive oil in a large skillet over medium heat. Add the diced pheasant breast and cook until browned on all sides. Remove the pheasant from the skillet and set aside.

In the same skillet, add the butter and sauté the chopped onion until translucent. Add the minced garlic and sliced wild mushrooms, cooking until the mushrooms are tender and fragrant.

2. Stir in the arborio rice, allowing it to absorb the flavors for a couple of minutes. Pour in the dry white wine and cook until it is mostly evaporated. Begin adding the chicken broth, one ladle at a time, stirring frequently. Allow each addition of broth to be absorbed by the rice before adding more. Continue this process until the rice is creamy and tender.

3. Return the cooked pheasant to the skillet, mixing it into the risotto. Stir in the grated Parmesan cheese and chopped fresh thyme, ensuring everything is well combined. Season with salt and black pepper to taste. Remove the skillet from heat and let the risotto rest for a few minutes before serving.

4. Garnish the risotto with freshly chopped parsley. Serve hot, paired with a crisp white wine or a light salad to balance the rich flavors of the pheasant and wild mushrooms.

Nutrition Values: Calories 620; Total Fat 23g; Saturated Fat 7g; Sodium 850mg; Total Carbohydrates 68g; Dietary Fiber 3g; Protein 34g; Potassium 720mg

Braised Squirrel in Red Wine Sauce

Preparation Time: 25 minutes
Cooking Time: 2 hours
Servings: 2

INGREDIENTS

- 2 squirrel legs, cleaned and trimmed
- 1 cup red wine
- 1 cup chicken broth
- 1 small onion, finely chopped
- 2 cloves garlic, minced
- 1 carrot, diced
- 1 celery stalk, diced
- 2 tbsp olive oil
- 1 tbsp tomato paste
- 1 tsp dried thyme
- 1 bay leaf
- Salt and black pepper to taste
- Fresh parsley, chopped for garnish

DIRECTIONS

1. Heat the olive oil in a Dutch oven over medium heat. Season the squirrel legs with salt and black pepper, then brown them on all sides in the hot oil. Remove the squirrel legs from the Dutch oven and set them aside. Add the chopped onion, garlic, carrot, and celery to the pot, sautéing until the vegetables are softened.
2. Stir in the tomato paste, cooking for a minute to incorporate it with the vegetables. Pour in the red wine, using a wooden spoon to scrape up any browned bits from the bottom of the pot. Allow the wine to reduce by half, then add the chicken broth, dried thyme, and bay leaf. Return the squirrel legs to the pot, ensuring they are submerged in the liquid.
3. Bring the mixture to a simmer, then cover the Dutch oven and transfer it to a preheated oven at 300°F (150°C). Braise the squirrel legs for about 1.5 to 2 hours, or until the meat is tender and falling off the bone. Check occasionally to ensure there is enough liquid, adding more broth if necessary.
4. Once cooked, remove the squirrel legs from the pot and keep them warm. Discard the bay leaf and blend the sauce with an immersion blender until smooth, if desired. Return the sauce to the stovetop and simmer until slightly thickened.
5. Serve the braised squirrel legs with the red wine sauce drizzled over the top. Garnish with freshly chopped parsley and accompany with mashed potatoes or crusty bread to soak up the rich sauce.

Nutrition Values: Calories 480; Total Fat 24g; Saturated Fat 6g; Sodium 700mg; Total Carbohydrates 20g; Dietary Fiber 4g; Protein 38g; Potassium 850mg

Pan-Seared Dove Breasts with Herb Butter

Preparation Time: 15 minutes
Cooking Time: 10 minutes
Servings: 2

INGREDIENTS

- 4 dove breasts
- 2 tbsp olive oil
- 3 tbsp unsalted butter
- 2 cloves garlic, minced
- 1 tsp fresh rosemary, chopped
- 1 tsp fresh thyme, chopped
- Salt and black pepper to taste
- Fresh lemon wedges for serving
- Fresh parsley, chopped for garnish

DIRECTIONS

1. Heat the olive oil in a large skillet over medium-high heat. Season the dove breasts with salt and black pepper on both sides. Once

the oil is hot, add the dove breasts to the skillet. Cook them for about 2-3 minutes on each side until they are golden brown and cooked through but still tender. Remove the dove breasts from the skillet and set them aside to rest.

2. Reduce the heat to medium and add the unsalted butter to the skillet. Allow the butter to melt and start to foam. Add the minced garlic, chopped rosemary, and thyme to the skillet, stirring to combine with the melted butter. Cook the herb butter for about 1-2 minutes, until the garlic is fragrant and the herbs are well incorporated.

3. Return the dove breasts to the skillet, spooning the herb butter over them to coat evenly. Cook for an additional minute to ensure the dove breasts are well-flavored with the herb butter. Remove the skillet from heat.

4. Serve the pan-seared dove breasts hot, drizzled with the remaining herb butter from the skillet. Garnish with freshly chopped parsley and serve with lemon wedges on the side for an extra burst of freshness. This dish pairs beautifully with a light salad or roasted vegetables.

Nutrition Values: Calories 350; Total Fat 24g; Saturated Fat 10g; Sodium 180mg; Total Carbohydrates 2g; Dietary Fiber 0g; Protein 30g; Potassium 380mg

Spicy Hare Stew with Root Vegetables

Preparation Time: 20 minutes
Cooking Time: 1 hour 30 minutes
Servings: 2

INGREDIENTS

- 1 hare, jointed into pieces
- 2 tbsp olive oil
- 1 onion, finely chopped
- 2 cloves garlic, minced
- 2 carrots, diced
- 2 parsnips, diced
- 1 potato, diced
- 1 can diced tomatoes (14 oz)
- 2 cups chicken broth
- 1 tbsp tomato paste
- 1 tsp smoked paprika
- 1 tsp ground cumin
- 1 tsp ground coriander
- 1/2 tsp cayenne pepper (adjust to taste)
- 1 bay leaf
- Salt and black pepper to taste
- Fresh cilantro, chopped for garnish

DIRECTIONS

1. Heat the olive oil in a large pot over medium-high heat. Season the hare pieces with salt and black pepper, then brown them in the hot oil. Remove the browned hare pieces and set them aside.

2. Add the chopped onion and minced garlic to the pot, sautéing until they become translucent and fragrant. Stir in the diced carrots, parsnips, and potato, cooking for a few minutes until they begin to soften.

3. Mix in the tomato paste, smoked paprika, ground cumin, ground coriander, and cayenne pepper. Cook for another minute to allow the spices to release their aromas.

4. Pour in the diced tomatoes and chicken broth, stirring to combine all ingredients. Add the bay leaf to the pot, then return the browned hare pieces to the mixture. Bring the stew to a simmer, then reduce the heat to low.

5. Cover the pot and let the stew cook slowly for about 1 hour and 30 minutes, or until the hare is tender and the flavors have melded together. Stir occasionally and adjust seasoning with salt and black pepper as needed.

6. Once cooked, remove the bay leaf and discard it. Serve the spicy hare stew hot, garnished with freshly chopped cilantro. This hearty stew pairs well with crusty bread or a side of steamed rice.

Nutrition Values: Calories 420; Total Fat 20g; Saturated Fat 4g; Sodium 850mg; Total Carbohydrates 32g; Dietary Fiber 7g; Protein 35g; Potassium 1100mg

Roasted Partridge with Cranberry Glaze

Preparation Time: 20 minutes
Cooking Time: 1 hour
Servings: 2

INGREDIENTS

- 2 partridges
- 2 tbsp olive oil
- Salt and black pepper to taste
- 1/2 cup fresh cranberries
- 1/4 cup honey
- 1/4 cup orange juice
- 1/4 cup chicken broth
- 1 tbsp balsamic vinegar
- 1 tsp fresh thyme, chopped
- 1 clove garlic, minced
- Fresh parsley, chopped for garnish

DIRECTIONS

1. Preheat the oven to 375°F (190°C). Rub the partridges with olive oil, then season them with salt and black pepper. Place the partridges on a roasting pan and set aside.
2. In a small saucepan, combine the fresh cranberries, honey, orange juice, chicken broth, balsamic vinegar, fresh thyme, and minced garlic. Bring the mixture to a simmer over medium heat, stirring occasionally. Cook until the cranberries have burst and the sauce has thickened, about 10 minutes. Remove from heat and let it cool slightly.
3. Brush the partridges generously with the cranberry glaze, ensuring they are well-coated. Place the roasting pan in the preheated oven and roast the partridges for about 45-50 minutes, basting with the glaze every 15 minutes. The partridges are done when the skin is golden brown and crispy, and the internal temperature reaches 165°F (74°C).
4. Remove the partridges from the oven and let them rest for a few minutes before carving. Serve the roasted partridges with any remaining cranberry glaze drizzled on top. Garnish with freshly chopped parsley for a burst of color and added freshness. This dish pairs beautifully with roasted vegetables or a side of wild rice.

Nutrition Values: Calories 480; Total Fat 24g; Saturated Fat 6g; Sodium 300mg; Total Carbohydrates 32g; Dietary Fiber 3g; Protein 34g; Potassium 600mg

Baked Woodcock with Garlic and Thyme

Preparation Time: 15 minutes
Cooking Time: 45 minutes
Servings: 2

INGREDIENTS

- 2 woodcocks
- 3 tbsp olive oil
- 4 cloves garlic, minced
- 1 tbsp fresh thyme leaves, chopped
- Salt and black pepper to taste
- 1/2 cup chicken broth
- 1/4 cup dry white wine
- 1 lemon, sliced
- Fresh thyme sprigs for garnish

DIRECTIONS

1. Preheat the oven to 375°F (190°C). Rinse the woodcocks under cold water and pat them dry with paper towels. Rub the woodcocks all over with olive oil, then season generously with salt and black pepper.
2. In a small bowl, combine the minced garlic and chopped thyme leaves. Rub this mixture

evenly over the woodcocks, ensuring the flavors penetrate the skin.

3. Place the seasoned woodcocks in a baking dish. Pour the chicken broth and dry white wine around the birds. Arrange the lemon slices on top and around the woodcocks for added flavor and moisture during baking.

4. Cover the baking dish with aluminum foil to retain moisture and bake in the preheated oven for 30 minutes. Remove the foil and continue baking for an additional 15 minutes, or until the woodcocks are golden brown and the internal temperature reaches 165°F (74°C).

5. Remove the woodcocks from the oven and let them rest for a few minutes before serving. Garnish with fresh thyme sprigs for an aromatic touch. Serve the baked woodcock with garlic and thyme alongside roasted potatoes or a fresh garden salad for a complete meal.

Nutrition Values: Calories 520; Total Fat 32g; Saturated Fat 8g; Sodium 400mg; Total Carbohydrates 8g; Dietary Fiber 2g; Protein 40g; Potassium 600mg

Grilled Pigeon with Balsamic Reduction

Preparation Time: 20 minutes
Cooking Time: 25 minutes
Servings: 2

INGREDIENTS

- 2 pigeons
- 3 tbsp olive oil
- Salt and black pepper to taste
- 1/4 cup balsamic vinegar
- 2 tbsp honey
- 1 tbsp Dijon mustard
- 1 clove garlic, minced
- 1 sprig fresh rosemary, chopped
- Fresh rosemary sprigs for garnish

DIRECTIONS

1. Begin by preparing the pigeons. Rinse them under cold water and pat them dry with paper towels. Rub the pigeons all over with olive oil, then season generously with salt and black pepper.

2. In a small saucepan, combine the balsamic vinegar, honey, Dijon mustard, minced garlic, and chopped rosemary. Bring the mixture to a simmer over medium heat, stirring occasionally. Reduce the heat to low and let it cook until the sauce thickens and reduces by half, about 10-15 minutes. Set aside to cool slightly.

3. Preheat a grill to medium-high heat. Once hot, place the pigeons on the grill, breast side down. Grill for about 8-10 minutes on each side, or until the internal temperature reaches 165°F (74°C) and the skin is crispy and golden brown.

4. While the pigeons are grilling, baste them occasionally with the balsamic reduction to enhance the flavor and keep the meat moist.

5. Remove the pigeons from the grill and let them rest for a few minutes before serving. Drizzle the remaining balsamic reduction over the pigeons for an extra burst of flavor. Garnish with fresh rosemary sprigs and serve with a side of grilled vegetables or a fresh salad for a balanced meal.

Nutrition Values: Calories 480; Total Fat 28g; Saturated Fat 6g; Sodium 320mg; Total Carbohydrates 16g; Dietary Fiber 1g; Protein 40g; Potassium 550mg

Quail Eggs Benedict with Truffle Hollandaise

Preparation Time: 15 minutes
Cooking Time: 20 minutes
Servings: 2

INGREDIENTS

- 8 quail eggs
- 2 English muffins
- **Preparation Time:** 15 minutes
- **Cooking Time:** 20 minutes
- **Servings:** 2

INGREDIENTS

- 8 quail eggs
- 2 English muffins, split and toasted
- 4 slices Canadian bacon or ham
- 1 tbsp white vinegar
- 1 tbsp butter
- **For the Truffle Hollandaise Sauce:**
- 3 egg yolks
- 1/2 cup unsalted butter, melted
- 1 tbsp fresh lemon juice
- 1 tsp truffle oil
- Salt and pepper to taste

DIRECTIONS

1. Start by preparing the Truffle Hollandaise Sauce. In a heatproof bowl, whisk the egg yolks and lemon juice until the mixture is thick and doubled in volume. Place the bowl over a saucepan of gently simmering water, making sure the bottom of the bowl does not touch the water. Slowly drizzle in the melted butter while continuously whisking. Once the butter is fully incorporated and the sauce is smooth, remove from heat. Stir in the truffle oil, and season with salt and pepper. Keep the sauce warm.
2. In a large skillet, heat the butter over medium heat and cook the Canadian bacon or ham slices until browned and heated through. Keep warm.
3. To poach the quail eggs, fill a small saucepan with about 2 inches of water and bring to a gentle simmer. Add the white vinegar. Crack each quail egg into a small bowl, then carefully slide them into the simmering water. Poach for about 2-3 minutes until the whites are set but the yolks remain runny. Remove the eggs with a slotted spoon and drain on paper towels.
4. To assemble the dish, place two halves of toasted English muffin on each plate. Top each muffin half with a slice of Canadian bacon or ham. Place two poached quail eggs on top of each muffin half. Generously spoon the warm Truffle Hollandaise Sauce over the eggs. Serve immediately, garnished with a sprinkle of fresh herbs if desired.

Nutrition Values: Calories 540; Total Fat 40g; Saturated Fat 20g; Sodium 870mg; Total Carbohydrates 20g; Dietary Fiber 1g; Protein 20g; Potassium 220mg

Smoked Grouse with Honey Mustard Glaze

Preparation Time: 30 minutes
Cooking Time: 1 hour 30 minutes
Servings: 2

INGREDIENTS

- 2 grouse breasts
- 1/4 cup honey
- 1/4 cup Dijon mustard
- 1 tbsp apple cider vinegar
- 2 cloves garlic, minced
- 1 tsp smoked paprika
- Salt and pepper to taste
- Wood chips for smoking (hickory or applewood recommended)

DIRECTIONS

1. Begin by preparing the honey mustard glaze. In a small bowl, mix together the honey, Dijon mustard, apple cider vinegar, minced garlic, and smoked paprika. Season with salt and pepper to taste. Set aside half of the glaze for serving.
2. Season the grouse breasts with salt and pepper, then brush a generous amount of the honey mustard glaze onto each breast, ensuring they are evenly coated.
3. Prepare your smoker by soaking the wood chips in water for at least 30 minutes. Preheat the smoker to a temperature of 225°F (110°C). Once the smoker is ready, drain the wood chips and place them in the smoker box or directly on the coals.
4. Place the grouse breasts on the smoker rack. Smoke the grouse for approximately 1 hour 30 minutes, or until the internal temperature reaches 165°F (75°C) and the meat is tender and juicy. During the smoking process, periodically brush the grouse with additional honey mustard glaze to build up a flavorful crust.
5. Remove the smoked grouse from the smoker and let it rest for a few minutes before slicing. Serve the grouse breasts drizzled with the reserved honey mustard glaze for added flavor.

Nutrition Values: Calories 450; Total Fat 12g; Saturated Fat 2.5g; Sodium 620mg; Total Carbohydrates 35g; Dietary Fiber 1g; Protein 50g; Potassium 600mg

Wild Rabbit Ragu with Pappardelle

Preparation Time: 20 minutes
Cooking Time: 1 hour 40 minutes
Servings: 2

INGREDIENTS

- 1 wild rabbit, cleaned and cut into pieces
- 1 onion, finely chopped
- 2 cloves garlic, minced
- 1 carrot, finely chopped
- 1 celery stalk, finely chopped
- 1 cup dry red wine
- 1 can (14 oz) crushed tomatoes
- 1 cup chicken broth
- 2 tbsp olive oil
- 1 bay leaf
- 1 sprig fresh rosemary
- 1 tsp dried thyme
- Salt and pepper to taste
- 200g pappardelle pasta
- Freshly grated Parmesan cheese for serving

DIRECTIONS

1. Begin by heating olive oil in a large pot or Dutch oven over medium heat. Add the rabbit pieces and brown them on all sides, ensuring they are well-seared. Remove the rabbit from the pot and set aside.
2. In the same pot, add the chopped onion, garlic, carrot, and celery. Sauté until the vegetables are softened and the onion is translucent, about 5-7 minutes. Add the red wine to the pot, stirring to deglaze and scrape up any browned bits from the bottom. Let the wine simmer for a few minutes to reduce slightly.
3. Return the rabbit pieces to the pot. Add the crushed tomatoes, chicken broth, bay leaf, rosemary, and thyme. Season with salt and pepper to taste. Bring the mixture to a boil, then reduce the heat to low, cover the pot, and let it simmer for about 1 hour and 30 minutes, or until the rabbit meat is tender and falls off the bone.
4. Once the rabbit is cooked, remove the meat from the pot and let it cool slightly. Shred the meat, discarding any bones, and return the shredded meat to the pot. Stir the ragu to combine and let it simmer for an additional 10-15 minutes to meld the flavors.
5. While the ragu is simmering, cook the

pappardelle pasta according to the package instructions until al dente. Drain the pasta and add it directly to the pot with the ragu, tossing to coat the pasta evenly with the sauce.

6. Serve the wild rabbit ragu with pappardelle in warm bowls, garnished with freshly grated Parmesan cheese.

Nutrition Values: Calories 650; Total Fat 18g; Saturated Fat 4g; Sodium 780mg; Total Carbohydrates 75g; Dietary Fiber 6g; Protein 45g; Potassium 950mg

CHAPTER 3
BIRD RECIPES FOR EVERY OCCASION

Citrus-Glazed Duck Breast

Preparation Time: 15 minutes
Cooking Time: 25 minutes
Servings: 2

INGREDIENTS

- 2 duck breasts
- 1 orange, zested and juiced
- 1 lemon, zested and juiced
- 2 tablespoons honey
- 1 tablespoon soy sauce
- 2 garlic cloves, minced
- 1 tablespoon fresh thyme leaves
- Salt and pepper to taste
- 1 tablespoon olive oil

DIRECTIONS

1. Score the skin of the duck breasts in a criss-cross pattern, being careful not to cut into the meat. Season the breasts with salt and pepper on both sides. Heat a skillet over medium-high heat and add the olive oil. Place the duck breasts skin-side down in the skillet and cook until the skin is crispy and golden brown, about 6-8 minutes. Flip the duck breasts and cook for an additional 4-5 minutes for medium-rare, or longer if desired.

2. In a small bowl, combine the orange zest, orange juice, lemon zest, lemon juice, honey, soy sauce, and minced garlic. Mix well to create the glaze. Remove the duck breasts from the skillet and set aside to rest. Pour off any excess fat from the skillet, leaving about a tablespoon. Add the glaze mixture to the skillet and cook over medium heat until it thickens slightly, about 2-3 minutes.

3. Return the duck breasts to the skillet, turning them in the glaze to coat well. Cook for another 2 minutes, ensuring the duck is fully coated and heated through. Slice the duck breasts thinly and drizzle with the remaining glaze. Garnish with fresh thyme leaves before serving.

Nutrition Values: Calories 580; Total Fat 38g; Saturated Fat 12g; Sodium 400mg; Total Carbohydrates 18g; Dietary Fiber 1g; Protein 43g; Potassium 550mg

Honey-Soy Marinated Quail

Preparation Time: 15 minutes
(plus 2 hours marinating)
Cooking Time: 25 minutes
Servings: 2

INGREDIENTS

- 2 whole quails
- 3 tablespoons soy sauce
- 2 tablespoons honey
- 1 tablespoon olive oil
- 2 cloves garlic, minced
- 1 tablespoon fresh ginger, grated
- 1 tablespoon rice vinegar
- 1 teaspoon sesame oil
- Salt and pepper to taste
- Fresh cilantro for garnish

DIRECTIONS

1. In a medium bowl, combine the soy sauce, honey, olive oil, garlic, ginger, rice vinegar, and sesame oil to create the marinade. Mix well until all ingredients are fully incorporated. Rinse the quails under cold water and pat them dry with paper towels. Place the quails in a shallow dish or a resealable plastic bag. Pour the marinade over the quails, ensuring they are fully coated. Cover the dish with plastic wrap or seal the bag and refrigerate for at least 2 hours, turning occasionally to ensure even marination.
2. Preheat your oven to 375°F (190°C). Remove the quails from the marinade and place them on a baking sheet lined with aluminum foil. Season the quails with salt and pepper. Reserve the remaining marinade.
3. Bake the quails in the preheated oven for 20-25 minutes, basting with the reserved marinade halfway through the cooking process. The quails are done when the skin is golden brown and the internal temperature reaches 165°F (74°C). Remove the quails from the oven and let them rest for a few minutes before serving.
4. Garnish with fresh cilantro and serve hot, accompanied by your choice of side dishes.

Nutrition Values: Calories 450; Total Fat 25g; Saturated Fat 7g; Sodium 1200mg; Total Carbohydrates 20g; Dietary Fiber 1g; Protein 35g; Potassium 450mg

Roasted Partridge with Sage and Apple Stuffing

Preparation Time: 20 minutes
Cooking Time: 50 minutes
Servings: 2

INGREDIENTS

- 2 whole partridges, cleaned
- 1 apple, peeled, cored, and chopped
- 1 small onion, finely chopped
- 2 cloves garlic, minced
- 2 tablespoons fresh sage, chopped
- 1/2 cup breadcrumbs
- 1/4 cup chicken broth
- 2 tablespoons butter, melted
- Salt and pepper to taste
- 1 tablespoon olive oil

DIRECTIONS

1. Preheat your oven to 375°F (190°C). In a bowl, combine the chopped apple, onion, garlic, sage, breadcrumbs, and chicken broth. Mix well until the ingredients are fully incorporated. Season with salt and pepper to taste.
2. Stuff the cavity of each partridge with the apple and sage mixture, ensuring it is evenly distributed. Tie the legs of the partridges together with kitchen twine to secure the stuffing.
3. Place the stuffed partridges in a roasting pan. Brush them with melted butter and drizzle

with olive oil. Season the outside of the birds with additional salt and pepper.

4. Roast the partridges in the preheated oven for 45-50 minutes, or until the skin is golden brown and the internal temperature reaches 165°F (74°C). Baste occasionally with the pan juices to keep the meat moist.

5. Once cooked, remove the partridges from the oven and let them rest for 5-10 minutes before serving. This allows the juices to redistribute throughout the meat, ensuring a tender and flavorful result.

Nutrition Values: Calories 650; Total Fat 35g; Saturated Fat 12g; Sodium 550mg; Total Carbohydrates 30g; Dietary Fiber 5g; Protein 50g; Potassium:700mg

BBQ Pigeon with Spicy Bourbon Sauce

Preparation Time: 30 minutes
Cooking Time: 40 minutes
Servings: 2

INGREDIENTS

- 2 whole pigeons, cleaned
- 1/2 cup bourbon
- 1/2 cup ketchup
- 1/4 cup apple cider vinegar
- 1/4 cup brown sugar
- 2 tablespoons Worcestershire sauce
- 1 tablespoon Dijon mustard
- 2 cloves garlic, minced
- 1 teaspoon smoked paprika
- 1/2 teaspoon cayenne pepper
- Salt and pepper to taste
- 2 tablespoons olive oil

DIRECTIONS

1. In a medium saucepan, combine the bourbon, ketchup, apple cider vinegar, brown sugar, Worcestershire sauce, Dijon mustard, minced

garlic, smoked paprika, and cayenne pepper. Stir well to combine. Bring the mixture to a simmer over medium heat, then reduce the heat to low and let it cook for 15-20 minutes, stirring occasionally, until the sauce thickens. Season with salt and pepper to taste and set aside.

2. Preheat your grill to medium-high heat. Rub the pigeons with olive oil and season generously with salt and pepper. Place the pigeons on the grill, breast side down. Grill for 5-7 minutes on each side, or until the skin is crispy and the internal temperature reaches 165°F (74°C).

3. During the last 10 minutes of grilling, brush the pigeons generously with the spicy bourbon sauce, allowing it to caramelize and create a glaze. Continue to turn and baste the pigeons frequently to ensure they are well coated.

4. Once cooked, remove the pigeons from the grill and let them rest for a few minutes before serving. Serve the pigeons with additional spicy bourbon sauce on the side for dipping.

Nutrition Values: Calories 720; Total Fat 28g; Saturated Fat 6g; Sodium 810mg; Total Carbohydrates 45g; Dietary Fiber 2g; Protein 45g; Potassium 650mg

Cranberry and Orange Pheasant

Preparation Time: 20 minutes
Cooking Time: 1 hour
Servings: 2

INGREDIENTS

- 2 pheasant breasts
- 1/2 cup fresh cranberries
- 1/4 cup orange juice
- 1/4 cup chicken broth
- 1 tablespoon honey

- 1 tablespoon olive oil
- 1 teaspoon orange zest
- 1 small onion, finely chopped
- 2 cloves garlic, minced
- Salt and pepper to taste
- Fresh rosemary for garnish

DIRECTIONS

1. In a small saucepan, combine the fresh cranberries, orange juice, chicken broth, honey, orange zest, and a pinch of salt. Bring to a boil over medium heat, then reduce the heat and let it simmer for about 10-15 minutes, or until the cranberries have burst and the sauce has thickened slightly.
2. Preheat your oven to 350°F (175°C). Season the pheasant breasts with salt and pepper. In an oven-safe skillet, heat the olive oil over medium-high heat. Add the pheasant breasts and sear them for 3-4 minutes on each side, or until they are golden brown.
3. Add the chopped onion and minced garlic to the skillet, stirring them around the pheasant breasts. Pour the cranberry and orange sauce over the pheasant, making sure they are well coated. Transfer the skillet to the preheated oven and roast for 25-30 minutes, or until the pheasant is cooked through and reaches an internal temperature of 165°F (74°C).
4. Remove the skillet from the oven and let the pheasant rest for a few minutes. Serve the pheasant breasts topped with the cranberry and orange sauce and garnished with fresh rosemary.

Nutrition Values: Calories 420; Total Fat 15g; Saturated Fat 3g; Sodium 320mg; Total Carbohydrates 25g; Dietary Fiber 3g; Protein 45g; Potassium 650mg

Lemon-Herb Grilled Goose

Preparation Time: 30 minutes
Cooking Time: 1 hour
Servings: 2

INGREDIENTS

- 2 goose breasts
- Juice of 2 lemons
- 2 tablespoons olive oil
- 2 cloves garlic, minced
- 1 tablespoon fresh thyme, chopped
- 1 tablespoon fresh rosemary, chopped
- Salt and pepper to taste
- Lemon slices and fresh herbs for garnish

DIRECTIONS

1. In a bowl, combine the lemon juice, olive oil, minced garlic, chopped thyme, and rosemary. Season the goose breasts with salt and pepper, then place them in the bowl with the marinade, ensuring they are well coated. Cover and refrigerate for at least 30 minutes, or up to 2 hours for a deeper flavor.
2. Preheat the grill to medium-high heat. Remove the goose breasts from the marinade and let any excess drip off. Place the breasts on the grill and cook for about 6-8 minutes on each side, or until they reach an internal temperature of 165°F (74°C) and are nicely charred.
3. Remove the goose breasts from the grill and let them rest for 5 minutes before slicing. Serve the grilled goose breasts garnished with lemon slices and fresh herbs for an extra touch of flavor and presentation.

Nutrition Values: Calories 480; Total Fat 18g; Saturated Fat 5g; Sodium 3240mg; Total Carbohydrates 6g; Dietary Fiber 1g; Protein 65g; Potassium 750mg

Moroccan-Spiced Squab

Preparation Time: 20 minutes
Cooking Time: 40 minutes
Servings: 2

INGREDIENTS

- 2 squab (young pigeons), cleaned and patted dry
- 2 tablespoons olive oil
- 1 teaspoon ground cumin
- 1 teaspoon ground coriander
- 1 teaspoon ground cinnamon
- 1 teaspoon ground paprika
- 1 teaspoon ground ginger
- 2 cloves garlic, minced
- Juice of 1 lemon
- Salt and pepper to taste
- Fresh cilantro and lemon wedges for garnish

DIRECTIONS

1. Combine olive oil, ground cumin, coriander, cinnamon, paprika, ginger, minced garlic, lemon juice, salt, and pepper in a small bowl to create the marinade. Rub the marinade thoroughly over the squab, making sure to coat the inside cavity as well. Allow the squab to marinate for at least 20 minutes at room temperature or up to 2 hours in the refrigerator for a more intense flavor.
2. Preheat the oven to 375°F (190°C). Place the marinated squab on a roasting pan, breast side up. Roast in the preheated oven for about 35-40 minutes, or until the internal temperature reaches 165°F (74°C) and the skin is golden brown and crispy.
3. Remove the squab from the oven and let them rest for 5 minutes before serving. Garnish with fresh cilantro and lemon wedges. Serve alongside couscous or a fresh salad for a complete Moroccan-inspired meal.

Nutrition Values: Calories 570; Total Fat 34g; Saturated Fat 8g; Sodium 780mg; Total Carbohydrates 5g; Dietary Fiber 1g; Protein 55g; Potassium 600mg

Wild Duck Cassoulet

Preparation Time: 30 minutes
Cooking Time: 2 hours
Servings: 2

INGREDIENTS

- 2 wild duck breasts, skin on
- 2 cups cooked white beans (cannellini or Great Northern beans)
- 1 cup diced tomatoes
- 1 cup chicken broth
- 1 small onion, diced
- 2 cloves garlic, minced
- 2 slices of bacon, chopped
- 1 small carrot, diced
- 1 celery stalk, diced
- 1 sprig fresh thyme
- 1 bay leaf
- 1 tablespoon olive oil
- Salt and pepper to taste
- Fresh parsley for garnish

DIRECTIONS

1. Preheat the oven to 325°F (165°C). In a large oven-safe pot or Dutch oven, heat the olive oil over medium heat. Add the chopped bacon and cook until it starts to brown. Remove the bacon and set aside, leaving the rendered fat in the pot.
2. Season the duck breasts with salt and pepper. Place the duck breasts skin side down in the pot and sear until the skin is golden brown and crispy. Flip the breasts and sear the other side for about 2 minutes. Remove the duck breasts and set aside.
3. In the same pot, add the diced onion, carrot, and celery. Cook until the vegetables are

softened. Add the minced garlic and cook for another minute. Stir in the diced tomatoes and chicken broth, then add the cooked white beans, thyme, and bay leaf. Bring the mixture to a simmer.

4. Nestle the seared duck breasts back into the pot, skin side up. Transfer the pot to the preheated oven and bake, uncovered, for about 1.5 to 2 hours, or until the duck is tender and the flavors have melded together.

5. Remove the pot from the oven and let it rest for a few minutes. Discard the thyme sprig and bay leaf. Garnish with fresh parsley before serving. Serve the Wild Duck Cassoulet hot, accompanied by crusty bread if desired.

Nutrition Values: Calories 680; Total Fat 32g; Saturated Fat 9g; Sodium 980mg; Total Carbohydrates 40g; Dietary Fiber 10g; Protein 58g; Potassium 1400mg

Maple-Balsamic Glazed Cornish Game Hen

Preparation Time: 20 minutes
Cooking Time: 1 hour
Servings: 2

INGREDIENTS

- 2 Cornish game hens
- 1/4 cup maple syrup
- 2 tablespoons balsamic vinegar
- 2 cloves garlic, minced
- 1 tablespoon Dijon mustard
- 1 tablespoon olive oil
- Salt and pepper to taste
- Fresh rosemary sprigs for garnish

DIRECTIONS

1. Preheat the oven to 375°F (190°C). In a small bowl, whisk together the maple syrup, balsamic vinegar, minced garlic, Dijon mustard,

olive oil, salt, and pepper until well combined. Set aside.

2. Rinse the Cornish game hens under cold water and pat them dry with paper towels. Place the hens on a roasting rack in a baking dish. Brush each hen generously with the maple-balsamic glaze, ensuring to cover all sides. Reserve some glaze for basting later.

3. Place the hens in the preheated oven and roast for about 30 minutes. Baste the hens with the remaining glaze and continue roasting for another 30 minutes, or until the internal temperature reaches 165°F (74°C) and the skin is golden brown and crispy.

4. Remove the hens from the oven and let them rest for 10 minutes before serving. Garnish with fresh rosemary sprigs and serve with your favorite side dishes.

Nutrition Values: Calories 560; Total Fat 30g; Saturated Fat 8g; Sodium 620mg; Total Carbohydrates 22g; Dietary Fiber 0g; Protein 48g; Potassium 560mg

Garlic and Herb Roast Woodcock

Preparation Time: 15 minutes
Cooking Time: 45 minutes
Servings: 2

INGREDIENTS

- 2 woodcocks, cleaned and plucked
- 3 cloves garlic, minced
- 2 tablespoons fresh rosemary, chopped
- 2 tablespoons fresh thyme, chopped
- 1 lemon, zested and juiced
- 2 tablespoons olive oil
- Salt and pepper to taste
- 1/4 cup white wine

DIRECTIONS

1. Preheat the oven to 375°F (190°C). In a small bowl, combine the minced garlic, chopped rosemary, chopped thyme, lemon zest, lemon juice, olive oil, salt, and pepper. Mix well to form a marinade.
2. Rinse the woodcocks under cold water and pat them dry with paper towels. Rub the garlic and herb marinade all over the birds, making sure to coat them evenly.
3. Place the woodcocks on a roasting rack in a baking dish. Pour the white wine into the bottom of the dish to keep the birds moist during roasting. Roast the woodcocks in the preheated oven for about 45 minutes, or until the internal temperature reaches 160°F (71°C) and the skin is golden brown and crispy.
4. Remove the woodcocks from the oven and let them rest for 10 minutes before serving. Serve with roasted vegetables or a fresh salad for a complete meal.

Nutrition Values: Calories 520; Total Fat 28g; Saturated Fat 7g; Sodium 380mg; Total Carbohydrates 3g; Dietary Fiber 1g; Protein 57g; Potassium 540mg

CHAPTER 4
EXOTIC AND UNIQUE GAME CREATIONS

Alligator Tail with Spicy Cajun Sauce

Preparation Time: 20 minutes
Cooking Time: 30 minutes
Servings: 2

INGREDIENTS

- 1 pound alligator tail meat, cut into medallions
- 2 tablespoons olive oil
- 1 lemon, juiced
- 2 garlic cloves, minced
- 1 teaspoon smoked paprika
- 1 teaspoon cayenne pepper
- 1 teaspoon dried oregano
- 1 teaspoon dried thyme
- Salt and black pepper, to taste
- 1 cup heavy cream
- 1/2 cup chicken broth
- 1/4 cup chopped green onions
- 2 tablespoons chopped fresh parsley

DIRECTIONS

1. Combine olive oil, lemon juice, minced garlic, smoked paprika, cayenne pepper, oregano, thyme, salt, and black pepper in a bowl. Add the alligator tail medallions, ensuring they are well-coated with the marinade. Cover and refrigerate for at least 1 hour. Heat a large skillet over medium-high heat and add the marinated alligator tail medallions. Cook for 3-4 minutes on each side until golden brown and cooked through. Remove from the skillet and set aside. In the same skillet, add the chicken broth and bring to a simmer, scraping up any browned bits from the bottom. Reduce the heat to medium and stir in the heavy cream, allowing the sauce to thicken for 5-7 minutes. Add the cooked alligator tail medallions back to the skillet and coat them with the spicy Cajun sauce. Cook for an additional 2-3 minutes until everything is heated through. Garnish with chopped green onions and parsley before serving.

Nutrition Values: Calories 520; Total Fat 34g; Saturated Fat 14g; Sodium 980mg; Total Carbohydrates 5g; Dietary Fiber 1g; Protein 46g; Potassium 780mg

Smoked Kangaroo Loin with Plum Glaze

Preparation Time: 30 minutes
(plus 1 hour marinating)
Cooking Time: 1 hour 30 minutes
Servings: 2

INGREDIENTS

- 1 pound kangaroo loin
- 2 tablespoons olive oil
- 2 garlic cloves, minced
- 1 tablespoon fresh rosemary, chopped
- Salt and black pepper, to taste
- 1 cup plum jam
- 1/4 cup balsamic vinegar
- 1/4 cup soy sauce
- 1 tablespoon honey
- 1 teaspoon ground ginger
- Wood chips for smoking

DIRECTIONS

1. Rub the kangaroo loin with olive oil, minced garlic, rosemary, salt, and black pepper. Let it marinate for at least 1 hour in the refrigerator. Prepare the smoker with wood chips and preheat to 225°F (107°C). Place the marinated kangaroo loin in the smoker and smoke for about 1 hour or until it reaches an internal temperature of 135°F (57°C) for medium-rare. While the kangaroo is smoking, prepare the plum glaze by combining plum jam, balsamic vinegar, soy sauce, honey, and ground ginger in a small saucepan. Heat over medium heat, stirring occasionally, until the glaze is smooth and slightly thickened. Once the kangaroo loin is done smoking, brush it generously with the plum glaze. Increase the smoker temperature to 350°F (177°C) and cook for an additional 30 minutes, basting with the glaze every 10 minutes. Remove the kangaroo loin from the smoker and let it rest for 10 minutes before slicing and serving.

Nutrition Values: Calories 510; Total Fat 16g; Saturated Fat 4g; Sodium 1280mg; Total Carbohydrates 44g; Dietary Fiber 2g; Protein 52g; Potassium 850mg

Grilled Ostrich Steaks with Garlic Butter

Preparation Time: 15 minutes
Cooking Time: 15 minutes
Servings: 2

INGREDIENTS

- 2 ostrich steaks (about 6 ounces each)
- 2 tablespoons olive oil
- Salt and black pepper, to taste
- 4 tablespoons unsalted butter, softened
- 3 garlic cloves, minced
- 1 tablespoon fresh parsley, chopped
- 1 teaspoon lemon juice
- Zest of 1 lemon

DIRECTIONS

1. Brush the ostrich steaks with olive oil and season with salt and black pepper on both sides. Preheat the grill to medium-high heat. In a small bowl, combine the softened butter, minced garlic, chopped parsley, lemon juice, and lemon zest, mixing well to create the garlic butter. Set aside. Grill the ostrich steaks for about 3-4 minutes per side, or until they reach your desired level of doneness. Transfer the steaks to a plate and immediately top each with a generous dollop of garlic butter, allowing it to melt over the meat. Let the steaks rest for a few minutes before serving to absorb the flavors of the garlic butter.

Nutrition Values: Calories 490; Total Fat 28g; Saturated Fat 10g; Sodium 420mg; Total Carbohydrates 2g; Dietary Fiber 0g; Protein 52g; Potassium 650mg

Crocodile Kebabs with Pineapple and Peppers

Preparation Time: 20 minutes
Cooking Time: 10 minutes
Servings: 2

INGREDIENTS

- 8 ounces crocodile meat, cut into 1-inch cubes
- 1 cup fresh pineapple chunks
- 1 red bell pepper, cut into 1-inch pieces
- 1 yellow bell pepper, cut into 1-inch pieces
- 2 tablespoons soy sauce
- 1 tablespoon honey
- 1 tablespoon olive oil
- 1 garlic clove, minced
- 1 teaspoon grated ginger
- Salt and black pepper, to taste
- Wooden skewers, soaked in water for 30 minutes

DIRECTIONS

1. In a medium bowl, combine the soy sauce, honey, olive oil, minced garlic, and grated ginger. Add the crocodile meat cubes to the marinade, ensuring they are well-coated, and let them marinate for at least 15 minutes. Thread the marinated crocodile meat onto the soaked wooden skewers, alternating with pineapple chunks and bell pepper pieces. Preheat the grill to medium-high heat. Place the kebabs on the grill and cook for about 10 minutes, turning occasionally, until the crocodile meat is cooked through and the vegetables are slightly charred. Serve the crocodile kebabs hot, garnished with any remaining marinade that has been boiled for safety.

Nutrition Values: Calories 450; Total Fat 12g; Saturated Fat 2g; Sodium 960mg; Total Carbohydrates 40g; Dietary Fiber 4g; Protein 45g; Potassium 780mg

Elk Tartare with Quail Egg

Preparation Time: 20 minutes
Cooking Time: None
Servings: 2

INGREDIENTS

- 6 ounces elk loin, finely diced
- 2 quail eggs
- 1 tablespoon capers, finely chopped
- 1 small shallot, finely diced
- 1 teaspoon Dijon mustard
- 1 tablespoon extra virgin olive oil
- 1 teaspoon Worcestershire sauce
- Salt and freshly ground black pepper, to taste
- Fresh chives, finely chopped, for garnish
- Microgreens, for garnish
- Lemon wedges, for serving

DIRECTIONS

1. In a mixing bowl, combine the finely diced elk loin with the chopped capers, shallot, Dijon mustard, extra virgin olive oil, and Worcestershire sauce. Season the mixture with salt and freshly ground black pepper to taste, ensuring all ingredients are well incorporated. Divide the elk tartare mixture between two plates, shaping it into a neat mound in the center of each plate. Carefully crack a quail egg over each portion of tartare, letting the yolk sit atop the meat. Garnish the tartare with finely chopped fresh chives and a handful of microgreens. Serve immediately, accompanied by lemon wedges for a fresh burst of acidity.

Nutrition Values: Calories 320; Total Fat 20g; Saturated Fat 4g; Sodium 420mg; Total

Carbohydrates 2g; Dietary Fiber 0g; Protein 30g; Potassium 450mg

Reindeer Meatballs in Creamy Dill Sauce

Preparation Time: 20 minutes
Cooking Time: 30 minutes
Servings: 2

INGREDIENTS

- 8 ounces ground reindeer meat
- 1 small onion, finely chopped
- 1 clove garlic, minced
- 1 egg
- 1/4 cup breadcrumbs
- 1 tablespoon fresh dill, finely chopped
- Salt and pepper, to taste
- 1 tablespoon olive oil
- 1/2 cup heavy cream
- 1/4 cup sour cream
- 1 teaspoon Dijon mustard
- 1 tablespoon lemon juice
- Extra fresh dill, for garnish

DIRECTIONS

1. In a mixing bowl, combine the ground reindeer meat, finely chopped onion, minced garlic, egg, breadcrumbs, fresh dill, salt, and pepper. Mix well until all ingredients are thoroughly combined. Shape the mixture into small meatballs, about the size of a walnut. Heat the olive oil in a large skillet over medium heat. Add the meatballs to the skillet, cooking them until they are browned on all sides and cooked through, which should take about 10 minutes. Remove the meatballs from the skillet and set aside.
2. In the same skillet, reduce the heat to low and add the heavy cream, sour cream, Dijon mustard, and lemon juice. Stir the sauce until it is smooth and begins to thicken, about 5 minutes. Return the meatballs to the skillet,

spooning the creamy dill sauce over them to ensure they are well-coated. Let the meatballs simmer in the sauce for an additional 5 minutes, allowing the flavors to meld. Serve the reindeer meatballs hot, garnished with extra fresh dill. Pair with mashed potatoes or a light salad for a complete meal.

Nutrition Values: Calories 540; Total Fat 36g; Saturated Fat 15g; Sodium 620mg; Total Carbohydrates 8g; Dietary Fiber 1g; Protein 38g; Potassium 450mg

Barbecued Snake with Honey-Lime Marinade

Preparation Time: 20 minutes
Cooking Time: 30 minutes
Servings: 2

INGREDIENTS

- 1 pound snake meat, cleaned and cut into pieces
- 3 tablespoons honey
- 2 tablespoons lime juice
- 1 tablespoon soy sauce
- 2 cloves garlic, minced
- 1 teaspoon ground cumin
- 1/2 teaspoon smoked paprika
- Salt and pepper, to taste
- 2 tablespoons olive oil

DIRECTIONS

1. In a medium bowl, combine honey, lime juice, soy sauce, minced garlic, ground cumin, smoked paprika, salt, and pepper. Mix well to create the marinade. Add the snake meat pieces to the marinade, ensuring each piece is well-coated. Cover the bowl and let it marinate in the refrigerator for at least 1 hour, allowing the flavors to infuse the meat.
2. Preheat the grill to medium-high heat. Lightly oil the grill grates to prevent sticking.

Remove the snake meat from the marinade and place it on the grill. Cook the meat, turning occasionally, until it is cooked through and slightly charred, about 15-20 minutes. Brush the snake meat with any remaining marinade during the grilling process for added flavor. Once cooked, remove the snake meat from the grill and let it rest for a few minutes before serving.

3. Serve the barbecued snake hot, garnished with fresh lime wedges for an extra burst of citrus flavor. This dish pairs well with a side of grilled vegetables or a crisp salad.

Nutrition Values: Calories 520; Total Fat 22g; Saturated Fat 5g; Sodium 940mg; Total Carbohydrates 23g; Dietary Fiber 1g; Protein 52g; Potassium 650mg

Bison and Blueberry Sausage Patties

Preparation Time: 15 minutes
Cooking Time: 20 minutes
Servings: 2

INGREDIENTS

- 1/2 pound ground bison
- 1/4 cup fresh blueberries
- 1 small onion, finely chopped
- 1 clove garlic, minced
- 1 tablespoon fresh thyme, chopped
- 1 tablespoon fresh sage, chopped
- 1/2 teaspoon salt
- 1/4 teaspoon black pepper
- 1 tablespoon olive oil

DIRECTIONS

1. In a mixing bowl, combine the ground bison, fresh blueberries, finely chopped onion, minced garlic, chopped thyme, chopped sage, salt, and black pepper. Mix the ingredients thoroughly until well combined. Form the mixture into four equal-sized patties.

2. Heat olive oil in a skillet over medium heat. Once the oil is hot, add the bison patties to the skillet. Cook the patties for about 5-7 minutes on each side, or until they are browned and cooked through. Be sure to flip the patties carefully to avoid breaking them apart. The blueberries will add a subtle sweetness to the savory patties, creating a unique and delicious flavor combination.

3. After the patties are cooked, remove them from the skillet and place them on a paper towel-lined plate to drain any excess oil. Let the patties rest for a few minutes before serving to allow the juices to redistribute.

4. Serve the bison and blueberry sausage patties hot, paired with a side of roasted vegetables or a fresh green salad for a complete meal. These patties also make a great breakfast option when served with eggs and toast.

Nutrition Values: Calories 320; Total Fat 18g; Saturated Fat 5g; Sodium 540mg; Total Carbohydrates 6g; Dietary Fiber 1g; Protein 30g; Potassium 450mg

Pan-Seared Yak Medallions with Red Wine Reduction

Preparation Time: 15 minutes
Cooking Time: 20 minutes
Servings: 2

INGREDIENTS

- 8 ounces yak tenderloin, cut into medallions
- Salt and black pepper, to taste
- 2 tablespoons olive oil
- 1 shallot, finely chopped
- 1 clove garlic, minced
- 1 cup red wine
- 1/2 cup beef broth

- 1 tablespoon unsalted butter
- 1 sprig fresh thyme

DIRECTIONS

1. Season the yak medallions with salt and black pepper on both sides. Heat the olive oil in a skillet over medium-high heat until shimmering. Add the yak medallions to the skillet and sear for about 3-4 minutes on each side, or until they reach your desired level of doneness. Remove the medallions from the skillet and set aside, keeping them warm.

2. In the same skillet, add the finely chopped shallot and minced garlic. Sauté until the shallot becomes translucent and the garlic is fragrant, about 2 minutes. Pour in the red wine, using a wooden spoon to scrape up any browned bits from the bottom of the skillet. Add the beef broth and fresh thyme sprig, bringing the mixture to a simmer. Let it reduce by half, which should take about 10 minutes.

3. Once the sauce has reduced, remove the thyme sprig and stir in the unsalted butter until the sauce is glossy and smooth. Return the yak medallions to the skillet, turning them in the sauce to coat well. Allow them to warm through for an additional minute.

4. Serve the yak medallions drizzled with the red wine reduction, pairing them with roasted vegetables or a creamy mashed potato for a balanced and sophisticated meal.

Nutrition Values: Calories 460; Total Fat 20g; Saturated Fat 7g; Sodium 600mg; Total Carbohydrates 5g; Dietary Fiber 0g; Protein 56g; Potassium 850mg

Venison Wellington with Mushroom Duxelles

Preparation Time: 30 minutes
Cooking Time: 45 minutes
Servings: 2

INGREDIENTS

- 8 ounces venison loin
- Salt and black pepper, to taste
- 2 tablespoons olive oil
- 1 tablespoon Dijon mustard
- 1 sheet puff pastry, thawed
- 1 egg, beaten
- **For the Mushroom Duxelles:**
- 8 ounces cremini mushrooms, finely chopped
- 1 shallot, finely chopped
- 2 cloves garlic, minced
- 2 tablespoons unsalted butter
- Salt and black pepper, to taste
- 1 teaspoon fresh thyme leaves
- 1/4 cup dry white wine

DIRECTIONS

1. Season the venison loin with salt and black pepper. Heat olive oil in a skillet over medium-high heat. Sear the venison for about 2-3 minutes on each side until browned. Remove from the skillet and let cool. Once cooled, brush the venison with Dijon mustard and set aside.

2. To prepare the mushroom duxelles, melt the unsalted butter in a skillet over medium heat. Add the finely chopped shallot and garlic, sautéing until fragrant and translucent. Add the finely chopped cremini mushrooms and fresh thyme leaves. Cook until the mushrooms release their moisture and become dry, about 10 minutes. Deglaze the skillet with dry white wine and cook until the liquid

evaporates. Season with salt and black pepper to taste. Let the mixture cool.

3. Preheat the oven to 400°F (200°C). Roll out the puff pastry on a lightly floured surface. Spread the mushroom duxelles in the center of the pastry. Place the seared venison on top of the duxelles. Fold the pastry over the venison, sealing the edges to form a neat package. Brush the pastry with beaten egg.

4. Place the wrapped venison on a baking sheet lined with parchment paper. Bake in the preheated oven for about 20-25 minutes, or until the pastry is golden brown. Let the Wellington rest for 10 minutes before slicing and serving.

Nutrition Values: Calories 640; Total Fat 36g; Saturated Fat 12g; Sodium 720mg; Total Carbohydrates 42g; Dietary Fiber 2g; Protein 38g; Potassium 650mg

CHAPTER 5
SWEET AND SAVORY SIDES

Honey-Glazed Carrots with Thyme

Preparation Time: 10 minutes
Cooking Time: 20 minutes
Servings: 2

INGREDIENTS:

- 4 medium carrots, peeled and cut into sticks
- 2 tablespoons honey
- 1 tablespoon butter
- 1 teaspoon fresh thyme leaves
- Salt and pepper to taste
- 1 cup water

DIRECTIONS:

In a medium saucepan, combine the carrot sticks and water. Bring to a boil over medium heat and cook until the carrots are tender, about 10 minutes. Drain the carrots and return them to the pan. Add the honey, butter, and thyme leaves to the pan with the carrots. Cook over low heat, stirring frequently, until the carrots are glazed and the honey and butter form a shiny coating, about 5-7 minutes. Season with salt and pepper to taste. Serve warm, garnished with a few extra thyme leaves if desired.

Nutrition Values: Calories 180; Total Fat 8g; Saturated Fat 5g; Sodium 190mg; Total Carbohydrates 28g; Dietary Fiber 4g; Protein 1g; Potassium 500mg

Maple-Roasted Butternut Squash

Preparation Time: 10 minutes
Cooking Time: 40 minutes
Servings: 2

INGREDIENTS:

- 1 small butternut squash, peeled, seeded, and cut into 1-inch cubes
- 2 tablespoons olive oil
- 2 tablespoons maple syrup
- 1 teaspoon ground cinnamon
- Salt and pepper to taste

DIRECTIONS:

Preheat the oven to 400°F (200°C). In a large bowl, toss the butternut squash cubes with olive oil, maple syrup, and ground cinnamon until evenly coated. Season with salt and pepper to taste. Spread the squash in a single layer on a baking sheet lined with parchment paper. Roast in the preheated oven for 35-40 minutes, stirring halfway through, until the squash is tender and caramelized. Serve warm, drizzled with any remaining glaze from the pan.

Nutrition Values: Calories 220; Total Fat 10g; Saturated Fat 1.5g; Sodium 10mg; Total Carbohydrates 35g; Dietary Fiber 4g; Protein 2g; Potassium 600mg

Cranberry-Walnut Wild Rice Pilaf

Preparation Time: 10 minutes
Cooking Time: 45 minutes
Servings: 2

INGREDIENTS:

- 1/2 cup wild rice
- 1 cup vegetable broth
- 1/4 cup dried cranberries
- 1/4 cup chopped walnuts
- 1 small shallot, finely chopped
- 1 tablespoon olive oil
- 1 teaspoon fresh thyme leaves
- Salt and pepper to taste

DIRECTIONS:

Rinse the wild rice under cold water. In a medium saucepan, heat the olive oil over medium heat and sauté the shallot until it becomes translucent. Add the wild rice and stir to coat the grains with the oil. Pour in the vegetable broth and bring to a boil. Reduce the heat to low, cover, and simmer for 45 minutes or until the rice is tender and the liquid is absorbed. Stir in the dried cranberries, chopped walnuts, and fresh thyme leaves. Season with salt and pepper to taste. Fluff the rice with a fork and serve warm.

Nutrition Values: Calories 360; Total Fat 16g; Saturated Fat 2g; Sodium 240mg; Total Carbohydrates 48g; Dietary Fiber 5g; Protein 8g; Potassium 450mg

Truffle-Infused Mashed Potatoes

Preparation Time: 15 minutes
Cooking Time: 20 minutes
Servings: 2

INGREDIENTS

- 2 large russet potatoes, peeled and cubed
- 1/4 cup heavy cream
- 2 tablespoons unsalted butter
- 1 teaspoon truffle oil
- Salt and pepper to taste
- Chopped fresh chives for garnish

DIRECTIONS

1. Place the cubed potatoes in a large pot and cover with cold water. Bring to a boil over high heat, then reduce to a simmer and cook until the potatoes are tender, about 15-20 minutes. Drain the potatoes and return them to the pot. Add the heavy cream and butter, then mash until smooth and creamy. Stir in the truffle oil and season with salt and pepper to taste. Garnish with chopped fresh chives before serving.

Nutrition Values: Calories 420; Total Fat 22g; Saturated Fat 14g; Sodium 200mg; Total Carbohydrates 49g; Dietary Fiber 3g; Protein 5g; Potassium 800mg

Garlic-Parmesan Green Beans

Preparation Time: 10 minutes
Cooking Time: 10 minutes
Servings: 2

INGREDIENTS

- 200 grams fresh green beans, trimmed
- 2 tablespoons olive oil
- 2 cloves garlic, minced
- 1/4 cup grated Parmesan cheese
- Salt and pepper to taste
- 1 tablespoon chopped fresh parsley for garnish

DIRECTIONS

1. Blanch the green beans in a pot of boiling salted water for 2-3 minutes until they are bright green and tender-crisp. Drain and immediately transfer to a bowl of ice water to stop the cooking process. In a large skillet, heat the olive oil over medium heat. Add the minced garlic and sauté until fragrant, about 1 minute. Add the blanched green beans to the skillet and toss to coat in the garlic oil. Cook for an additional 2-3 minutes, stirring frequently. Remove from heat and sprinkle with grated Parmesan cheese. Season with salt and pepper to taste. Garnish with chopped fresh parsley before serving.

Nutrition Values: Calories 200; Total Fat 15g; Saturated Fat 3g; Sodium 150mg; Total Carbohydrates 12g; Dietary Fiber 4g; Protein 6g; Potassium 300mg

Sweet Potato and Apple Gratin

Preparation Time: 20 minutes
Cooking Time: 45 minutes
Servings: 2

INGREDIENTS

- 1 large sweet potato, peeled and thinly sliced
- 1 large apple, peeled and thinly sliced
- 1/2 cup heavy cream
- 1/4 cup grated Gruyere cheese
- 1 tablespoon butter, divided
- 1 teaspoon fresh thyme leaves
- Salt and pepper to taste
- 1/4 teaspoon ground nutmeg

DIRECTIONS

1. Preheat the oven to 375°F (190°C). Grease a small baking dish with half the butter. Arrange a layer of sweet potato slices at the bottom of the dish, followed by a layer of apple slices. Sprinkle with a pinch of salt, pepper, nutmeg, and thyme. Repeat the layers until all the sweet potato and apple slices are used, finishing with a layer of sweet potatoes. In a small saucepan, heat the heavy cream over medium heat until it begins to simmer. Pour the cream evenly over the layered sweet potatoes and apples. Dot the top with the remaining butter and sprinkle with the grated Gruyere cheese. Cover the dish with foil and bake for 30 minutes. Remove the foil and bake for an additional 15 minutes, or until the top is golden brown and the sweet potatoes are tender. Let it cool slightly before serving.

Nutrition Values: Calories 480; Total Fat 28g; Saturated Fat 17g; Sodium 220mg; Total Carbohydrates 52g; Dietary Fiber 7g; Protein 6g; Potassium 780mg

Herb-Butter Sautéed Wild Greens

Preparation Time: 10 minutes
Cooking Time: 15 minutes
Servings: 2

INGREDIENTS

- 2 cups mixed wild greens (such as dandelion, nettles, and mustard greens), washed and chopped
- 2 tablespoons unsalted butter
- 1 garlic clove, minced
- 1 teaspoon fresh thyme leaves
- 1 teaspoon fresh rosemary, finely chopped
- Salt and pepper to taste
- 1 tablespoon lemon juice

DIRECTIONS

1. Melt the butter in a large skillet over medium heat. Add the minced garlic and sauté until fragrant, about 1 minute. Add the fresh thyme and rosemary, stirring to combine. Add the wild greens to the skillet, tossing to coat them evenly with the herb-butter mixture. Cook for 5-7 minutes, stirring occasionally, until the greens are wilted and tender. Season with salt and pepper to taste. Remove the skillet from the heat and drizzle with lemon juice. Serve immediately.

Nutrition Values: Calories 180; Total Fat 14g; Saturated Fat 8g; Sodium 200mg; Total Carbohydrates 8g; Dietary Fiber 4g; Protein 4g; Potassium 500mg

Caramelized Pear and Blue Cheese Salad

Preparation Time: 15 minutes
Cooking Time: 10 minutes
Servings: 2

INGREDIENTS

- 2 ripe pears, sliced
- 1 tablespoon unsalted butter
- 1 tablespoon brown sugar
- 4 cups mixed salad greens (such as arugula, spinach, and watercress)
- 1/4 cup crumbled blue cheese
- 1/4 cup toasted walnuts
- 2 tablespoons balsamic vinaigrette
- Salt and pepper to taste

DIRECTIONS

1. Melt the butter in a skillet over medium heat. Add the sliced pears and sprinkle with brown sugar. Cook the pears, turning occasionally, until they are golden and caramelized, about 5-7 minutes. Remove from heat and let cool slightly. In a large bowl, toss the mixed salad greens with balsamic vinaigrette until evenly coated. Divide the greens between two plates. Top each salad with the caramelized pears, crumbled blue cheese, and toasted walnuts. Season with salt and pepper to taste. Serve immediately.

Nutrition Values: Calories 450; Total Fat 26g; Saturated Fat 9g; Sodium 320mg; Total Carbohydrates 47g; Dietary Fiber 8g; Protein 9g; Potassium 600mg

Chestnut and Sage Stuffing

Preparation Time: 20 minutes
Cooking Time: 30 minutes
Servings: 2

INGREDIENTS

- 1 cup cooked and peeled chestnuts, roughly chopped
- 2 cups cubed day-old bread
- 1/2 cup chicken or vegetable broth
- 1/4 cup unsalted butter
- 1 small onion, finely chopped
- 1 celery stalk, finely chopped
- 1 tablespoon fresh sage, finely chopped
- 1 teaspoon fresh thyme, finely chopped
- Salt and pepper to taste

DIRECTIONS

1. Preheat the oven to 350°F (175°C). In a skillet, melt the butter over medium heat. Add the onion and celery, cooking until softened, about 5 minutes. Stir in the sage and thyme, cooking for another minute until fragrant. In a large bowl, combine the bread cubes and chopped chestnuts. Pour the onion and celery mixture over the bread and chestnuts, tossing to combine. Gradually add the broth until the stuffing is evenly moistened but not soggy. Season with salt and pepper to taste. Transfer the stuffing mixture to a small baking dish, cover with foil, and bake for 20 minutes. Remove the foil and bake for an additional 10 minutes, or until the top is golden brown and crispy. Serve hot.

Nutrition Values: Calories 400; Total Fat 20g; Saturated Fat 9g; Sodium 640mg; Total Carbohydrates 48g; Dietary Fiber 5g; Protein 7g; Potassium 400mg

Spiced Pumpkin Soup

Preparation Time: 15 minutes
Cooking Time: 30 minutes
Servings: 2

INGREDIENTS

- 2 cups pumpkin puree
- 1 small onion, finely chopped
- 2 garlic cloves, minced
- 1 tablespoon olive oil
- 1 teaspoon ground cumin
- 1/2 teaspoon ground cinnamon
- 1/4 teaspoon ground nutmeg
- 2 cups vegetable broth
- 1/2 cup coconut milk
- Salt and pepper to taste
- Pumpkin seeds and fresh parsley for garnish

DIRECTIONS

1. In a medium pot, heat the olive oil over medium heat. Add the chopped onion and cook until translucent, about 5 minutes. Stir in the minced garlic, ground cumin, ground cinnamon, and ground nutmeg, cooking for another minute until fragrant. Add the pumpkin puree and vegetable broth, stirring to combine. Bring the mixture to a boil, then reduce the heat and let it simmer for 20 minutes. Stir in the coconut milk and season with salt and pepper to taste. Use an immersion blender to blend the soup until smooth, or transfer it to a blender in batches. Serve hot, garnished with pumpkin seeds and fresh parsley.

Nutrition Values: Calories 280; Total Fat 18g; Saturated Fat 10g; Sodium 640mg; Total Carbohydrates 27g; Dietary Fiber 7g; Protein 5g; Potassium 650mg

INDEX OF RECIPES

Made in United States
Troutdale, OR
01/04/2025

27496353R00101